D1604126

The Zinzendorf — Muhlenberg Encounter:

A Controversy in Search of Understanding

By

Walter H. Wagner

A Moravian Historical Society Publication

Printed in the United States of America
Cover design by Kathryn M. Fiandaca

Library of Congress Control Number: 2002105162

ISBN 0-9719060-0-9

Made possible by the
Margaret McKee Williams and Henry L. Williams
Publication Fund
of the Moravian Historical Society
Nazareth, Pennsylvania 18064

CONTENTS

Introduction   i

Chapter One   From Westphalia to Philadelphia   1

Chapter Two   Orthodoxy and Pietism in Seventeenth   11
                     and Eighteenth Century Germany

Chapter Three   Aspects of Pennsylvania's Contexts   22
                     Prior to 1742

Chapter Four   Zinzendorf Prior to his Arrival in   40
                     the Colonies

Chapter Five   Muhlenberg Prior to his Arrival in   75
                     the Colonies

Chapter Six   Zinzendorf in Pennsylvania   89

Chapter Seven   Muhlenberg in Pennsylvania   105

Chapter Eight   The Confrontation   118

Chapter Nine   Aftermaths, Understandings and   144
                     Implications

Bibliography of Works Cited   163

Index   167

INTRODUCTION

On December 30, 1742 the Reverend-Count Nicholas Ludwig von Zinzendorf und Thürnstein and the Reverend Mr. Heinrich Melchior Muhlenberg met for the first and last time in Stephen Benezet's Philadelphia parlor. The stormy meeting was clouded by personal animosities, mutual suspicion, and conflicting understandings of the church and its future in America. The meeting has had both little effect and tremendous effect on Lutheran and Moravian churches, perhaps even on the shape of denominational relations in America. The traditional Moravian version is benign — and misleading. According to August Spangenberg, Zinzendorf's confidant:

> a Lutheran preacher [Muhlenberg] arrived from Germany, and began to act against the Count. For though the Lutherans in Pennsylvania had been left without a preacher, notwithstanding their repeated request, yet a different view of the matter was taken of the subject after the Count had devoted himself to them. By this means, a separation took place among the Lutherans. The newly arrived clergyman, who was an able and talented man, soon formed a party; whilst those to whom the Count's ministry had been blessed adhered to [Zinzendorf]. The result at length was that the Count thought it best to let the preacher above mentioned, and his subsequent assistants, act as they pleased; being satisfied if only Christ were preached.[1]

On the other hand, the Lutheran account is malign — and misleading. Muhlenberg ended his report with a word to the reader:

> Now I leave it to any Christian and intelligent mind to judge and consider whether the Count exhibited anything of the mind of Christ or the apostles or our dear father Luther. The congregations in New Hannover and Providence the Count could not capture because they were too smart for him ... The Count did try it in both congregations and won over a few, but the people felt that he acted like a fox which is as skillful in luring the hens as a cock, and when they are near enough to him, he gobbles them up. What good is it to be able to speak ever so sweetly of the Saviour and the Lamb when along with it thine eye be evil? So since the Count could get nowhere with these two country congregations, he granted them to me without any contradiction whatsoever, saying that he had no objection, for he has no desire for what he cannot get.[2]

Moravians generally ignore the incident, yet wonder why American Lutherans seem disdainful and even hostile toward the Brethren whom Luther embraced and the Count who insisted that he was an ordained Lutheran pastor. For their part, American Lutherans considered

Zinzendorf an ecclesiological misfit and his followers theologically shallow. The Philadelphia controversy is the source for these American attitudes. While one side forgets the incident, the other considers it unforgettable. Might a historical examination assist Zinzendorf's and Muhlenberg's ecclesiastical descendants to understand the event as important yet not final to their future existences in North America? Obviously, this study answers "Yes."

Two developments and a gap prompt an examination of the event and the persons involved. The first development is the ecumenical arrangement entered into by the Moravian Church in America and the Evangelical Lutheran Church in America called "Full Communion" in 1998–1999.[3] In the course of the bilateral dialogues (1992–1997) which preceded the actions of the churches, the dialoguers re-opened the doors to Benezet's parlor to re-hear and re-view what went on that night. The second development has been the tercentenary of Count Zinzendorf's birth. His thought, influence and legacy are being appreciated anew in a time that may be more receptive to his theological content and style. The gap is the virtual silence about the broader social and political contexts in which the encounter took place. The War of the Austrian Succession, the natures of Pennsylvania's settlers and government, the Great Awakening, and the rush of events around that evening heightened the tensions and raised the stakes for both men and for what they represented. To understand the controversy and its aftermath, we need to consider the contextual as well as the personal dynamics involved.

The study's first three chapters set the historical and religious scenes in Germany and Pennsylvania prior to the meeting. Chapter Four traces Count Zinzendorf's development and activities until his arrival in British North America. Chapter Five deals with Muhlenberg from his early years to his arrival in the colonies. Chapters Six and Seven examine their respective progresses to Mr. Benezet's parlor. The text of Muhlenberg's version of the face-to-face confrontation with my exchange-by-exchange analysis of its rhetoric and intended impact is covered in Chapter Eight. The concluding chapter surveys a number of the controversy's aftermaths, then moves to posit several understandings, and concludes with drawing some implications for today.

Because the encounter was the culmination of converging events and personalities — a veritable collision — I track both men with careful attention to where they are and when. The approach raises the issues of the accuracy of dates in sources and the differences in calendars used. As may be expected, on occasion one source may cite an incident as occurring on one day while another gives a different date. Generally, the results are inconsequential, but readers ought be aware of occasional discrepancies. The other issue, the British retention of the Julian Calendar and the continental use of the Gregorian Calendar, may have contributed to some of the variations in dating.

The Gregorian calendar replaced its Julian counterpart in Catholic Europe from 1582–87. By 1700 western Europe, with the exception of Britain and its dependencies, followed the New Style (NS) calendar. The British maintained the Julian or Old Style (OS) until 1752 when what would have been September 3 OS was reckoned as September 14 NS, a difference of eleven days. When in continental Europe, Zinzendorf and Muhlenberg used NS dating. In British North America, dates from Brethren sources prefer New Style and the Brethren looked to the liturgical dating that their brothers and sisters used in Germany in order to celebrate and pray together. For example, Zinzendorf used NS and followed the religious calendar according to those dates when observing the 1741 Christmas Eve service in Bethlehem on December 24 NS, with the Old Style date of December 13.[4] Muhlenberg, on the other hand, switched from New Style to Old Style a few days after arriving in England. He used Old Style from that point in the *Journals* until the official change in 1752.[5] I use the following procedure:

1. When events are noted and both men are in continental Europe where the Gregorian Calendar is used, the dates are New Style usually without specific designation.

2. When events are cited in British North America prior to and independent of Muhlenberg and Zinzendorf, the dates are Old Style without specific designation.

3. When Muhlenberg and Zinzendorf are in England, the dates are cited Old Style unless the context requires clarification.

4. When both are in British North America the dates are cited as Old Style/New Style (OS/NS), e.g., Zinzendorf arrived in Philadelphia on November 29/December 10, 1741, the first Pennsylvania Synod was held from January 1–2/12–13, and the encounter took place on December 30, 1742/January 10, 1743.

In the notes at the end of each chapter, I cite the authors' names and, where appropriate, an abbreviated form of the work indicated. Full citations are in the Bibliography of Works Cited.

This study of the encounter grew out of the bilateral dialogues. I was the Lutheran co-chair and was partnered with the Rt. Rev. Dr. Arthur

Freeman, bishop of the Unity and at that time Professor of New Testament and Spirituality at the Moravian Theological Seminary, Bethlehem, Pennsylvania. Fittingly, when the dialogue began, I was a faculty member at Muhlenberg College, Allentown, Pennsylvania. By the end of the process I was an adjunct professor at Moravian Theological Seminary in addition to being the senior pastor of Christ Evangelical Lutheran Church, Allentown. Bishop Freeman has since published his study of Zinzendorf's theology, and I managed a tentative examination of the Philadelphia meeting.[6] Papers delivered to the Friends of the Moravian Archives and the Zinzendorf Tercentenary Celebration sponsored by the Center for Moravian Studies at Moravian Theological Seminary in 2000 led Ms. Susan Dreydoppel, executive director of the Moravian Historical Society, to encourage my return to that verbally stormy night in Philadelphia.

Since the reader and I will be together for some time, permit some personal observations about history and what you will encounter in this account. History involves more than recounting things done by human beings. History extends into attempting to interpret, on the basis of available evidence, why persons in the past acted and thought as they did. While the events of the past do not change, interpretations change because history engages people in the present to consider what those words and deeds have come to mean up to the present and what they may mean in the future. We are about to examine an event that lasted less than two hours. Yet the events and dynamics that led to it help explain why it happened the way it did and what resulted from it. It is necessary to engage the historical contexts and the key individuals involved in the expectation that the pieces will come together to form a comprehensible as well as comprehensive whole. This study also has an added element. We will look beyond the immediate aftermaths of those few minutes in Philadelphia. Unlike the men and women in Mr. Benezet's parlor, we know what happened to the main characters and their successors. We, therefore, can attempt some understandings of the knots of action and arguments as these may be seen in our time. Obviously, we are limited to our present; future historians and readers will judge the accuracy and adequacy of the points presented here. Nevertheless, I will venture some implications or projections about what may yet happen with the encounter-controversy as understandings and events continue to develop.

I cheerfully acknowledge the assistance and patience of Ms. Dreydoppel and her associates at the Moravian Historical Society; the Rev. Vernon Nelson, director of the Moravian Archives; the Rev. J. Thomas Minor, director, and the staff of the Reeves Library of Moravian

College and Moravian Theological Seminary; Bishop Freeman; and Moravian Theological Seminary's Professor Otto Dreydoppel, Jr.

The work before you is dedicated to my faculty colleagues and students at Moravian Theological Seminary, and my wife, Deborah.

Walter H. Wagner
Bethlehem, Pennsylvania

Endnotes to the Introduction

1 Spangenberg, *Life,* pp. 298–299.
2 *Journals*, Vol. 1, p. 80.
3 Wagner and Freeman.
4 *The Bethlehem Diary*, *1742–1744*, Vol. 1, p. 128.
5 See *Journals*, Vol. 1, entry for April 17, 1742 (NS), p. 18. He continued to follow the liturgical calendar aligned with Old Style until the transition in 1752. The *Journals* do not cover the last portion of 1752. By the time the *Journal* resumes, he is using New Style. The Tappert and Doberstein edition of the *Journal* inserts the *Hallesche Nachrichten, Selbstbiographie* and other items to make up gaps, indicating the added materials with notes and brackets. In addition to these sources is *Correspondence, Vol. 1, 1740–1747* and *Korrespondenz.*
6 Freeman. See also Wagner.

Chapter One

FROM WESTPHALIA TO PHILADELPHIA

The social and political context in which Muhlenberg and Zinzendorf lived was compounded by bursts of confusion and confessionalism. Western Christendom never recovered from the Papal Captivity and the Triple Schism (1302–1415). Jan Hus' execution-martyrdom heralded persistent resistance to the ecclesiastical and doctrinal authority of the papacy and the governments which supported it. Devout persons throughout the Empire compounded their disillusionment with repulsion when dealing with the church's traditional structures and leaders. For whatever legacy Luther and other Protestant reformers left, their actions threatened to overthrow civil and religious institutions, thereby setting societies on the courses of war and unrest. Religious diversity, except when labeled schism and heresy, had always existed among Christians, sparking searching, debate and flexible co-existence with perceived orthodoxies. The Reformation provided opportunities for illuminati, repristinators, charismatics, mystics, iconoclasts, anti-trinitarians, apocalypticists and, occasionally, atheists to emerge and develop, even if only temporarily. Governments, frequently urged by Catholic, Lutheran and Reformed church officials, attempted to restore order and uniformity. But even the semblance of religious unity had been shattered by the end of the sixteenth century.

Virtually ceaseless political and military turmoil, abetted and stoked by religion and growing nationalism, culminated in the Thirty Years War (1618–1648). Appeals to confessional loyalties mingled with secular ambitions wreaked physical and spiritual havoc in German-speaking lands. The Peace of Westphalia legitimated the principle "as the ruler, so the people" in order to avert further carnage. In addition, the Peace attempted to prevent future declines and disorder by recognizing the legal status of the three churches, each within its own boundaries with careful provisions to discourage shifts in those boundaries. In this manner Catholics, Lutherans and Reformed supposedly could observe geographic conformity and confessional monopolies in order to preserve order. As sensible as the arrangement seemed to those who exercised political and religious authority, it could not halt the rise and spread of dissenting movements and believers — except by the coercive methods of punishment, banishment and death.

Within territories governed by Lutheran and Reformed rulers, the prospect of recognizing the legal status of any other ecclesiastical group as a distinct "church" was regarded with dread. Such a step would violate the Peace, arouse the ire of the territorially established church, and risk military responses from powerful Catholic neighbors who were eager to recover souls for the Catholic Church and territory for themselves. Should an ecclesial community surface, it would be prudent for that community to be sheltered under the legally established umbrella of one of the sanctioned churches. On the other hand, the established church's leaders would be wary of and even hostile toward such a community's claims and leaders.

The Thirty Years War itself was permeated with other struggles, e.g., the English Civil War, Ottoman aggression, and a Swedish-Danish War (1643–1645). In geopolitical and dynastic terms the Peace of Westphalia set the stage for future conflicts, e.g., the War of the League of Augsburg (1688–1697). The forces of France's Sun King, Louis XIV (reigned 1643–1715), moved into the Rhineland, provoking a Grand Alliance composed of Emperor Leopold I (reigned 1658–1705) of the Holy Roman Empire, the electors of Bavaria, Saxony and the Palatinate, together with the kings of Sweden and Spain. Almost simultaneously the Dutch Statholder, William of Orange (later William III of England), organized an offensive coalition against French designs on the Lowlands and Germany. In 1689 Savoy (until 1696), Britain and the Netherlands joined the alliance. Franco-German hostility at the end of the seventeenth century would lead to the Wars of the Spanish Succession (1701–1714).

The Thirty Years War resulted in Sweden's emergence as one of Europe's great powers. Charles X Gustav (reigned 1654–1660) conquered most of Poland and triumphed briefly over Denmark. Charles XI (reigned 1660–1697) and Charles XII (reigned 1697–1718) sought to expand and consolidate Swedish gains, thereby precipitating the Great Northern War (1700–1718) that pitted Sweden against Russia, Poland and Denmark. During the conflict Swedish troops occupied sections of Pomerania (including the cities of Stralsund and Greifswald) and invaded Saxon-ruled Lusatia. A Swedish detachment had a surprise encounter with the child-count Zinzendorf at prayer (1706). Later, the adult Count traveled to Stralsund for a theological examination involving faculty from the University of Greifswald.

In 1713 Prussia joined the attack on Sweden and humiliated Charles XII. His death in a battle against the Norwegians (1718) effectively ended the Vasa dynasty. The Swedish Diet elected Ulrika Eleonora as her brother's successor. She abdicated two years later in favor of her husband, Frederick of Hessen. He reigned as Frederick I until 1751. At first friendly toward Pietism and Zinzendorf, his attitude reversed by 1735. In 1735, rebuffed in Sweden and facing mounting opposition, the Count addressed to Frederick a lengthy statement of faith based on the Augsburg Confession.

The Peace of Nysted (1721) ended the Great Northern War, leaving Sweden so weakened that its monarchs were forced to yield to parliamentary initiatives; Sweden's so-called "Age of Greatness" was over. The Dutch had ended the dream for a New Sweden in the Americas decades earlier, and since 1664 transplanted Swedish settlers and institutions accommodated themselves to British rule.

The Peace of Westphalia brought neither political coherence nor an end to hostilities for the German-speaking states. Prussia-Brandenburg, as it was then called, challenged the Holy Roman Empire through gaining economic and military power under the Elector, Frederick Wilhelm (reigned 1640–1688). His successor, Frederick III (reigned 1688–1713), forced Emperor Leopold I to confer on him the title of king (1701) and was subsequently styled Frederick I of Prussia. Leopold had little choice if he wanted Prussian aid in the impending Wars of the Spanish Succession. The Holy Roman Empire was pulled and pushed into increasingly debilitating wars and concessions. The Peace of Westphalia had rendered it a loose association of states that included the duchies of Austria, Styria, Carinthia and Krain; the county of Tyrol; the kingdom of Bohemia, Moravia and Silesia; and the kingdom of Hungary. Conflicts in the Balkans seemed incessant. Ottoman invasions overran most of the Balkans and Hungary, and led to the siege of Vienna (July – September, 1683). Combined forces from Saxony, Bavaria, Franconia and Poland under John III (Jan Sobieski), king of Poland, routed the Ottomans. Austria recovered Hungary (1686), and the Treaty of Carlowitz (1699) pushed the Turks temporarily further back. Nevertheless, the Empire was losing ground steadily in the Balkans. A series of Ottoman-Russian wars from 1677–1711 gave the Empire some respite. If western Europe breathed easier as the Ottoman threat receded, new dynastic struggles plunged it into war again.

The death of Spain's weak and childless Charles II (1700) set in motion that conglomeration of conflicts called collectively the War of the Spanish Succession (1701–1714). Charles II had willed all his possessions to Philip, the Duke of Anjou, the Bourbon grandson of Louis XIV. Installed as king and designated Philip V, he ruled from 1700–1746. Louis XIV immediately moved troops into the Spanish Netherlands and parts of Italy, then recognized Philip as his successor to the French throne.

The specter of French hegemony stretching from Iberia, into the Low-lands and Italy as well across the Atlantic to New Spain and New France was a cause for war. In 1701 Hannover, Brandenburg-Prussia, Savoy and the Empire opened hostilities against the French and their allies, Bavaria and Electoral Cologne. In 1702 Holland and Britain joined the anti-French Grand Alliance. Britain's withdrawal (1712) led to the Treaty of Utrecht (1713) and other agreements that concluded the conflict. The Spanish Empire was partitioned with the Hapsburg Archduke Charles designated as the next monarch of Spain, Austria in control of the former Spanish Netherlands, and French recognition (at least temporarily) of the legitimacy of the 1701 Act of Settlement in Great Britain. The Act recognized the validity of William III and Mary II's acccssion to the British throne. In the midst of the Spanish War, Leopold died and was succeeded by Joseph I (reigned 1705–1711). Now the struggle over succession moved from Spain to Vienna.

When Joseph I died, he left female but not male offspring. The electors chose his brother, the last Hapsburg of the Spanish line, to be the next emperor. Charles VI (reigned 1711–1740) also had no surviving sons. In 1713 he issued a decree that came to be called the Pragmatic Sanction. Through it, he specified that the Empire was an indivisible unity. He continued that his daughters or, if they died without male issue, their descendants would succeed to the throne. If his daughters died childless, the line of succession would pass to the daughters of his deceased brother, Joseph I, and their descendants. Between 1717–1724 Charles VI and his empress had three daughters, the oldest of whom was Maria Theresa (born 1717). The Pragmatic Sanction was recognized and accepted in all Hapsburg territories, by Britain (1732) and, after initial opposition, by Saxony (1732). The Saxon Elector, Augustus the Strong, was offered and accepted the throne of Poland in 1697 under the condition that he become a Roman Catholic. His death in 1733 led to the short conflict called the War of the Polish Succession. It concluded in 1735 with his Saxon son-successor, like his father a nominal Catholic, ruling Poland as well as Saxony. He was known in Poland as Augustus III. In 1733–1734 France, Sardinia and Spain attacked Austria. In the settlement, the French agreed to recognize the Pragmatic Sanction in return for concessions in the Rhineland. Then, in 1740, death struck.

Within five months of each other, Emperor Charles VI and the Prussian king, Frederick I, died. Frederick II (the Great, reigned 1740–1786) succeeded his father. He was willing to support the election of Maria Theresa's husband, the Hapsburg Duke of Lorraine, Francis Stephen, as

4

emperor for a price: Maria Theresa's ceding Silesia to Prussia. If she complied, Maria Theresa would have been subject to increased pressures from Frederick and others — and she would give away the source of the Empire's best soldiers and a strategic location. To acquiesce meant strengthening her greatest future rival. To refuse meant war. And war it was. The War of the Austrian Succession (1740–1748) reversed previous loyalties and alliances. France, Bavaria and Spain joined Prussia to dismember Austria. By 1742 French troops occupied Upper Austria, Bohemia and parts of Hannover. Civilian travelers from Hannover had to pass French military checkpoints on their ways to Holland and England — as Muhlenberg discovered. Initially Saxony allied itself with Austria's enemies, but switched to support the Empire out of the realization that Prussia was determined to dominate its neighbors and more distant nations. Austria was aided directly by Hungary, Hannover, Saxony, Britain, Sweden and Russia. Support came less out of loyalty to the Empire than out of anxiety about Prussia's rising power. In April, 1741, as Muhlenberg ministered to the orphaned and poor at Grosshennersdorf, and Zinzendorf prayed with the Pilgrim Congregation in Geneva, imperial forces won an unexpected victory at Mollwitz. Instead of selecting Maria Theresa's husband, the electors proclaimed Charles Albert of Bavaria as Emperor Charles VII. At Charles VII's death (1745), Francis Stephen was finally elected emperor, but the war ground on until the treaties of Dresden and Aix-la-Chapelle were signed. By the time Muhlenberg left Europe, Hannover, Saxony, Sweden and Britain united to support the empress and to oppose France and Spain. Consequently, Spanish and British ships engaged in mutual hostilities and hostage-taking on the high seas, Spanish soldiers stationed in Florida pillaged Georgia settlements, and Swedish churchmen in Pennsylvania were positively disposed toward Hannoverians.

Britain played critically important roles prior to and following Westphalia. Of particular note is the network of marriages that wove and tangled persons and politics in the seventeenth and eighteenth centuries. England's James I (reigned 1603–1625) married Anne, the second daughter of Frederick II, king of Denmark.[1] The marriage connected Lutherans and Danes to British royalty. They had several surviving children: Charles, James, Elizabeth, and Henrietta Anne. Elizabeth was married to Frederick V, duke-elector of the Palatinate. Their twelfth-born child, Sophia (1630–1714) was wed to Ernst Augustus, duke of Brunswick who later became the elector of Hannover. Their daughter was named Anne. Anne's son, born in 1660, was Georg Ludwig. He became elector of Hannover on his father's death (1698). In 1682 he married Sophia Dorothea, but divorced and imprisoned her in 1694 for adultery. By the time of her incarceration, she and Georg had two children. Their son, named Georg for his father, remained in Hannover and their daughter, Sophia, later became the queen of Prussia and the mother of Frederick II.

James I's son, Charles, was married to Henrietta Maria, the Catholic sister of Louis XIV. James I's death (1625) brought Charles to the throne. His struggles with the House of Commons and religious reformers, magnified by Catholic-Protestant conflicts in the Thirty Years War, led to the two-phased English Civil War (1642–1646 and 1648 respectively) and ended with his execution (January, 1649). Charles I and Henrietta had three children: Charles, James and Mary Henrietta Sophia. He arranged the marriage of his daughter, then nine years old, to the fifteen-year-old William (later William II) of Orange. A dozen years later and on the day her husband died, she gave birth to a son, naming him William. He grew to be William III of Orange — and, through the complexities of marriage, William III of Great Britain.

A spate of ineffectual parliamentary attempts to govern the realm (1649–1653), led to the Protectorate (1653–1659), and finally to the restoration of the House of Stuart (1660). In the Restoration Settlement, Charles II (reigned 1660–1685) agreed to make allowances for those of tender conscience as long as those consciences did not belong to Catholics, anti-trinitarians or disrupters of Anglican ecclesiastical order. In 1662 the king married the Portuguese princess, Catherine of Bragauza, a devout Catholic. Spurts of repression directed against dissenters and members of unauthorized conventicles gradually yielded to an unofficial policy of benign indifference that gave Catholics, especially those connected to the royal house, room to practice their faith. Henrietta Anne, James I's daughter and Charles II's sister, was married to the brother of Louis XIV. In a 1670 secret protocol to the marriage agreement, Charles agreed to declare himself a Catholic at an appropriate time. That time was on his deathbed, but many Britons suspected that he was a functional Catholic long before he died. In 1673 Charles' younger brother, James, Duke of York, converted to Catholicism.

Through the Anglo-Dutch Wars (1664–1667 and 1672–1674), Britain gained the Dutch colony of New Amsterdam (New York) and what came to be called New Jersey and Delaware. In 1681 William Penn was rewarded for financial services to the crown through an extensive land grant to establish an experimental proprietary colony, Pennsylvania. Penn's

6

"Frame of Government" (1682) guaranteed religious freedom to all "who confess and acknowledge the one Almighty and Eternal God… and hold themselves obliged, in conscience, to live peaceably and justly in civil society." A governor in the colony ruled on behalf of the Quaker proprietors. An Assembly, dominated by Quakers from 1682–1756, was responsible for originating legislation and raising revenues. Penn along with other representatives solicited widely in the Palatinate and Hannover as well as other German states for persons to settle in the colony. The Swedes welcomed the British and fine relationships were established between the Swedish Church (Lutheran) and the Anglican Church in Pennsylvania, southern New Jersey and Delaware.

Although Charles fathered at least fourteen children by various mistresses, he and Catherine had no surviving offspring of their own. Realizing James' Catholicism heightened fears about a restoration of Catholicism, Charles attempted to assure his subjects that an Anglican would become monarch. So, he became a matchmaker with James' children. The Duke of York and his first wife, Anne Hyde, had two daughters, Mary (born 1662) and Anne (born 1665). James wanted Anne to wed the then-unmarried but not-yet elector of Hannover, Georg Ludwig. King Charles had other plans. In 1683, he matched Anne to the colorless George, younger brother of Christian V, king of Denmark.[2] Prince George moved to England. As a Lutheran, he requested and was granted the appointment of German chaplain-court preachers at the St. James Chapel. Through the recently established Society for the Propagation of Christian Knowledge (SPCK), a request for such a chaplain was made to a German member of the SPCK, August Francke of Halle. Francke sent one of his former students, Anton Wilhelm Bohme (1673–1722). He served until his death. During his ministry, he translated German Pietist writings into English and English puritan and evangelical writings into German. He also served as an effective liaison for German-speaking refugees and others who sought to travel to or settle in British North America. He was followed in 1723 by another "Halle man," Friedrich Michael Ziegenhagen (1664–1773). Ziegenhagen played a major role in the controversy between Zinzendorf and Muhlenberg.

Charles II's efforts to insure his brother's accession to the throne included agreeing to a series of Test Acts with Parliament, especially that of 1673. The latter virtually excluded all non-Anglicans from public offices and university positions. But persistent suspicions and rumors of Catholic treachery haunted the Stuart brothers. These were heightened when Charles temporarily allied Britain with France against the United

Provinces (1670) and when the totally non-existent "Popish Plot" of 1678 was "exposed." In that context (1677) Charles had James' daughter, Mary, marry the architect of the anti-French and anti-Catholic Grand Alliance, William of Orange, now Statholder of the United Provinces. Mary crossed the channel to be with her Dutch spouse, William. She would return with him in 1689.

Continuing political-religious fears about creeping Romanism clouded the coronation and brief reign of James II (1685–89). In 1688 James and his second wife, Maria of Modena, surprised themselves and dismayed British Protestants by parenting a son, James Francis Edward Stuart. The prospect of a continuation of Catholic monarchs in a realm where the ruler was to be the head of the Church in England moved many to oppose the continuance of James' reign. James blundered repeatedly, turning possible supporters into foes. Several key leaders "invited" William of Orange to "investigate" the paternity of baby James. Actually, they requested the Hollander to bring his Dutch army with him to drive James from the throne. William bargained shrewdly. The Declaration of Rights, 1689, stipulated that Mary (as Mary II) and William (as William III) would be joint sovereigns but William was to be "sole administrator." The Declaration also held that future monarchs were to be members of the Church of England, and that if William and Mary died childless, Anne would become queen.

The "Protestant Winds" of October – November, 1688 prevented James' ships from leaving port and aided the Dutch landing. James II fled with his wife and son to Louis XIV's France, and William and Mary entered London. Louis XIV immediately backed James II, declaring that his successor should be James Francis. William's major interest in gaining the crown was to use British manpower and wealth to oppose France. His plans were delayed because James II made a French-supported and abortive attempt to raise a rebellion against William and Mary (1690), and William then "pacified" Ireland and Scotland. Personally unpopular and cold, his reign (1689–1702) nevertheless advanced Britain's world position as a naval-military power and defender of Protestantism.

James II's departure (December 18, 1688), however, left the Church of England in a quandary. Was he or were William and Mary rulers by the Divine Right and who could command the obedience that was required of loyal subjects and good Christians? Could an act of Parliament express the will of God on so crucial a matter? Granted that James was a Catholic, but William was a Calvinist. While most Anglican clergy took the oath of loyalty to William and Mary, eight bishops and four hundred other clergy refused. Although the "Non-Jurors" were re-absorbed into the Church of England after 1746, their statements of conscience raised issues related to the nature of the church and pluralism in church and society. In the course of the Non-Jurors' struggles, numerous Anglicans, especially High Churchmen, felt the divisions among Christians could be healed through worship and prayer. Some advocated cooperation among Anglicans, Lutherans and Moravians. Moravian-Anglican relationships, begun in the seventeenth century, were expanded to the point that the Anglican Church and Parliament Lords came the conclusion in 1749 that the Unity was indeed an "antient Protestant Episcopal Church."[3] The Edict of Toleration (1689) granted non-conformists the rights of their own teachers and preachers, but disqualified them from public office. Foreigners and non-conformists could have their own clergy, chapels and "study houses." The designation "church" was restricted to Anglican centers of worship.

Mary II died in 1694, and in 1700 the only surviving child of Anne Stuart and Prince George died. The Declaration of Rights (1689) was now re-asserted through the Act of Settlement, 1701: Anne Stuart would become queen on William III's death, but Danish Prince George would not become king. If she died without surviving issue, the succession would pass to Sophia of Brunswick-Hannover or her child (Anne) or Anne's oldest son, Georg Ludwig. Many felt James II's death (1701) ended his immediate family's claims to the throne, although numerous royalists felt they would rather have James II's son, James Francis — known to his supporters as James III and to his later detractors as the "Old Pretender," rather than the sullen Dutchman, insipid Dane or German boor.

Anne, crowned in 1702, ruled through politically and militarily treacherous times until 1714. Throughout her reign, Britain grew in power, influence and colonial wealth. Upon her death and in accord with the 1701 Act of Settlement, the British turned to the House of Hannover for a new, if related, royal family. The Lutheran Hannoverians moved across the channel. The Old Pretender attempted a French-supported landing and uprising in 1715. He was defeated and driven out of Britain. Four years later, he married Clementina Sobieski, granddaughter of the Polish king who defeated the Ottoman forces besieging Vienna in 1683. Their son, Charles Edward Louis Philip Casimir (1720–1788), called tauntingly by the Hannoverians "the Young Pretender" and by Jacobins "Bonnie Prince Charlie," went on to the disastrous battle of Culloden (1746).[4]

9

The Hannoverians retained their rule over Hannover when Georg Ludwig became George I of England (ruled from 1714–1727). Although he never understood the English language or the British people, he and his ministers maneuvered the realm through the risks and conflicts that involved the rise of Prussia, the ambitions of Saxony, and the declines of Sweden and Austria. He quarreled bitterly with his son and successor, Georg (1683–1760). Whether through choice or lack of interest, the Hannoverian Lutheran-become-Anglican left the Church of England alone.

The first George was followed by his German-raised son, George II (reigned 1727–60). George II, monarch during the War of the Austrian Succession, threw his support to the Austrians under the condition that if Hannover were invaded by Prussia, the other imperial allies would come to the aid of his Fatherland. When Hannover was attacked, George II demonstrated his considerable personal courage in 1743 by leading a British force in battle at Dettingen in conjunction with his soldier-son, Wilhelm, Duke of Cumberland.

From 1648 to the 1740s Austrian-Hungarian policies included trapping dissenters so that they could not remain unmolested in their homes in Bohemia, Moravia or Salzburg, yet they could not emigrate legally. They had to leave their possessions behind them, cross borders surreptitiously, and begin anew. Lutherans, Reformed and Moravians fled their homelands, taking refuge in Saxony, Prussia, Poland, Scandinavia, Britain, the Danish West Indies and British North America. Pennsylvania was especially attractive and hospitable.

Endnotes to Chapter One

1 Their cool relationship worsened when she converted from being a Lutheran to being a Catholic.

2 Charles is reported to have said, "I have tried him drunk, and I have tried him sober, and drunk or sober there is nothing in him." A more critical source wrote after Anne became queen, "He is very fat, loves news, his bottle and the queen... He hath neither friends nor enemies." Quoted in Van der Zee, p. 354. The latter statement is from John Macy, *Memories of the Secret Service* (London: no publisher, 1733).

3 See Podmore, *Conversations*, pp. 72–79. For a more detailed examination see his *Moravian Church*, pp. 228–265.

4 Clementina divorced the charming, mistress-chasing, dissolute and alcoholic James III. James died in Italy.

Chapter Two

ORTHODOXY AND PIETISM IN
SEVENTEENTH AND EIGHTEENTH CENTURY GERMANY

As do earthquakes, the Protestant Reformation of the sixteenth century released pent-up tensions and movements. Multiple upheavals forecast by rumblings were followed by severe after-shocks. European politics, economics, jurisprudence, education, art and literature were as involved as were theological doctrines, liturgies, hermeneutics, ecclesiologies, moralities, and spiritualities. The so-called "medieval synthesis" was an uneasy and poorly disguised bundle of contradictions and paradoxes. Reason and revelation, human free will and God's grace, clergy authority and lay expectations, biblical renewal and authoritarian interpretations, resurgent "heresies" and enforced orthodoxies are merely a few issues that burst through the crust of assumptions and traditions. Shifts accelerated by the Reformation continued in new forms, attitudes, expectations and anxieties. And, as in other human affairs, the post-Reformation structures and dynamics contained elements of the old problems compounded by energies in different contexts.

Luther's Ninety-five Theses (1517) began with a challenge to prevailing doctrines and practices that proved important in later Lutheran Orthodoxy and Pietism:

1. When our Lord and Master Jesus Christ said, "Repent," he willed the entire life of believers to be one of repentance.

2. This word cannot be understood as referring to the sacrament of penance, that is, confession and satisfaction, as administered by the clergy.

3. Yet it does not mean solely inner repentance; such inner repentance is worthless unless it produces various outward mortifications of the flesh.[1]

From its beginnings, the Lutheran Reformation called for an on-going inner renewal which ought transform the believer's external actions, alter the relationships between clergy and laity as well as among laypersons, and challenge traditional liturgies. Luther went on to develop the three "onlys," (Scripture alone, Grace alone, and Faith alone), the priesthood of all believers, a revolutionary understanding of Christian vocation, and a Christocentric vision of the Christian life. All these became core components of later evangelical Pietism. At the same time, the Wittenberg professor and his colleagues considered themselves to be unquestionably orthodox in the method and content of their theologies. They sought to ground their spirituality, church order, scholarship, and personal lives on the bedrock of Scripture, creeds, reason — and polemics. All these became core components of what came to be known as Lutheran Orthodoxy. In fairness to those who have been tagged as such by friends and foes, almost all Pietists were committed to being doctrinally orthodox, and almost all Orthodoxists were deeply pious.

After Luther's death (1546), the Lutheran movement fractured. In the wake of later imperial battlefield victories and diplomatic efforts, Lutherans scrambled for survival, integrity and time. Two major camps emerged among the late great Reformer's erstwhile colleagues: the Philippists (supporters of Philip Melanchthon) and the Gnesio-Lutherans or self-styled "True Lutherans." In general, the Philippists provided perspectives that were absorbed into Pietism, while the Gnesio-Lutherans were the forerunners of Lutheran Orthodoxy. In an attempt to reconcile the major parties and several splinter groups and to settle some unsettling theological battles among second generation Lutherans, several leaders negotiated the Formula of Concord, then collated a body of earlier and important documents into the Book of Concord (1580).[2] German Lutheran clergy were required to subscribe to these confessional writings in order to retain their positions, and candidates for ordination likewise were to agree to teach and preach in accordance with the "Confessions," as the works in the Book of Concord came to be called. The most important of these Confessions were the Unaltered Augsburg Confession and Luther's Small Catechism. The development of the Book of Concord and the tone of the Formula reflect animosities toward Roman Catholicism and Calvinism.

While the Enlightenment played significant roles in eroding the claims of revealed religions throughout the seventeenth and eighteenth centuries, and influenced theological methodology, scholarship, homiletical styles and evaluations of tradition, the major tensions relevant to this study may be characterized in terms of Orthodoxy and Pietism. Each was itself a cluster of often contrasting attitudes, expectations and determined personalities.

Sketches of Orthodoxy and Pietism, while superficial, will be helpful. First Orthodoxy. Robert Preus summarized its mind:

> Orthodoxy is more than a mere attitude or spirit. The concrete feature of Lutheran orthodoxy is its doctrinal platform, a definite and permanent doctrinal position based on Scripture as interpreted by the Lutheran Confessions and (in harmony with the Confessions) by the ancient creeds, the church fathers, and Luther. Since theology is based solely on God's written Word, its content does not change; Law and Gospel

and the articles of faith remain the same, being the summation of God's unchangeable Word to man. This confessional and doctrinal constant is to the old dogmaticians more than a mere statement of belief and platform for action; it is an expression of the very Gospel, a power that controls and changes lives and ideas and movements in history. Lutheran orthodoxy is utterly convinced of this.[3]

Preus made several other points. First, Orthodox theologians were reluctant to break with the past while trying to face new situations and issues. Second, they held that piety was to be formed on the basis of doctrine supported by Luther's writings and their interpretations of his theology. Third, such zeal for doctrine led to animosity to all heresies and suspicions of heterodox positions. This in turn led to polemical and disputatious engagements among the orthodox and between those Christians who had differing expressions of faith.

The University of Wittenberg became a bastion of Lutheran Orthodoxy. Although Luther and Melanchthon spent their careers there, its stature was diminished as a result of controversies involving Philippists and Gnesio-Lutherans as well as through the defeats sustained by the Lutheran princes in the middle of the sixteenth century. Beginning in 1590, however, Duke Friedrich Wilhelm set about to recover the university for pure Lutheranism. He and his successors appointed leading Orthodoxists to the faculty. The last significant Orthodox theologian to teach there was Valentin Löscher (1673–1749). An astute student of Luther, he was convinced that there was a single body of teaching that could be called "pure doctrine" and that Luther was its chief exponent and interpreter. Löscher, accordingly, was considered a *Luther revividus*. He became the implacable opponent of Hallesian-style Pietism, publishing from 1701 onward the anti-pietist periodical *Unschuldige Nachrichten*. He became the superintendent of the Dresden Consistory. The terms "inspector" and "superintendent" were essentially synonymous. Many Lutherans did not want to revive the term "bishop" because of its Roman Catholic connotations. Basically, inspectors and superintendents were overseers of the congregations and clergy under their jurisdiction. They certified the acceptability of candidates for ordination and authorized their being called to and installed as pastors in congregations.

Pietism, according to Ernst Stoeffler, insisted on:

the need for, and the possibility of, an authentic and vitally significant experience of God on the part of individual Christians; the religious life as a life of love for God and man, which is marked by social sensitivity and ethical concern; utter confidence with respect to the issues of life and death, in the experientially verifiable authenticity of God's revelation in Christ, as found in the biblical witness; the church as the community of God's people which must ever be renewed through the transformation of individuals, and which necessarily transcends all organizationally required boundaries; the need for the implementation of the Reformation understanding of the priesthood of all believers through responsible participation in the various concerns of the Christian enterprise; a ministry which is sensitized, trained and oriented to respond to the needs and problems of a given age; and, finally, the continued adaptation of ecclesiastical structures, practices, and verbal definitions to the mission of the church.[4]

The central theme is a personal and vibrant experience of God's presence which unites God's gracious love with human acceptance in faith, and growth in transforming one's life through discipling attitudes and actions. The heart-experience was usually referred to as "rebirth."[5] Reborn believers knew themselves as children of God (*Kinder Gottes aus der neuen Geburt*). They had a heart-consciousness of the Holy Spirit who assured them of salvation. For most Pietists, the awareness of God's presence and consequent rebirth involve the person's realizing his or her deep need for repentance; Luther's first three Theses were essential for the Pietist grasp of the believer's life. Repentance was not only a repetitive act for one's specific sins; it was a life-long and soul-filled turning toward God. Through repentance and rebirth, understood as expressions of God's grace through Jesus and unmerited by sinners, Pietism centered on the individual and then from the individual to relationships with other believers, the immediate society and the world. Engagement with the Bible, prayer, and devotional readings in the family and in small groups of fellow believers were hallmarks of the Pietist way of life. The true church was not the external institution (*Gesamtkirche*) — although most cherished it and sought to reform it — but a community of the children of God united in the Spirit. Far from being isolated individuals or remaining in self-absorbed clusters, most Pietists saw their wider goal as *Weltverwandlung durch Menschenverwandlung*, transforming the world through transforming individuals.

Pietism became "the most important development of Protestant spirituality."[6] A complex cross-fertilization of influences and relationships made Pietism an international, inter-confessional movement. Pietism's Lutheran forms sought to remain within the several geographically-politically established churches. A significant and recurring problem was the suspicion that the Pietists' "heart religion" would lead to gross emotionalism, theological error and ecclesiastical ruptures. While these aberrations occasionally occurred, the main thrust and major leaders remained in their churches of origin. Nevertheless, the proliferation of new movements, spurred by dynamic leaders, played important, if subsidiary, roles in Europe and America. What is called "Radical Pietism" is a factor especially for Zinzendorf's development and his ministry in Pennsylvania.[7]

In the mid-1680s, however, the words "Pietism" and "Pietist" were being used derisively to describe censorious attitudes, disordered emotions, legalistic rules, schismatic tendencies and previous heterodoxies. Ironically, some who today are identified as part of the movement, such as Zinzendorf, sought to discredit others by labeling them as Pietists. By 1730, in order to thwart the splintering of the established churches and the proliferation of dissident sects, especially in the wake of the Peace of Westphalia, several German states began to ban private conventicles for prayer and Bible study.

Obviously, Pietists and Orthodoxists were headed toward collisions. The doctrinal platforms and certainties about the pure teachings to which Orthodoxists gave first priority were present among Pietists but occupied a position below their personal heart-experience and life-changing commitments. In addition, Orthodoxists virtually posited the necessity of a doctrinal cadre, a *magisterium*, which would argue about, defend, and elucidate the "pure teaching" for the Christian community. In effect, the cadre was composed of eminent Orthodox theologians and pastors, thereby emphasizing the position of clergy in the life and organization of the church. Pietism, on the other hand, opted for the priesthood of all believers, emphasizing the laity in dealing with Scripture, teachings, spiritual growth, conduct, worship, mission and clergy accountability.

Conflict between Orthodoxists and Pietists was muddled by the strengths of each, the genuine religious devotion of partisans on each side, and divisions within each side. Among the several manifestations of Pietism were the apocalyptic hermeneutics of Johann Albrecht Bengel (1687–1752), the New Testament scholar in Württemberg, as well as the eventually mystical pietism of Tübingen's Friedrich Christoph Oetinger (1702–1782). Of immediate importance for the present study is the work of Philip Jacob Spener (1635–1705, the superintendent of the Frankfurt am Main Consistory), August Hermann Francke (1663–1727) and their successors at Halle. The conflict between Lutheran Orthodoxy and Pietism serves as the backdrop for the encounter in Philadelphia, but that encounter had to do more with rivalries and tensions among Pietists.

Spener's *Pia Desideria* (1675) began as a preface to a new edition of Johann Arndt's *True Christianity*. In that book-length preface Spener proposed an approach to reform the "true Protestant Christian Church." Spener urged what came to be hallmarks of German Pietism: Bible reading and study, reform of preaching, small groups that met in homes, development of close relationships between pastors and lay persons, a moratorium on theological controversies, and pious educational patterns for children and clergy.

As Arndt's and Spener's writings stimulated German Pietist authors to compose their own works and to translate into German those of their counterparts in France, Holland and England, others turned the fervor and proposals into institutions (*Stiftungen*) connected with the new University of Halle. Led by August Hermann Francke, Christian Thomasius (1655–1728), Justus Breithaupt (1658–1732), Paul Anton (1661–1730), Joachim Lange (1670–1744) and Johann Michaelis (1668–1738), Halle soon became a vibrant Pietist center. Francke was most influential among the faculty, students and supporters, combining the emphasis of *Bekehrung* (conversion) and *Wiedergeburt* (rebirth) with the Bible. Breithaupt was more volatile than the others and perhaps faster to repent his rashness than most other faculty. Anton was something of an anomaly with a doctrinal emphasis akin to that of the Orthodoxists, insistence on adherence to the Book of Concord and stress on Luther. Lange and Michaelis were biblical scholars. Michaelis was a skilled Hebraist.[8] In 1742 he was preaching at the German Chapel of St. James in London, and Muhlenberg was able to be with him for a short time.[9]

The connection with Britain developed when one of Francke's former students, Anton Wilhelm Bohme, became the chaplain at the St. James Chapel and Francke's direct contact with the Society for the Propagation of Christian Knowledge (SPCK) and British royalty.[10] Through Bohme, the SPCK sponsored two Halle-trained missionaries to the East Indies. Ziegenhagen, Bohme's successor, was involved in authorizing German-Lutheran missionaries to serve their fellow Germans in British colonies. Those whom he endorsed remained partially accountable to him. The SPCK, when needed and at a later date, was involved in assisting indigent German pastors.[11]

In good Lutheran style, pastors for congregations were "called" to their positions. The term "call" was used in ways that need to be distinguished. The Augsburg Confession, Article 14 reads: "It is taught among us that nobody should publicly teach or preach or administer the sacraments in the church without a regular call." One aspect of "call" involved certification by an official ecclesiastical consistory or directory that the person is spiritually prepared, doctrinally sound and personally suitable for the office of the ministry of Word and Sacraments. Another factor was the certification and approval by appropriate ecclesiastical authorities that the situation in which the person was to enter was a legitimate venue for the person to exercise the office. The third element was the actual extending of a local call, through a congregation's authorized leaders or other proper ecclesiastically approved source, to a person to be the pastor in that setting, and the person accepting that local call.

A natural route for supplying pastors and missionaries involved the Halle authorities ("Fathers") receiving a request from the foreign field and considering whether the situation could support a viable ministry. If the decision was affirmative, a suitable candidate was invited to undertake the task. The person, if willing, spent several months in England with Ziegenhagen to be oriented to the field, the English language, and local colonial society. The Anglican bishop of London was responsible for religious affairs in British North America. It appears that names were submitted by the German chaplain at the Court of St. James and the bishop would approve them routinely. The period in England also served to give the candidate further theological instruction and practice in preaching. The Court Chaplain, when satisfied, provided the person with appropriate credentials. The individual then took ship for the colony. In instances where congregations were already established, those congregations' leaders issued a formal local call — or declined to do so. Upon arriving in the field, the pastor made the rounds of various church and governmental officials, informing them of his presence and purpose. At least that was the theory; conditions in British North America sometimes differed in practice.

The Halle *Stiftungen* included a plethora of schools and institutions. These included orphanages for boys and girls, a *Paedagogium* for the education of the children of nobles, Latin School to prepare older boys for the University, separate schools for poorer and non-nobility boys and girls, and a training center for clergy with an emphasis on sending missionaries around the world to proclaim the Gospel. In addition there was a publishing center as well as several charitable foundations. Devout wealthy, often noble, men and women supported and emulated the work at Halle. Several opened orphanages on their estates, staffing these with Halle-trained teachers and pastors. Zinzendorf's family supported Halle's enterprises. Indeed, Spener was one of the Count's godfathers. Baroness

Henriette Sophie von Gersdorf, Zinzendorf's aunt, established an orphans' school at her estate at Grosshennersdorf — and engaged Heinrich Muhlenberg to head four of its departments.

What may be termed Radical Pietism had significant roles in shaping the perceptions and actions of the Pietistic movements. Just as the sixteenth century brought to the surface sublimated movements and generated new ones, so, too, did the seventeenth and eighteenth centuries' evangelical stirrings. The so-called radicals of both times highlighted the real and assumed religious indifference of the established churches, insisting on some kind of *Wiedergeburt* and personal renewal accompanied by holy conduct and new communal patterns for believers. Because of their spiritual intensity, the radical groups separated from the established churches, and frequently splintered among themselves. The Peace of Westphalia and the prevailing societal mind-set prevented them from achieving a legal status in Europe. The political and ecclesiastical authorities criminalized their meetings, organizations and leaders. Pennsylvania was a rare haven open to them.

Several Radical Pietists and related movements are important for our purposes.[12] Jacob Boehme (1575–1624) developed a Sophia-Adamatic theology that involved the side wounds of Christ, applied female imagery to the Divine, and advocated a spirituality that virtually jettisoned the material creation as well as the visible church. Jean de Labadie (1610–1674) withdrew first from the Jesuits (1650), was a Reformed pastor when he met Spener (1659), and established his own communities independent of Reformed churches beginning in 1668. His emphasis on the centrality of *ecclesiolae in ecclesia* may have influenced Spener. Some Labadieists emigrated to Surinam and Maryland. The groups dwindled and disbanded by the end of the eighteenth century. Gottfried Arnold (1666–1714) studied at both Wittenberg and Halle. He developed further Boehme's Sophia theology, regarded the established churches as the heretics who persecuted and drove the genuine Christians underground, and advocated a sanctification-based union with God.

A trio of Radical Pietist movements that utilized Boehme, Labadie and Arnold emerge especially for Zinzendorf. First, the Philadelphia Movement. The English widow, Jane Leade (1623–1704), was given to visual and auditory revelations. Her basic teachings revolved around an eschatology that anticipated the restoration (*apokatastasis*) of all things based on God's love. Jesus was expected to return to begin the physical-spiritual thousand-year kingdom on the basis of the first resurrection. That reign would start when a truly "Philadelphia church," based on

Revelation 3:7–13, was established on earth. Leade sounded the "Philadelphia Alarm": The end was near! True believers ought to shun external church structures and rituals to focus on a true awakening of their hearts. Disunity among believers, she insisted, must cease. In place of fragmented and established churches, awakened believers must strive for unity based on mutual love in expectation of Jesus' physical and spiritual return. Christians, Leade claimed, were already united through the Spirit.

Leade's writings were translated into German. Among those who spread her ideas was Ernst Christoph Hochmann von Hohenau (1670–1721), sometime steward to Zinzendorf's maternal grandmother. A friend of Gottfried Arnold, he was converted under the ministrations of August Francke at Halle (1693). Later, while a member of the *ecclesiola* at Ebersdorf, he appears to have influenced Erdmuth Dorothea von Reuss, Zinzendorf's first wife. Jailed over thirty times for his activities, he eventually advocated adult believer baptism. A Philadelphiaist, Johann Petersen (1649–1727), traveled with his "spiritual wife," Johanna Eleanora von Merlan, to Halle where they impressed August Francke. Zinzendorf and Petersen met in Leipzig in 1726. A Radical Pietist of a different stripe, Alexander Mack (1679–1735) and his adherents were the seventeenth and eighteenth centuries' version of the pacifist Anabaptists, and they suffered a similar although less bloody fate. They practiced immersion believer baptism beginning in 1711. As did their forebears, they refused to take oaths, interpreted the Bible literally, sought to separate themselves both from the established churches and sinful brethren, and practiced mutual aid to one another. Their love and unity as well as their discipleship were rooted in attempts to recover the assumed purity of New Testament Christianity. Eventually they came to be called the Church of the Brethren. Hochmann was one of Mack's and the Brethren's supporters. The Brethren were regularly hounded out of their German, Swiss and Dutch surroundings. Most Brethren emigrated to British North America, particularly to Pennsylvania, between 1719–1740. A number settled in Philadelphia, spread through the countryside to Reading and westward toward Lancaster and York. Individuals and congregations took root in places such as Skippack, Falckner's Swamp, and Conestoga.

Johann Conrad Beissel (1690–1768) wove his way among the radical groups but eventually established his own theology and community. He spent time in Halle, but Frankean Pietism and its dedication to reforming the established Lutheran churches did not suit his spiritual needs. He had on-again, off-again relations with Mack and the Brethren. For a time he associated with the Church of the Inspirationalists, knew several Philadelphiaists, and was drawn to the French Camisards. Increasingly his Boehmist tendencies furthered his speculations on Sophia and Adamatic humanity. Based on his readings of patristic sources, he claimed celibacy was superior to matrimony. In 1720 he arrived in Boston and moved quickly to the Conestoga-Lancaster, Pennsylvania area where he reestablished contact with the Brethren. He helped establish and then served briefly as the pastor of a fledgling Brethren congregation. As the result of a personal spiritual crisis (1724), he spent some time as a hermit, adopted seventh day Sabbath observance, and went on to establish a community between Reading and Lancaster, calling it "Ephrata." On the basis of his revelatory experiences, distinctive interpretations of the Scriptures and Boehmist-based considerations, Beissel's community gave priority to the Solitaries (those covenanted to celibacy) over the married householders, proxy baptism for the dead, and a disciplined life similar to some monastic orders. Ephrata was soon a center for printing, music and distinctive art. A number of Germans attracted initially to Ephrata left for reasons ranging from disenchantment with Beissel to doctrinal disagreements. Among these one-time adherents was Conrad Weiser (1696–1760), Zinzendorf's guide in Indian country, justice of the peace, member of the Tulpehocken Lutheran congregation and eventually Muhlenberg's father-in-law. Other radical German communal groups such as the Holy Woman (as in Revelation 12) and Wissahickon Saints settled in Philadelphia and its environs, exciting the disdain of the members of established churches and non-believers. On their part, Radical communalists suspected that any spokesperson associated with the churches would attempt to lure them back to what they regarded as priestcraft and superstition.

The spread of various forms of Pietism aroused the concern of political leaders and the ire of the Orthodoxists. Löscher and others regarded Halle as largely responsible for the perceived heterodoxies, heresies and schisms that haunted Christianity. The Halle divines recognized the abuses committed in the name of heart-felt religion and were determined to thwart further disunity while attempting to restore doctrinal and ecclesial order on the mission fields as well as at home. As their roads to Philadelphia became increasingly crowded, Zinzendorf and Muhlenberg bumped into some movements, persons, misconceptions and attitudes that formed their views of each other and their visions for the future.

Endnotes to Chapter Two

1   *Luther's Works*, Vol. 31, p. 25.

2   The documents in the Book of Concord, in addition to the Apostles', Nicene and Athanasian Creeds, are the Augsburg Confession, Apology of the Augsburg Confession, Smalcald Articles, Treatise on the Power and Primacy of the Pope, Small Catechism, Large Catechism, and the Formula of Concord. The Latin and German texts of the Augsburg Confession presented at the Diet of Augsburg (1530) are not known. Melanchthon revised the Confession several times. The "Altered" versions were tilted, said foes, toward a Calvinist understanding of the Sacrament of the Altar. Both Orthodoxists and Pietists came to rely on what was deemed as the "Unaltered" version.

3   Preus, Vol. 1, p. 30. The rest of the sketch is based on points made by Preus, Vol. 1, pp. 27–44. He observed that the Orthodox came to appreciate Melanchthon's orderly articulation of Luther's theology. The disputes between Melanchthon and his contemporary Gnesio-Lutherans revolved around his views of the Sacrament of the Altar, possible modifications of Luther's views about the corruption and helplessness of the human will, willingness to compromise with Catholics in the aftermath of Lutheran military defeats, the realities of imperial politics, and his alterations of the Augsburg Confession.

4   Erb, *Pietists*, p. 7. The quotation is from Stoeffler's *German Pietism During the Eighteenth Century* (Leiden: Brill, 1973), p. ix.

5   See Schmidt and Jannasch, pp. ix–xlviii.

6   Erb, *Pietists*. The Introduction is by Stoeffler. See p. xii.

7   See Erb, *Pietists*, pp. 11–17.

8   See the following references in the *Journals:* Breithaupt, II, p. 598 and III, p. 724; Anton (sometimes Anthon), I, p. 499; II, pp. 134, 201, 437, 473, 598; III, p. 379; Lange, I, p. 22, II, p. 421; Michaelis, I, pp. 18–20, 462; II, p. 761; III, p. 50, 72, 82, 85, 575. See also Snyder, pp. 56–72.

9   Muhlenberg refers to each of these as his teachers and resources for his religious and intellectual development. Zinzendorf surely knew and may have studied directly under Francke, Anton and Lange.

10 In 1698 Francke became a member of the newly established SPCK.

11 A "legacy" or home for such ministers was established at Providence before and during the Revolution.

12 Further and intertwined discussions of Boehme, de Labadie, Arnold, Leade, Mack, and Beissel are available in Erb, *Pietists*; Durnbaugh (especially pp. 8–102); Erb, *Beissel* (especially pp. 3–37); and Nielsen, Vol. I, (especially pp. 9–52 for Jane Leade and the Philadelphia Movement).

Chapter Three
ASPECTS OF PENNSYLVANIA'S CONTEXTS
PRIOR TO 1742

Pennsylvania was different. Charles II (reigned 1660–1685) opened the Charter of Pennsylvania (1681):

> Whereas our trusty and well-beloved subject, William Penn, esquire, son and heir of Sir William Penn, deceased (out of a commendable desire to enlarge our English empire, and promote such useful commodities which may be of benefit to us and our dominions, as also to reduce the savage natives, by gentle and just manners, to the love of civil society and Christian religion), has humbly besought leave of us to transport an ample colony unto a certain country hereinafter described, in the parts of America not yet cultivated and planted, and has likewise so humbly besought Our Royal Majesty to give, grant, and confirm all the said country, with certain privileges and jurisdictions, requisite for good government and safety of the said country and colony to him and his heirs forever.[1]

Penn (1644–1718) and his heirs owned Pennsylvania and had almost complete authority and power over the inhabitants, trade, land distribution, governmental structure, and social life. The son of Charles I was careful to include provisions that demanded the loyalty of proprietors and settlers to the crown. Penn sought the inclusion in the Charter of a clause that granted broad religious freedom, but settled for a provision that if twenty inhabitants petitioned the Bishop of London for an Anglican preacher or preachers to "reside within the said province without any denial or molestation whatsoever," the Bishop would endeavor to meet their request. Instead of the Charter's specifying the establishment of a church, Article XXXV of Penn's first (draft) Charter of Liberties (1681, also known as the first Frame of Government) provided that everyone living within the province who "confess and acknowledge the one almighty and eternal God to be the creator, upholder, and ruler of the world, and that hold themselves obliged in conscience to live peaceably and justly in civil society, shall in no ways be molested or prejudiced for their religious persuasion or practice in matters of faith and worship, nor shall they be compelled at any time to frequent or maintain any religious worship, place or ministry whatever."[2]

The Royal Charter and the draft Charter of Liberties set a tone and provided the conditions that puzzled and provoked Zinzendorf and Muhlenberg. Religious, social and economic conditions in several other colonies indicate that Pennsylvania was significantly different. With the exception of Rhode Island, the New England colonies restricted political and overt social power to those devout white men who shared in the Puritan spectrum of theology and morality. The New England socio-economic base centered in nucleated villages and outlying farms, pre-supposed an English ethnic commonality, and, because of the scarcity of arable land for subsistence farming, depended on commercial activity. New England, therefore, did not encourage dissenters, continentals, non-English Britishers, or land-seekers. South Carolina, established to grow food for the sugar-producing Barbados settlements, developed a planta-tion-based society dependent on general agriculture, rice and cattle. Given the climate, malarial conditions in the swampy coastlands and high levels of other diseases, whites preferred to obtain African slaves to labor, of-ten literally to death. The white colonists usually did not come in family units, but often were unattached male fortune-seeking minor aristocrats.

Because of the perceived and genuine reality of attacks from Spanish Florida, Britain found it expedient to charter the last of its Atlantic colo-nies, Georgia. General James Oglethorpe (1696–1785) obtained the char-ter for a proprietary colony in 1732. Oglethorpe, well-disposed toward the Moravians and Lutherans, encouraged their settling in the colony. The philanthropist-general intended to found a well-ordered experiment-colony whose moral codes and government reformed the behavior of marginalized persons and transported criminals. He sought to include Salzburg Lutheran and Moravian refugees in order to provide diligent, honest and pious leaven in the colonial mixture. In 1740 and 1742 the General launched successful attacks against Florida. Oglethorpe's ex-pectation that Moravians would join his armed forces weighed in the Moravian settlers' decision to leave Georgia for Quaker Pennsylvania.

Penn's pamphlets covered and his representatives canvassed Britain and the German states, encouraging responsible individuals and families to be part of Pennsylvania. Promises of cheap land and freedom from as well as for religious affiliations attracted thousands. As a result, the colony had the third largest and most ethnically and religiously diverse population in British North America. It was a country of family farms and businesses. Although one might serve a two or three years inden-ture to pay for passage across the Atlantic, the conditions under which persons worked and the final settlement on completion of service made Pennsylvania the "richest poor man's land." From 1710 to 1760 the colony's population went from 24,400 to 184,000. In the same period, Philadelphia grew from fewer than 9,000 to 16,000 inhabitants. Be-tween 1727 and 1742 some ninety-five shiploads of German immigrants arrived through the port of Philadelphia alone. Forty thousand Germans and thirty thousand Scotch-Irish arrived between 1726 and 1755. Many of the Germans came from the Palatinate and Hannover. The influx of Germans fueled suspicions that an ethnic and political advantage that favored the Anglo-Americans would be lost. In 1727 colonial leaders required arriving immigrants to take an oath of loyalty to the crown and colonial authorities before disembarking. A 1728 act to tax all foreign immigrants forty shillings, clearly aimed against the Germans, was repealed in 1730.

Safety and stability also marked Pennsylvania. Georgia and South Carolina had to cope with threats, real and imagined, from Florida. Charleston may have been the Atlantic colonies' richest city, but when Muhlenberg passed through it (1742), South Carolina was still reeling from devastating Indian attacks and a slave rebellion. The city was emerging from a justified siege mentality, its commerce crippled. New York and New England were jittery over French menaces based in Canada. Conflicts among Indian tribes in those colonies caused migratory dislocations that the white authorities did not fully comprehend. Penn established essentially peaceful relationships with the dominant Iroquois Confederacy. The Moravians gained the Indians' respect and friendship, thereby helping to make Pennsylvania peaceful.

Penn's Quaker commitments extended into political, social and economic structures and attitudes. If each person has the Inner Light, then there can be no restrictions on a person's religious expressions as long as the expressions are not treasonous, harmful to others or blasphemous toward God. There would be neither an official religion nor established church in the colony, although the 1682 Charter of Liberties assumed that office holders would believe in Jesus (Article XXXIV). Penn's 1681 draft of the Charter of Liberties reflected Charles II's expectations about a profitable, loyal and peaceful colony and Penn's vision of the Holy Experiment based on freedom of religious expression and practice.[4]

Penn's vision and practice had two effects. The first opened Pennsylvania to a panoply of religious groups. Along with German Reformed, Moravians and Lutherans, came Catholics, Jews, Schwenkfelders, Mennonites, various adult baptizing groups, sabbatarians, illuminati, and adventists. Anglicans and Quakers were supplemented by English Presbyterians, Congregationalists, baptists and unitarians. The second result was unintended: the development of the "Pennsylvania Religion," indifference toward and even hostility to all forms of religion. Europeans disillusioned with ecclesiastical politics and warfare or Enlightenment critics of Christian doctrines found they could avoid or disdain religion in general. They did not have to be part of any religious group or be subject to an established church. Others were too busy trying to eke out a living on the farms and in the shops of Pennsylvania. Indeed, Muhlenberg and Zinzendorf often encountered active hostility toward organized religion and particularly the heartfelt evangelical piety — and sobriety — they espoused. "Pietist" was a derisive term.

Both effects were heightened by the Great Awakening. It was extended in time (roughly from the 1720s to 1750) and broad in geographic scope, while being distinctive in particular localities yet sufficiently general to have overall characteristics. Influenced and nourished by continental Pietism, Anglo-American Puritanism and British Evangelicalism, it was marked by American versions of individualism and belief in personal moral agency. The Awakening promoted criticisms of established religious institutions and their clerical defenders. Emotional responses to fervent preachers and challenges posed by itinerant ministers roused opposition not only from settled pastors who felt threatened but also from articulate leaders concerned for doctrinal and ecclesiastical order. The Awakening united supporters and foes across theological boundaries. Among the Awakening's negative results were the fracturing of ecclesial communities, the development of still more Protestant splinters, and the growth of religious indifference.

Pennsylvania was not as agitated by revivals as were other colonies. Perhaps Pennsylvania's religious pluralism, language barriers among the inhabitants, and absence of numerous home-grown charismatic leaders contributed to the lower-key responses. But the colony did experience that Grand Itinerant, George Whitefield (1714–1770) and the local Presbyterian, Gilbert Tennent (1703–1764). German and Swedish Pennsylvanians were moved by the Awakening to a far lesser degree than their British counterparts. Largely because of his involvement with Moravians in England and Georgia even before finalizing the plans that led to the establishment of Nazareth, Pennsylvania, Whitefield was Stephen Benezet's houseguest (May, 1740), turning down an invitation to lodge with his Philadelphia printer, Benjamin Franklin (1706–1790).

By 1742 the Awakening was waning and in disarray. Anglican and other pulpits were closing to Whitefield, himself an Anglican priest. His American fellow-traveler, Gilbert Tennent, preached and published his inflammatory sermon, "The Danger of An Unconverted Ministry," in 1740, thereby making himself and Whitefield unwelcome in most congregations. Whitefield adroitly adapted the British Evangelical-

Methodist practice of proclaiming his message in city public places and rural fields. The existence of sincere as well as unscrupulous itinerant clergy and of shady figures claiming ministerial standing preceded the Awakening. German Lutherans were being served and occasionally bilked by itinerants of dubious, often discredited credentials.

Swedes were provoked by Lars Tollstadius (died 1706). So certain was he that he would be assigned to a pastoral post in New Sweden, when the appointment did not materialize, he went to the congregations anyway. He asserted, falsely, that he was sent by the Swedish king and Church to replace Pastor Andrew Rudman in southern Jersey. Tollstadius' deception, even when revealed by the arrival of the officially appointed replacement, did not prevent his inserting himself into an already troubled congregation. His alleged immorality and other scrapes with the law terminated when he drowned accidentally.[5] Ever afterward, Swedish authorities were suspicious of persons who claimed to be pastors but who were unable to produce their official documents. That suspicion influenced Swedish attitudes toward itinerants generally and toward Zinzendorf and Muhlenberg specifically. Growing animosity over itinerancy, attacks on the regular clergy, and emotional excesses in the late 1730s and early 1740s colored the religious-political-social context of the colony when Muhlenberg and Zinzendorf met in Philadelphia.

The Philadelphia area is the stage for the encounter. Broadly, the only Reformed and Lutheran congregations in Philadelphia shared the same building on Arch Street, then called Mulberry Street. There was a Reformed congregation and a Lutheran congregation about five miles away in Germantown. The Lutheran congregations in Providence and New Hannover were in close proximity to each other and about a day's ride from Philadelphia. A scattering of other Lutheran and Reformed congregations dotted the landscape north and west of the city. Plainly, the overwhelming majority of German immigrants, whether Lutheran or Reformed, had neither the inclination nor time to establish congregations and to engage in churchly activities. Certainly their Fatherlands' religious wars, polemics and stodgy ministry as well as Enlightenment-spurred rejections of organized religion played significant roles in the dismal state of congregational development in the colonies.

The Moravian immigrants were different; they came as religious communities for the purpose of living their faith. While that could mean settling together in Herrnhut-like communities, they also could be the Lord's leaven in the lumps of other congregations. The Brethren were serious about carrying on missionary work among the Indians and in assisting fellow Christians to deepen their devotion to the Savior. Because of Zinzendorf's influence, the Moravians preferred to be part of existing congregations rather than to establish rival or parallel worshiping communities. From the perspective of the Reformed, Lutheran and other Protestant bodies, to mix metaphors, Moravian leaven could appear as wolves in sheep's clothing or agents gradually subverting congregations into Moravian fellowships.

More specifically, the context discloses sets of relationships and places that are essential to understanding the 1742 controversy. Included in the British 1664 seizure from the Dutch were the remnants of New Sweden in what is now northern Delaware and southern New Jersey contiguous to Philadelphia.[3] Five Swedish Lutheran churches and several preaching points remained in 1742, and were served by clergy sent from the homeland. The Germans who entered Pennsylvania rarely came from Saxony or Prussia. The earliest arrivals who had religious commitments often were associated with groups that separated from the official Lutheran and Reformed churches. Because of their communal organization and antipathy toward clerical authority as well as traditional ceremonialism, they managed their own worship and other spiritual needs through articulate lay leaders who were not reluctant to argue with either ordained clergy or visiting noblemen. The Reformed and Lutheran settlers also spread into the countryside, although a significant number resided in the larger towns and cities as artisans, tradespersons, merchants, etc. Many Germans gathered in what came to be called "Germantown." In spite of the absence of officially-trained and sanctioned German-speaking pastors and catechists, lay persons gathered for prayers, worship and communal observances in what developed into congregations. How these Reformed and Lutheran persons and groups were to be served by pastors became a pressing issue for them and influenced the colony as well.

The Lutheran Amsterdam Consistory handled the certification and sending of pastors to New York. In 1725 the Consistory sent Wilhelm Christopher Berkenmeyer (1686–1755) to serve especially in the Hudson and Raritan river valleys. Diligent and tough, he was especially hostile toward imposter-pastors, that is, those who claimed falsely to be accredited ministers of Word and Sacraments. A few of these men might serve faithfully and well, or at least not cause serious trouble. Others were incompetent or unbalanced or even swindlers and lechers. Berkenmeyer developed collegial relationships with the Swedish clergy in what had been New Sweden (southern New Jersey, northern Delaware and "Wicaco," a section of Philadelphia now part of what is called "south

Philadelphia"). By 1735 Berkenmeyer adapted the Reformed-influenced Amsterdam Consistory pattern for congregational polity to fit the colonial situation. On the whole, Berkenmeyer's adaptation was used by Lutheran congregations in Pennsylvania until Muhlenberg altered the pattern in 1762. Berkenmeyer's pattern provided for a local congregational consistory or council composed of a pastor, lay deacons and elders. In practice the lay deacons and elders were appointed by the pastor for life or until resignation or removal. In the absence of a called pastor, the existing lay deacons and elders selected other congregational members to be part of the consistory. Congregations did not vote to call a pastor; the lay deacons and elders did.[6]

Philadelphia's German Lutherans often sought to have their spiritual needs met through German-speaking Swedish priests (the Swedish Lutheran term for pastors) at Wicaco. In 1726 Peter Tranberg (d. 1748) and Andreas Windrufwa arrived from Sweden, but the latter died within two years. Tranberg ministered to the Swedish congregations at Penns Neck (New Jersey), Christiana (Delaware) and Wicaco. In the last named congregation, Johannes Dylander was the priest in charge from 1737 to his untimely death in November, 1741, and had the archbishop of Uppsala's authority to ordain pastors. Olaf Malander, a candidate for ordination, helped the Lutheran priests. Dylander died before Malander could be ordained, and Tranberg did not assume that the archbishop's authority devolved on him. Malander, suspected of Moravian sympathies and later imprisoned for a short time for debt, left the colony for Rhode Island in 1742 and eventually joined the Brethren. Dylander and Tranberg developed highly positive relationships with the Anglican clergy and the German Lutherans and Reformed. The overworked Swedish priests often served to lead worship for the Anglicans at Christ Church. Tranberg regularly held services in Wicaco in Swedish, German and English. Dylander proposed to Philadelphia's German Lutherans and Reformed that they jointly acquire a building in which to hold their separate services so that they would not have to trudge to Wicaco for worship. Dylander also married the daughter of the wealthy Swedish merchant, Peter Koch. Koch became the chief lay leader of the Wicaco congregation and Muhlenberg's firm supporter and close friend. He also infuriated Zinzendorf. Tranberg, officially the rector of the Christiana congregation, was challenged by laymen in that congregation concerning his authority in temporal affairs. He knew that this could be the first step to a more general challenge to his ministerial authority and a prelude to schism. He and Koch were, therefore, sensitive toward any movements

28

and persons who attempted to question the roles and legitimacy of the clergy.

Germans, both ordained and unordained, began to arrive and function among their *Landsleute* (fellow countrymen). Anton Jacob Henkel (1668–1728) probably was ordained before he arrived in 1717. He settled as a farmer near New Hannover. He organized what became the first German Lutheran congregation in Pennsylvania (New Hannover), and may have organized the congregations in Providence and Germantown. He was known among the Philadelphia Lutherans and had a hand in organizing them into a congregation. In addition, he urged the Germans at Tulpehocken (west of what is now Reading) to build a church (1727). Before his death from a fall from his horse, he was challenged by the imposter-hunting Berkenmeyer, accused before the civil authorities of performing weddings illegally, jailed briefly, and publicly humiliated. The congregations at New Hannover, Providence, Philadelphia and Tulpehocken became the relevant flash points in the 1742 controversy.

The situations of the Lutheran congregations changed with the arrival in 1728 of two Johann Casper Stövers (also given as Stiver in Moravian sources and Stober sometimes by Muhlenberg), Senior (d. 1738) and Junior (1704?–1779) and, in 1732, Johann Christian Schultz (also Schultze, 1701–1744?). The Stövers were close relatives of the Orthodox theologian, Johann Fresenius of Darmstadt, a vociferous opponent of the Moravians, Zinzendorf and anyone associated with the Hallesians. As far as Stöver the Younger was concerned, the terms Pietism, Halle, Moravian and Zinzendorf were interchangeable. For years he accused Muhlenberg of being a secret Moravian who was out to subvert Lutheranism in order to Moravianize Lutheran congregations. The senior Stöver served in Virginia and North Carolina, apparently becoming well-to-do and entangled in an immoral relationship. He returned to Germany to raise funds for the mission among the Germans and to buy books for the Lutheran congregationally-sponsored schools. He died at sea on the return journey (1738).

Both Stövers came under Schultz's influence and direction. The latter claimed to have been ordained privately as a Lutheran missionary for Pennsylvania on behalf of the Darmstadt Consistory, but he never produced the documents attesting to his call and ordination. Once he obtained the local call to be pastor of the Lutheran congregations in Philadelphia, New Hannover and Providence, he proposed that two laypersons from the congregations accompany him on a fund-raising expedition to Britain and Germany to bolster the congregations' missions. The three congregations raised a substantial sum to support him and pay for the passage to Europe. Immediately before his departure, he privately ordained both Stövers in a barn at Providence (1733).[7] Stöver, probably at Schultz's suggestion, urged the Philadelphia, New Hannover and Providence congregations to unite in seeking a single pastor from German sources. Schultz and his companions departed with letters of recommendation from the colony's governor, Patrick Gordon. They arrived in London, where Ziegenhagen helped them raise money. Schultz ran into undefined legal problems, was arrested, left for Germany and vanished with most of the cash. A report from Halle indicated that he died in 1744.[8] Naturally, the congregations were embittered but were not unwilling to apply for another pastor from Schultz's supposed source of authority, the Darmstadt Consistory. They also turned to Halle.

In 1734 the United Congregations, as they called themselves, petitioned the Halle Fathers for a pastor. The Fathers responded with a set of conditions before they would attempt to locate a pastor: he would have

> to be ordained before leaving Germany after receiving a call from the congregations according to a form which [the Halle authorities] provided. The duties of the congregations to pastors are enumerated and especially enjoined on [the congregations]. A fixed compensation in money must be promised in advance, as the payment of the salary in tobacco or produce would involve the pastor in secular business. In the form of call, not only necessary sustenance is pledged, but also traveling expenses to Germany, should a pastor desire to return.[9]

Given colonial realities, which were beyond the Halle Fathers' ken, these were stringent conditions, yet given the risks a pastor would undertake and the likelihood of a congregational default, perhaps understandable. The United Congregations remonstrated that they were unable to meet the requirements, pled poverty, the instability of the times, and cited the example of Schultz. In 1737, they addressed an angry letter to Ziegenhagen, expressing their dismay that "It looks as if money had more power than any spiritual principle has to urge you to labor for the spreading of the kingdom of God...."[10] The Fathers did not respond until they heard that the Count was in Pennsylvania. Then they waived all the previous stipulations as they dispatched Muhlenberg without a call and did not even notify the congregations that he was on the way. In the meantime, others were providing the congregations with pastoral ministry.

The temperature of the volatile mix of persons and interests increased even more on August 25, 1741 when the younger Stöver's former theological teacher, ex-Hallesian and defrocked Lutheran pastor, Valentin Kraft (1680–1751) arrived in Philadelphia. Muhlenberg described, probably accurately although with malice, Kraft's procedure and aims:

> Mr. Kraft had traveled through the whole province of Pennsylvania, appointed deacons and elders here and there, and established a general presbytery in the whole country, and a special presbytery, as he called it, in Philadelphia. And besides all this, he organized a consistory of which he was the president and Mr. Stöver the *assessor*…. The purpose of the presbytery was to make it possible for Valentin Kraft and his *assessor* to travel around the country and carry on his trade with the Holy Sacraments. The consistory served the purpose of letting him ordain a few more lazy and drunken schoolmasters and place them as preachers in vacant places. He enjoys great respect because our poor, ignorant Lutherans are pushed into the corner by the Moravians on the one hand, and on the other are duped by his windy boasting.[11]

Kraft claimed he was sent by a consistory to be the superintendent-inspector of all German Lutheran churches with the authority to ordain men to be pastors, and charged with organizing German Lutheran pastors into a ministerial consistory. Of course, he had no documents to prove these claims, but said they would arrive shortly from Germany. They never did. Stöver gladly allied himself with Kraft and was given the title of his adjunct or assessor. Kraft, as Muhlenberg quickly realized, was no friend of Pietism or Halle. By that August, the Philadelphia congregation was in an uproar because of an incident involving Zinzendorf and his adjunct. Kraft inserted himself into the Arch Street congregation's affairs. He also claimed authority over the New Hannover and Providence congregations. Stöver was involved in the turmoil at Tulpehocken as he supported one of his associates in a complex power play against the Count and the Moravians for pastoral leadership.[12]

Among the German Reformed, Johann Philip Böhm (also Böhme, 1683–1749), a teacher who arrived in the colony in 1720, began to hold services. An imposter-pastor challenged his credentials. Böhm responded by applying for ordination through the Dutch Reformed clergy in New York. The Amsterdam Classis had granted its Senior the authority to ordain qualified men. Böhm was ordained in Philadelphia on November 23, 1729. He was understandably vigilant in insuring that imposter-pastors and other unauthorized persons did not inveigle their ways into Reformed congregations. He served a large number of Reformed congregations in the Philadelphia area. Because of his heavy responsibilities, he held services only one Sunday a month in the building owned originally by Andrew Hamilton that the Reformed and Lutherans shared on Arch Street. [13] The Lutherans had its use for their services three times a month. Legally, the Lutherans were the lease-holders — a point that had later consequences. Böhm was highly respected by the English, Swedes and Germans, and thoroughly hostile toward the Brethren and the Count. He was alert to any movement either would make to wriggle their way into the Reformed congregations. [14]

The Reformed congregation in Germantown was led by a licensed lay preacher, Johann Bechtel (1690–1758). Bechtel, a carpenter-mechanic, served the congregation for sixteen years without remuneration, holding prayer meetings every day in his home. After a reluctant beginning, he became one of the Count's most ardent and valuable supporters. [15]

Pennsylvania's politics and personalities also added to the 1742 controversy. The founder set up a bicameral provincial system in which a 72-man Council, which included the proprietor-appointed governor, proposed and implemented laws, and an up to 200-man Assembly had the power to accept, reject or amend any legislation approved by the Council. It was a formula for gridlock. According to the colony's election procedures for the provincial Assembly, adopted in 1706, elections for the Assembly were held annually on October first by eligible freeholders, that is, male white citizens who owned property and paid taxes on that property in rural areas or who resided in urban areas and paid the taxes. If a person had both an urban residence and rural property, he could vote in both places. About a week before the elections, the list of qualified voters was drawn up and the persons so designated met in electoral districts to select election inspectors. The inspectors supervised the election process and monitored the activities of the often-disorderly crowds who turned out on election day to support candidates. Quaker influence and campaigning was evident and several Friends meetings urged members to vote only for fellow Friends or persons sympathetic to Quaker interests. On the whole, the Germans sided with the Quaker establishment, thereby allowing the Quakers to dominate the provincial Assembly. The situation in Philadelphia was more mixed, where an elected city council and board of aldermen worked with the mayor and his officials. The Provincial Assembly, dominated by a Quaker oligarchy known as the "Country Party," was loathe to vote any tax increases or allocate funds for what the commercial interests of Philadelphia were convinced was essential for the development of the city. Opposing the Country Party was the Philadelphia-based and Lancaster-supported "City" or "Gentleman's Party." As was Philadelphia's Council and Board of

Aldermen, the Gentlemen's Party was dominated by Anglican and Presbyterian merchants and artisans.

From the founder's death (1718) until her death (1727), Penn's second wife, Hannah, wielded enormous influence. Penn's three sons, John (d. 1746), Richard (d. 1771) and Thomas (d. 1775), repudiated their father's faith and became Anglicans. Their religious shift pitted the proprietors and the Quakers against each other in matters dealing with the fiscal, social and political futures of the colony. Since the proprietors appointed the governor, his relationships with the Assembly usually were acrimonious. The Provincial Council often proposed the raising of money for the erection of public buildings, but the Assembly refused approval or simply stalled. The governor was assailed by the Assembly and pressured by the proprietors. The impasse between governor, proprietors and Assembly was heightened by the personalities of the leaders involved, a troubled economy and the expectations of the Gentlemen's Party. Accusations of bribery led to the removal of William Keith by Hannah Penn in 1726. His forced departure was followed by serious Assembly election day riots in October. Again, the Germans, whether enfranchised or not, supported the Quakers overwhelmingly. Keith was succeeded by Patrick Gordon, 1726–1736.

During Gordon's administration, three Philadelphia-based men, dubbed the "Prominent Gentlemen," rose to and maintained eminence: Andrew Hamilton (d. 1741), William Allen (1704–1780) and Joseph Turner (1701–1783).[16] They were the wealthiest and among the most influential men in the colony — and among the most resented or at least held in wary regard by the Quakers and the Germans. Hamilton studied law in England and was admitted to the bar through Gray's Inn (1712–13). Apparently he made the acquaintance of the Penns while in London, and gained their confidence. He settled in Philadelphia where he quickly became the colony's attorney-general. As a reward for services rendered, the Penns granted him 153 acres of prime land in the heart of Philadelphia, including the site of what is now Independence Hall. In 1727, after Keith's removal from office, Hamilton was appointed recorder of deeds and prothonotary of the Pennsylvania Supreme Court — highly lucrative and influential positions that also allowed him to become a major land investor through his receiving first-hand information about newly surveyed and available territory. His real estate dealings made him one of the largest landowners in Bucks County. He served in the Provincial Assembly as a representative from Bucks. German suspicions about Hamilton were understandable; he wrote soon-repealed legislation that imposed an arrival tax on immigrants. Highly respected for his organizational and rhetorical skills, Hamilton was elected Speaker of the Assembly from 1729–32 and 1734–39.

Joseph Turner (1701–1783) was a British sea captain who settled in Philadelphia in 1713–14. In 1729 he became a city councilmen and in 1741 was a city alderman. Turner and Allen became partners in an import-export business originally owned by Allen's father. Together they bought and sold horses, slaves, rum, coaches and other commodities and invested heavily in Bucks County iron mines, exporting pig iron to England.

Allen was born to a Scotch-Irish family that immigrated to Philadelphia before William Allen's birth. He was baptized and remained a staunch Presbyterian for his whole life. His father was a wealthy merchant. He spent his youth and early manhood in Britain, attended Cambridge, and also studied law. On his father's death (1725), he returned to Philadelphia to take over the thriving family export-import business. Hamilton's daughter, Margaret, married Allen in 1733. On Hamilton's death (1741), his property passed to his daughter, that is, really to Allen. His holdings in Philadelphia included what came to be known as the Mount Airy section of the city.[17] The 1737 "Walking Purchase" gave men like Allen significant opportunities to purchase land questionably acquired from the Indians. Allen was never a man to miss an opportunity. As a result the new land together with his previous holdings in Philadelphia and Bucks County included what is presently most of Lehigh and Northampton Counties, including the land Allen later sold to George Whitefield at a handsome profit and on which Whitefield planned to settle the Moravians from Georgia. In 1739 Hamilton retired in disgust from public life, and Allen took his post as recorder.

In the wake of the 1726 election day riots, Allen was appointed to head a commission charged with reforming the system of selecting the election inspectors. His proposals were rejected by the Assembly largely because the Quakers did not trust him. If Allen's skills as a lawyer and judge (he was appointed judge of a special court in 1739 and chief justice in 1750) were arguable, his political influence and range of control were indisputable. He served as a representative to the Assembly from Philadelphia County (1731–1739), and mayor of Philadelphia (1735) in addition to recorder.

Thomas Penn, the proprietor who exercised authority over the colony, appointed George Thomas, a wealthy planter from Antigua, to be governor

(1738–1747). He struck a deal with the fiscally pressed Penns by which Governor Thomas was to pay them a stipulated annual amount or a percentage of the income he derived from his office. Thomas, however, did not make as much money as he expected from the fees and other emoluments for his expenses were greater than anticipated and the economy was in a decline. One cause for his disappointment was the Assembly's resistance to vote any taxes or funds for projects that the governor and others considered important for the economic advance and social development of the colony. The political support of non-Quaker immigrants was of great concern to those engaged in government.

A pressing issue was the proposal to raise troops for a militia. Along with raising troops was the necessity of raising funds to equip and train them. Attached to that issue was the question of whether or not militiamen from the proprietary colony of Pennsylvania would or ought to serve beyond the colony's borders in order to defend or otherwise fight in another colony. The so-called War of Jenkin's Ear (1739) and the declared war of Britain against France and Spain (1740) precipitated a crisis. Could Friends, in good conscience, finance the acquisition of weapons and countenance the training of men for the purpose of maiming and killing other men? Further, while other British colonies, proprietary and royal, were in danger of enemy attacks, most of Pennsylvania was not. Yet, the Charter bound the proprietors to be loyal to the king, and those other colonies were British, too. Generally, German voters and indentured servants were reluctant to agree to any arrangement which could be used as a precedent to establish conscription or governmentally-forced military service. Such military obligations, they thought, were left behind in their Fatherlands. Germans, then, tended to side with the Quaker-run Assembly on fiscal and military matters.

If Thomas were to overcome or neutralize the Quaker bloc, he had to wean the Germans from voting with the Friends. Intimidation might be an effective weaner. Allen, Turner and Hamilton had interests in virtually every potentially lucrative enterprise in Pennsylvania, so they also were deeply concerned to protect the colony from marauders and all British foes by land and sea, and their investments from Quaker rivals. The Gentlemen wanted and needed the militia. Allen felt that the Quakers used fear and trickery to make the German voters and those not yet able to vote think that conscription into a militia and that taxes laid to equip troops would be enacted if the Gentlemen gained power. The Germans backed the Country Party in the elections of 1739, 1740 and 1741. In addition, a 1740 British act eased the naturalization of Germans as citizens, thereby opening the way for increased numbers of Germans to the franchise. German voters were a key bloc in political considerations.

The winters of 1740–1742 were particularly harsh with deep snow-drifts and severe ice storms. A yellow fever epidemic stalked the colonies from New York to the Carolinas in the same years. Death and appeals to the divine Judge-Deliverer became part of the already-existing religious revivals. In the same period, Governor Thomas was forced to report to the proprietors that profits had fallen and the treasury was being rapidly depleted. Lean years were following the fat good times; there were bread riots in Philadelphia in 1739. Increasingly, provincial elections were charged with divisive rhetoric. When Hamilton withdrew from public life in 1739, and died in August 1741, Allen and other Gentlemen stepped aside from the October 1741 Assembly election. The result was a landslide victory for the Country Party. Allen, Mayor Clement Plumstead, William Till (mayor after October 1, 1742), Turner, and Thomas knew that the elections of 1742 would be difficult because rowdy crowds might take to the streets again. The Gentlemen's Party anticipated the renewal of an election reform act in time for the 1742 vote, but again hostility between the governor and the Assembly prevented the implementation of the renewal. Allen attempted to strike an agreement with some Quaker leaders that would have increased and balanced the number of inspectors between the two parties, but the night before the election, the Quakers rejected the proposal. That meant an inadequate number of election inspectors was on duty on October 1, 1742.

The election in Philadelphia was a disaster for the Gentlemen. The polling place was on the courthouse's second floor. While the details are unclear, Turner and John Sober were determined to drive the "broad-hats," as the Quakers were labeled, and their German supporters out of the building and intimidate others from voting. Sixty to eighty well-liquored sailors were hired to attack the Friends and their friends. The attempt failed miserably, as many shocked citizens changed their intentions and voted against the Gentlemen. Although Allen probably had no direct hand in the affair, the Assembly censured Allen, Turner and Sober for the riot.

Instead of using the stick to detach the Germans from the Quakers, Allen and the faction he headed promised the Germans that there would be no law requiring service in a militia unless England went to war against the traditional German foe, France, and Germans who opposed military service on the basis of religious scruples would be given the same exemption as was offered to Friends. The Governor, Allen and the Gentlemen also realized that if they were able to enlist the support of prominent and potentially prominent German leaders, those leaders might influence their constituents to follow suit. Pennsylvania politics, therefore, contributed to the reception given Muhlenberg by the Governor and city officials.

Given his knack to gather information and to take advantage of opportunities presented to him, Muhlenberg probably was well aware of the governor's precarious but still powerful position as he presented himself to Thomas. Zinzendorf had the same information and was active in the colony for a year, yet he did not appear to have perceived Thomas' need to achieve an advantage over the elected colonial Assembly while respecting their elected status.[18]

Thomas had to court the Germans, Swedes and other immigrant groups who had achieved voting status. Hannoverian immigrants were favorably disposed to George II, for he was also the ruler of their homeland and vowed to march to its defense. Nevertheless, rumors of the machinations of the Young Pretender made it necessary for the British authorities to require settlers to swear or affirm their loyalty to the English crown. Because Zinzendorf was officially a member of the Dresden court, he was accorded diplomatic status and was not required to take the oath. After a momentary demurral because he had already sworn fealty to George II as ducal-elector of Hannover, Muhlenberg quickly acceded to the formality on December 28, 1742.[19]

The governor, needing the support of the authority-respecting Germans and Swedes, would attempt to resolve any disputes among them quickly. On July 18, 1742, a serious and somewhat violent disturbance occurred at the building where the Lutheran and Reformed congregations worshiped, the Lutheran congregation fractured into two factions, and a law suit was brought by the Count's supporters. Thomas and Till would have to deal carefully with the Germans. By late December Thomas had met and listened to the Count and to Muhlenberg. He knew that the former planned to return to Europe in early 1743 and that Muhlenberg was committed to staying for at least three years. He also knew the newspaper diatribes for, against and by Zinzendorf. The personal agendas of Philadelphia's and the colony's leaders and political considerations became factors at least in Muhlenberg's mind in the controversy and the reports he gave of it.

Endnotes to Chapter Three

1 Soderlund, p. 41. Charles II was paying off a debt of £16,000.

2 Soderlund, p. 132. The approved 1682 Charter of Liberties is also known as the Frame of Government. Article XXXVIII had a number of qualifications and provisions such as reserving Sunday as a day of rest from "common daily labor" so that the people would be better disposed to worship God according to their "understandings." Article XXXVII banned and threatened severe punishments for "wildness and looseness," enumerating a catalogue of vices, violence and amusements.

3 Delaware was controlled by Penn until 1701 when it was chartered as a separate colony.

4 See Soderlund, pp. 98–99.

5 For a brief description of Tollstadius' activities and the Swedish situation, see Geissler, pp. 5–32.

6 See Nelson, pp. 53–55.

7 S. H. Gapp's entry for Stöver, Jr. in *A History of the Beginnings*, p. 161 is mistaken at several points. Gapp states that the ordination took place in a tavern. This appears to be residue from a report that has the ordination at "Trappe," another name for the Providence area. The popular etiology of Trappe was that a German merchant set up a store in a cave near the road. Liquor was among the wares sold to neighbors and travelers. Some said Stöver, who had a serious drinking problem, was a frequent customer, and the local people called the place a trap. More likely the name derived from the Anglicized version of the German word for step, that is *Treppe*. Gapp lists Stöver's death as occurring in 1734. Actually, he died while confirming children on Ascension Day (May 13) 1779. See *Journals*, Vol. 3, p. 242. Stöver went on to be a decidedly active, controversial and probably competent itinerant pastor. He was an almost life-time foe of Halle and Muhlenberg. He was reconciled to Muhlenberg and became part of the Muhlenberg-led Ministerium in 1763. The Ministerium did not require him to be ordained again.

8 Glatfelter, Vol. 1, p. 126.

9 Jacobs, p. 193.

10 Jacobs, pp. 194–195.

11 *Journals*, Vol. 1, p. 68.

12 The trouble in Tulpehocken involved Zinzendorf-appointed pastors, Kraft-Stöver candidates, and later Muhlenberg.

13 It was described variously as an unoccupied house, miserable shed, dilapidated butcher's house, old house, and leaky slaughterhouse. See Glatfelter, Vol. 1, p. 413.

14 See Reichel, pp. 30–35 and Glatfelter, Vol. 1, p. 21.

15 He was licensed not through the Amsterdam Classis but the University of Heidelberg, a Reformed center. This may have put him beyond Böhm's reach.

16 Hamilton's origins and birth date are obscure. He appears to have been raised in Virginia and then settled in Maryland. Throughout his life, he did not join a congregation of any type and seems to have pursued an independent religious attitude probably influenced by rationalism. After election to and service in the Maryland Assembly, Hamilton studied law in England and was admitted to the bar through Gray's Inn (1712–13).

17 The mansion, Mount Airy, was on the corner of what is now Germantown Avenue and Allen's Lane. Fittingly, the Lutheran Theological Seminary at Philadelphia is

located directly across the street from what had been the site of the mansion and is nicknamed "Mt. Airy Seminary." A large relief of Muhlenberg preaching to a rapt congregation stands at the main entrance of the seminary. For more details on Allen see Kistler, and Harle.

18 See Kelley, pp. 157–218.

19 *Journals*, Vol. 1, p. 75.

Chapter Four

ZINZENDORF PRIOR TO HIS ARRIVAL IN THE COLONIES

"I yield to no one, not even to the whole world," the Zinzendorf family motto, may serve as the theme for the life of Nicholas Ludwig, Count and Lord of Zinzendorf and Pottendorf; Lord of the Baronies of Freydeck, Schöneck, Thürnstein and the Vale of Wachovia; Lord of the Manor of Upper, Middle and Lower Berthelsdorf; and Hereditary Warden of the Chase to His Imperial Roman Majesty in the Duchy of Austria. The Zinzendorf coat of arms featured crowned knights' helmets, rampant wolves and lions, all surmounted by hunting horns. The array of titles and flamboyant *Wappen* (family crest) claimed importance and authority that outpaced the realities of a now minor noble house.[1] Nevertheless, the son of Baroness Charlotte Justine von Gersdorf (1684–1763) and Count Georg Ludwig von Zinzendorf (1662–1700) was shaped and burdened by the societal and familial perceptions of aristocratic prerogatives and responsibilities.[2] His lineage and relations helped steer him toward Benezet's home.

The Zinzendorfs traced their origins to 11th century Austria. Some members became Lutherans in 1552. Emperor Leopold raised the family to the degree of Counts of the Holy Roman Empire. Maximilian Erasmus von Zinzendorf (1633–1672), Georg Ludwig's father and Nicholas' grandfather, left Counter-Reformation Austria to settle in Franconia (1661). Maximilian's three daughters married into Franconian families; his son, Otto Christian (d. 1718) became a field marshal in the Saxon army and his second son, Georg Ludwig, a privy councilor to the Elector of Saxony, Johann Georg IV.

Zinzendorf's maternal grandparents, the von Gersdorfs, combined intellect and piety. Baron Nicholas von Gersdorf (d. 1702) was the chief magistrate of Upper Lusatia. His spouse, Henriette Catherine (d. 1726), was an artist, musician, and poet who read Hebrew and Greek and discussed sophisticated theological points. Spener, both Franckes, Anton and other Hallesians were frequent guests in her home, and Pietist prayer meetings were held there. Indeed, Spener was a godfather to the newborn Count. Henriette Catherine contributed to the Halle institutions and the Halle-like project which her daughter, Henriette Sophie, began in 1717. From 1739–41 several of the institution's departments were supervised by Muhlenberg. One of Henriette Catherine's brothers-in-law, Baron Carl Hildebrandt von Canstein (d. 1738), founded the Canstein Bible Institute at Halle (1710).[3] Nicholas Ludwig's mother, Charlotte

Justine, also engaged in theological discussions, and knew Greek and Latin. The von Gersdorf and Zinzendorf families took their noble privileges and responsibilities and deep personal commitments to Hallesian Pietism seriously.

Born on May 26, 1700, the future renewer of the Unity was left a half-orphan when his father died on July 9, 1700.[4] Georg Ludwig's will named his brother, Otto, guardian for his children by his first marriage and for his newborn son. The young widow resided with her parents. In 1702, her father, Nicholas, died. Henriette Catherine moved her daughters and two-year-old grandson to her ancestral home, the manor-castle of Grosshennersdorf in Upper Lusatia. In 1704, the child-count's mother married the Prussian field marshal, Dubislaw Gneomar von Natzmer. She and von Natzmer took up residence in Berlin, yet gave frequent advice on the manner in which her first-born son was to be raised. The couple had two sons (1705 and 1709). Nicholas Ludwig apparently was not close to either his older or younger half-siblings.

From at least the age of five, Zinzendorf was committed to Jesus as his Savior and acutely aware of matters related to sin and grace. As Swedish soldiers discovered in 1706, he was given to fervent prayer. The adult Count recalled that when Christian Ludwig Edeling, his tutor from 1703–1706, left the family's employ, Edeling "spoke a few words to me about the Saviour and his merits; and in what sense I belonged to him and to him only. These words made so deep and lively impression on me that I fell into a long protracted paroxysm of tears, during which I resolved to live for him alone, who had laid down his life for me. My very dear Aunt Henriette endeavored to keep me in this frame of mind by often speaking to me loving and evangelical words."[5]

"Tante Netty," as he called her, encouraged him to bare his inmost thoughts to her: "I opened all my heart to [her], and then we spread my case before the Lord in prayer. I was not in the least afraid of her. I freely told her all about myself, both bad and good. My open and candid intercourse with her was of so great benefit to me that I could never forget it. This confidential interchange of thought and feeling prompted all my endeavors in later years to establish bands or societies for mutual conference and edification."[6] Apparently that intimacy soured for in later years she told others, including Muhlenberg, uncomplimentary tales about him.

The Grosshennersdorf adults accepted the prevailing Pietist view that children were steeped in sin and needed to be disciplined so as to conform to God's will. As the ten-year-old went to the Halle Paedagogium, the family added that the boy was stubborn, proud and resistant to authority. For at least the first three of his six years at Halle (1710–1716), his private tutor, the Halle teachers and staff did their best to break his will, accusing him of lying, hypocrisy, vanity and assorted youthful transgressions. He was humiliated and punished in front of the other students. Nevertheless, Zinzendorf retained a life-long respect for the elder Francke but his relationship with Gotthilf, the younger Francke, was just the opposite. Not all of the problems concerned Zinzendorf's character. He opposed the Halle insistence on an invariable path to salvation that involved severe bouts of being convicted of one's sinfulness and helplessness prior to a convincing experience of God's grace. Zinzendorf felt that while the Halle pattern fit many persons, it was not universal and invariable.

In addition to being a fine student, he enjoyed being a leader among some serious and pietistically minded students. He formed several "bands" or small groups of students devoted to prayer, Bible study and missions. He realized the need for Christians to be in fellowship and communion with one another for mutual support and edification. His bands were called by names such as "Slaves of Virtue," "Confessors of Christ," and finally, the "Order of the Grain of Mustard Seed." Several members remained in close contact with Zinzendorf, and a few joined him in the renewed Unity. Friedrich von Watteville (1700–1777), son of a Swiss banker, proved to be a loyal colleague and eventually an in-law.[7]

From his early childhood onward, Zinzendorf sensed the Spirit's call to serve his Lord as an ordained Lutheran pastor. He understood himself to be a person sent out with God's commission to bring the gospel to others. The family decision-makers, however, countered him with their conviction that a nobleman's place was at the Saxon royal court, not in the pulpit. Implicitly, they may have considered him to be a headstrong youth who needed a hiatus from intense religious involvement. They decided and he agreed that he would attend the staunchly Orthodox University of Wittenberg to study law — with the further proviso that he not take courses in theology. In addition, he was to prepare for his future career in service to the Elector. Externally Zinzendorf complied with the family's instructions. From August, 1716 to April, 1719 he enrolled in the appropriate law courses and learned the social graces they expected. Internally, the Count walked his own way by maintaining his practices of fasting, praying and Bible reading. While he did not enroll in a theology course, he engaged in deep conversations with members of the theology faculty and came to know Löscher, by then the superintendent of the

Lutheran church in Saxony. The 1717 bicentennial of the beginning of the Lutheran Reformation sparked celebrations and studies of Luther and his colleagues. Zinzendorf immersed himself in his own study of the Reformer's writings. The anniversary impressed Zinzendorf with the fragmented state of Christianity and fissures within the Lutheran churches. In August of the celebratory year, Zinzendorf published a tract, *Thoughts On Peace To The Quarreling Lutheran Churches*. Encouraged by several Wittenberg faculty members, the seventeen-year-old student contacted the elder Francke about a meeting aimed at reconciling the differences between the proponents of Pietism and Orthodoxy. The scheme was aborted when his family learned of his activities. They ordered him to desist. In 1719, when he left Wittenberg, Zinzendorf tried again. The meeting between Löscher and Francke was civil, but no further sessions were held.

Upon leaving Wittenberg, Zinzendorf considered himself to be a sound interpreter of Scripture, a correct expositor of Luther, and a devotee of the Augsburg Confession. He regarded himself as a thorough-going Lutheran who had a heart relationship with the Savior and who extended an irenic hand to other Christians. By the time he departed from the university, he had shown himself already to be a devout, spiritually-aware and creative individual with a flair for writing, establishing organizations, and attracting persons to his causes. He was increasingly troubled about the divided state of Christianity, and he was stepping forward to bring about new understandings and new grounds for uniting Christians. Still convinced that God called him to the ordained ministry, he was seeing his as a ministry of reconciliation. Yet, he also was a man of the privileged classes and never divested himself of the assumption that he was entitled to be heard with deference, if not obedience.

Zinzendorf chafed under the determined will of superiors in his family and schools. From his earliest days, Zinzendorf's relationships with authority structures from family to church — and eventually government — were marked by tension and reciprocal resistance. His creativity and passion ran counter to their prevailing desires for continuity and stability. At times, he would acquiesce to the will of those in authority, but, increasingly, he either circumvented or ignored or acted contrary to established procedures and those responsible for enforcing those procedures. In addition, if part of an organization, the Count would seek to be its head. The young Zinzendorf was becoming convinced that God, not any human institution, had authorized him to bring others to Christ. He grew in his conviction that a specific dimension of his work was to bring about that reconciliation and unity among Christians that would advance the Kingdom beyond narrow ecclesiastical loyalties.

Zinzendorf undertook the traditional *Bildungsreise*, or educational Grand Tour (1719–1721). Since he was being groomed to serve as a councilor in the Saxon Elector's royal court, he studied international law at the University of Utrecht (May – September, 1719). He took the opportunity while in the United Provinces to meet leading members, both lay and clergy, of the Reformed, Lutheran and Roman Catholic churches along with like-minded members of the diplomatic corps posted to the Netherlands. The Jansenist controversy was still prominent in the United Provinces and France. He included persecuted French Protestants and Catholics in his daily prayers. Zinzendorf realized that the Jesuits worked mightily to secure the condemnations of Jansenius, his writings and those who continued to support resistance to papal policies against Jansenism. The *Bildungsreise's* next destination was Paris.

The importance of his sojourn in Paris (September, 1719 – May, 1720) is still to be addressed.[8] Four factors pertinent to the 1742 controversy may be cited. First, the complex political-ecclesiastical situations in France. The term "Jansenist" often was applied pejoratively to discredit an opponent and not with theological precision. Papal responses to Jansenism were sensitive to relationships with the French royal house and the often independent-minded Gallican church. Recognizing the theological quagmire into which the Catholic church could be drawn by what seemed to be a Calvinizing interpretation of Augustine by Cornelius Jansenius (d. 1638), popes from Paul V to Clement XI sought to muffle and then condemn Jansenius' ideas and those who supported them. Opposition by Jansenists and their supporters had political as well as religious implications especially in France. The Jesuits led the assault on Jansenism and sympathetic clergy. At first Louis XIV supported the papal pressures, but, for unrelated reasons, relations between Versailles and the Vatican deteriorated to the point that in 1673 the Sun King revived a provision of a concordat made between Leo X and Francis I (1516) that gave the French king the right to appoint all bishops and abbés in the kingdom. Innocent XI (1676–1689) opposed both the Sun King and Gallicanism, the traditionally independent-minded Gallican (French) church. Relations between Louis and Rome crumbled to the point that a royally convened General Assembly (1684) essentially declared the pope had no temporal jurisdiction over the French church or sovereign, but instead was subject to the decisions of church councils, and could not presume to infringe on the liberties of the Gallican church or the rights of the crown.

Those French laity and clergy who were prone to Jansenism or labeled as such were emboldened. [9] The wars and conflicts that embroiled the Empire, France, England and much of western Europe at the end of the seventeenth and beginning of the eighteenth centuries allowed Jansenism and similar movements to spread in France. The earlier popular writings of Father Pasquier Quesnel were used by his Jesuit critics to revive opposition to perceived Jansenistic positions. Louis demanded that Pope Clement XI (1700–1721) pressure French clergy to oppose forthrightly Quesnel's ideas and suspected Jansenism. Clement responded with the bull *Vineam Domini* (1705). A group of clergy and the lawyers for the Parlement of Paris refused to conform and they were supported by the cardinal archbishop of Paris, Louis-Antoine de Noailles (1651–1729).[10] Louis could not brook such open defiance and insisted on and received a more powerful bull, *Unigenitus* (1713). In it, the pope condemned 101 propositions drawn from Quesnel's 1671 *Summary of the Morality of the Gospel* and some brief comments on the New Testament. Cardinal de Noailles, who several years earlier commended the *Summary*, refused to publish the bull in the archdiocese. A number of bishops and priests appealed for a council to discuss the condemnations and the issues cited in the bull. They, therefore, are called the "Appellants." By 1720, while Zinzendorf was in Paris, Clement XI issued *Pastoralis Offici,* threatened to excommunicate all who disobeyed *Unigenitus,* and insisted that clergy sign a declaration of submission. In March 1720, under the pressures of failing health and Jesuit tactics, de Noailles came to a compromise agreement with Rome. On May 24, 1728, the old cardinal-archbishop submitted fully by signing a treatise to that effect. He died less than a year later.

A second factor concerns the role of the abbé in France. The French version was more flexible than a title for the head of a monastery.[11] The title also included a person who received the tonsure, even as a youth, and who could also receive abbatial revenues *in commendam* even though the individual did not proceed to holy orders. The abbé, then, could live off the largess of the church without really serving a charge or cure. Louis XIV appointed men to be abbés *in commendam* in such numbers that there were no real positions for them in the hierarchy.[12] The position attracted aristocratic and educated individuals, and drew many to Paris. They could associate with upper echelon officials in church and state, participate in Parisian high society, and engage in intellectual activities while drawing their incomes from the church. As they were relatively free from ecclesiastical supervision, the abbés could engage in commenting on and critiquing society and the church. Several wrote for journals under assumed names.

The third pertinent factor is the specific contacts Zinzendorf had during his stay in Paris. His association with religiously like-minded nobles in the diplomatic corps and social circles gave him entrée to Cardinal de Noailles, the Appellants and those associated with them. The Cardinal and the youthful Count developed a cordial relationship that lasted to the Cardinal's death. Whether or not the Cardinal was aware of his being listed among the godparents of two of Zinzendorf's sons, it certainly would not have enhanced his standing with his critics if it became known that a German Lutheran had so favored him.[13] Surviving correspondence shows a fervent Zinzendorf scolding the embattled ecclesiastic for the compromise on *Unigenitus*. After his return to Saxony and at the publishing enterprise established at Ebersdorf in Thuringia, Zinzendorf had printed Samuel de Beauval's translation into French of Johann Arndt's *True Christianity*, adding a laudatory dedication to the Cardinal. Friedrich de Watteville presented a copy to de Noailles, who received it kindly, but noted correctly that the French crown would ban it. Zinzendorf also worked on a hymnbook for use by Protestants and Catholics, and the unauthorized disclosure of an unsent letter to the pope proposing the use of the hymnal in furthering Christian understanding surfaced without Zinzendorf's permission and much to his embarrassment.

Did, as Weinlick suggests, an abbé-style of ministry influence Zinzendorf's emerging understanding of his future ministry?[14] Did the nineteen- and twenty-year-old Zinzendorf appreciate the Cardinal's and the Appellants' position? Did he realize that his statements and actions might aid the opponents of the men who befriended him? Did the French and Catholic connection rebound negatively on Zinzendorf and the Moravians once war broke out in 1740? These gestures may help explain why the British and British North Americans suspected the Count and the Moravians of being French agents and papist subversives.

A final *Bildungsreise* factor is Zinzendorf's continued negative experience with authority structures. Once again, he saw and interpreted the civil and ecclesiastical establishments as interfering with and, as he saw it, repressing the workings of the Spirit. He seems not to have recognized that de Noailles and the Appellants had an ecclesiology that revered the offices and procedures of the church while resisting, as long as feasible, the exertions of individual leaders. While Zinzendorf recognized the internal or invisible relationships that united believers to the Savior whatever their external institutional identities might be, he seems not to have seen that the procedures and regulations of the external or visible church had validity when he and they were in disagreement.

To complete the *Bildungsreise*, he traveled from France to Switzerland and several German cities before returning to Saxony. During those years, he met and became friends with Count Heinrich XXIV Reuss-Köstritz (1681–1748). In the course of his return to Hennersdorf in early 1721, Zinzendorf withdrew his suit for marriage with Theodora von Castell when he learned that Count Heinrich and she loved each other. Following the Castell-Reuss nuptials (spring, 1721), Zinzendorf undertook the steps that led to his September marriage to Erdmuth Dorothea von Reuss of Ebersdorf (1700–1756), Count Heinrich's sister. In the same eventful year, he bought the large estate, Berthelsdorf, from his now-aged maternal grandmother.

Zinzendorf and his spouse took up residence in Dresden and he began his service at the court of the Elector Augustus the Strong (1670–1733).[15] Augustus was a political opportunist with an immense libido. The moral tone of the Dresden royal court was low, and religious feeling had scant priority except as a political expedient. While Zinzendorf disdained the "worldly" activities of the royal court, the Elector and Superintendent Löscher tolerated the young couple's religious meetings in their Dresden apartment. These sessions included prayer, Bible study and the Count's discourses. Zinzendorf's interests were neither in serving Augustus the Strong at the Saxon royal court nor in managing the estates. He was involved in only a few cases during his Dresden years (1721–1727). He took several personally worthwhile trips to Sweden and Denmark through which he gained the acquaintance and friendship of highly placed persons in the government and church. While in Dresden, relegating Berthelsdorf's administration to his wife, the Count worked toward transforming Berthelsdorf into a religious center. The death of the resident pastor at Berthelsdorf gave him the opportunity to provide a call for his evangelically fervent pastor-friend, Johann Andreas Rothe, and to engage Johann Georg Heitz as steward. Around the same time he made the acquaintance of the pastor at Görlitz (in Silesia), Melchior Schaeffer, and persuaded von Watteville to come to Berthelsdorf. In 1722 Schaeffer introduced Zinzendorf to Christian David (1691–1751), the dedicated and problematic Moravian leader. Soon the Brethren, aided by Heitz, and then other persecuted believers began to settle on that section of the Berthelsdorf estate that they named Herrnhut.

In 1723 Zinzendorf created yet another version of his Order of the Grain of Mustard Seed, calling it the Covenant of the Four Brethren. Its members were Schaeffer, Rothe, von Watteville and himself. The Order's aims have been summarized as to

> seek the power of the Holy Ghost for their own renewal in holiness and for the exaltation of the actual and practical sway of Christ throughout the land, and purposed to attain their aim by personal correspondence, by securing the allegiance of pulpits pledged to seek to promote revivals of religion, by the publication of suitable literature, by the reformation of pastoral methods and of the inner life of churches, by the itinerancy of evangelists, and by the founding and maintenance of a college distinctively religious in its educational methods.[16]

Zinzendorf planned to locate the publishing house at Berthelsdorf, but Augustus' privy council refused to permit it to be established there. Count Heinrich agreed to set up the printing enterprise out of the reach of Saxon proscriptions at Ebersdorf, his estate in Thuringia. It was from here that the French translation of *True Christianity* was printed as well as an updated German rendition of Luther's Bible plus other works, including Zinzendorf's tracts. The covenanters' aspiration to establish a school was brought to fruition initially among the Moravian refugees who settled at Herrnhut. Von Watteville gave the endeavor sound organizational and economic bases along with spiritual guidance. The Count was intent on developing a school to educate pastors, catechists and missionaries.

Among the items that came from the Ebersdorf press was a weekly sheet, *The Dresden Socrates*. In thirty-two issues printed over the course of 1725–1726, anonymous *Socrates* railed against existing practices in the church, proposing reforms and renewals. One early issue was confiscated by the government. It soon became clear that "Socrates" was Zinzendorf's pen name. For a member of the Elector's privy council to engage in such criticisms was to court trouble. Superintendent Löscher had little choice but to ban the religious meetings in the Zinzendorf apartments (1726). Did the Count see himself as an abbé-like journalist while adding the gadfly Socrates to his roles?

The Count's career following 1723 was consonant with the Covenant's objectives. These also were inimical to the Orthodoxists, the Saxon consistory, and the Halle Fathers. Whether they intended to or not, the covenanters challenged the existing authorities of state, church and Hallesian Pietism and promoted embryonic new structures. After 1722 Zinzendorf moved further away from the Dresden royal court and his family of origin and closer to the refugees at Berthelsdorf-Herrnhut and his call to be a pastor. Both movements raised the levels of suspicion and opposition toward him from governmental, ecclesiastical, academic and familial authorities. The Count resisted yielding to anyone, except God. At Berthelsdorf-Herrnhut, Zinzendorf developed from being a hospitable provider of shelter to involved participant to recognized leader to renewer of the Unity. Through the mid-1720s the number and variety of persons, including Silesian Schwenkfelder refugees, seeking shelter and safety on his estate increased. The fervent preaching and energetic evangelicalism of Rothe at Berthelsdorf and Schaeffer at Görlitz attracted members of other parishes and earned the enmity of neighboring pastors as well as the critical attention of church authorities. The styles of both men stirred disagreements and factionalism among the Herrnhuters.

A journey into Austria to negotiate a better understanding with the ruling Catholic authorities over Protestant refugees from Bohemia, Moravia and Salzburg generated further criticisms from those authorities. Zinzendorf appeared the defender of heretics and troublemakers, scarcely the conduct the Austrian imperial authorities would tolerate from an official of the Saxon government. His travels to Denmark and Sweden were more productive, at least initially. He made excellent contacts with religiously awakened governmental leaders and a good impression on sympathetic church officials.

In 1727 Zinzendorf took a leave of absence from almost all his Dresden duties. He and the Countess returned to Berthelsdorf-Herrnhut. A series of crises of three types threatened the community's existence, yet resulted in the formation of a durable and renewed Unity. The first crisis concerned refugees who arrived in Herrnhut with strange ideas and tarnished reputations. Could those who had also suffered the loss of homeland and livelihood expel others from their midst? Yet some of these persons and groups were branded as heretical by Catholic and Protestant authorities. To provide them with shelter was illegal and even dangerous to the community. Some refugee leaders were deranged and/or antagonized the authorities with their inflammatory rhetoric. To allow them to remain would scandalize neighboring Christians and provoke the authorities to exile all the residents of Herrnhut.

The second crisis involved dissent among the Moravians and those who were devout members of the Herrnhut community. A cherished leader such as Christian David could be difficult and unpredictable. Did he and other original leaders have a vision for the community that was different from that of their patron, Count Zinzendorf? How would the Moravians handle disagreements and disharmony within their own ranks?

These two crises lurched toward resolution in May and July 1727 through the development of agreed-upon organizational documents that constituted the community as a Brotherhood with clearer procedures about jurisdictional matters. Sometime between July 22 and August 4, while in Silesia, Zinzendorf received a copy of the Ancient Unity's 1616 *Ratio Disciplinae*.[17] The crisis over leadership served as setting for a profound religious experience, the August 13, 1727 "Little Pentecost." The pattern that emerged was that in times of stress and when division threatened the unity of the community, the members would recall their faithful reliance on the Savior and covenantal relationship with each other. They strengthened their bonds through prayerful searching and sharing in the lovefeast.

The third crisis came in 1728 when Rothe urged that the Moravians formally join the official Lutheran church and forsake their distinctive heritage and traditions. The Ancient Church, that is the Bohemian-Moravian Brethren, had struggled through the seventeenth century with the problem of becoming part of Lutheran or Reformed churches. Generally, the leaders and members decided that they would maintain their distinctive communal and spiritual identities. Rothe actually raised again the persistent issue of identity: were the Moravians a separate church? Given the Westphalian settlement and the legal status of the recognized churches, Rothe put the Moravians in a theological and political quandary. The Moravians knew the price for non-conformity was persecution and exile, yet most refused to jettison their historic identity to become legal Lutherans. Zinzendorf wanted to preserve much of the devotion of the Ancient Moravian Church, genuinely thought the Brethren could be *ecclesiolae* in the Lutheran and Reformed churches, and realized that if they were another church, the Peace of Westphalia and Saxon law would be breached.

The situation led to some revisions in the 1727 Manorial Injunctions and Prohibitions that Zinzendorf drew up in that earlier crisis of leadership and discipline but which did not have a faith-confessing character. The changes provided for Herrnhut's adherence to Lutheran forms of belief, the Augsburg Confession and Lutheran liturgy while retaining customs from the Bohemian Brethren.[18] The affair seemed ended by the notarization of the revised document (August 12, 1729). Rothe, while remaining the pastor of the Lutheran congregation at Berthelsdorf, became increasingly testy toward Zinzendorf and distanced himself from the Herrnhuters. That raised concerns for providing ordained leadership at Herrnhut. Indeed, Rothe-style questions lurked within the Moravian community, for the Count had one understanding of the Unity's future with regard to other Christian bodies and a number of the Brethren had another.

In dealing with problems at Herrnhut, Zinzendorf acted with patience, persistence and prayer. The members of the community respected and even revered him for his devotion, spiritual depth and courageous integrity. While he could exercise his persuasive powers and implicitly his manorial authority, he and they turned to the Lord as their guide. Did he, however, presume that his vision for the church and the Unity's role in it would prevail even over the hopes of the Brethren? Did he consider that there were Brethren elsewhere in Europe who wanted a distinct ecclesial identity? On the other hand, his responses to detractors outside the Herrnhut community often were as aggressive and sharp as the attacks.

The spiritual and organizational life of the Brethren developed rapidly, if unevenly, after August 1727. The Nitschmann family, originally from Moravia, furnished important and sometimes controversial leaders in the Unity's ministry. Four members of the family were named "David": the Father (the father of Anna, Zinzendorf's second wife), the Martyr, the Syndic (moderator) and the Bishop (prior to his consecration as bishop in 1735 known as the Carpenter).[19] The September visit to Denmark by David the Syndic and Johann Nitschmann resulted in the Unity's foreign mission impulse to go to the Danish possessions of Greenland and the Virgin Islands. The missionary impulse also involved a European dimension. In September, 1727 Gottlieb Wriede and Andreas Beyer went through several German states and Liechtenstein. While in Jena they met and deeply impressed Augustus Gottlieb Spangenberg (1704–1792). Christian David and David Nitschmann (the Carpenter) went into Austria, Beyer continued his itinerancy into Silesia, and others went to Moravia and Hungary. Several were imprisoned in Austria, including David Nitschmann the Martyr who died in an Austrian jail in 1729.

The Moravian missionaries established prayer and Bible study groups that met in homes. Clearly, however, the established governmental and ecclesiastical authorities, sensitive to the widespread perception that Pietism often led to schism and disorder, were seeing the movement as schismatic, even heretical. Zinzendorf, however, denied that he and the Herrnhut community were Pietists; he reserved that term for the Hallesians and sneered that those associated with Halle were Pietists. Secular and church officials did not make the same discriminating definition, and traced religious unrest and confusion to Herrnhut and Zinzendorf. In territories such as Silesia where a Jesuit-led Counter-

Reformation was succeeding, as well as imperial Austria, the ruling authorities raised serious objections to the Saxon government based on the Peace of Westphalia. And Saxon court officials asked the same questions of the king. Soon tracts and treatises appeared, branding the Herrnhuters and the "Zinzendorfians" as distorters of doctrine, teachers of innovations and misleaders of the simple people.[20] The Count was becoming notorious and the Brethren were perceived as threats to public and ecclesiastical stability. August Francke moderated Hallesian criticism of Zinzendorf, but his death (1727) opened the way for Gotthilf Francke and others to sharpen and multiply their criticisms of Zinzendorf and to influence others to join their attacks. In 1728, Zinzendorf sent representatives to England to contact members of the SPCK, Anglican Church officers and the German Court chaplain, Ziegenhagen. Aware of his Halle colleagues' antipathy to their troublesome alumnus, Ziegenhagen was unreceptive to the Herrnhut visitors.

As the fiscal resources of the Count and Countess' estates dwindled, new disruptions rocked Herrnhut. In 1729–1730 separatists and radical mystics were drawn to the community. Earlier ideas voiced by the French Prophets and perhaps echoes of Jane Leade's Philadelphia movement challenged the community and the Count. At first he permitted unauthorized, clearly heterodox, if not heretical, persons to preach and teach in the religious meetings. His Saxon noble neighbors were deeply concerned and hostile. Their peasants absented themselves from the Lutheran services provided on those nearby estates, and were attending worship at Herrnhut. They returned imbued with the novel and perplexing ideas they heard both from the Brethren and the newly arrived preacher-teachers. Disruptive notions seemed to emanate from Zinzendorf's estates. Ultimately, Zinzendorf repudiated the radicals and gradually broke with the teachings of the more blatant inspirationalists and mystics such as Gottfried Arnold, Leade and Boehme. He saw in these a theology of glory in which the human will was the motivating force and not God's grace. Instead, Zinzendorf claimed that he was recovering a Lutheran theology of the cross centered on Jesus, his death and resurrection, and God's freely bestowed grace. Nevertheless, Berthelsdorf and its owner were becoming targets.

Denmark had attracted Zinzendorf because its ruling house was deeply religious and open to the Brethren's missions. The Count appears to have entertained hopes that he might be called to be Danish court preacher to Friedrich IV and consequently ordained in a setting that was suitable to his social rank.[21] When Friedrich died (October, 1730), Zinzendorf made plans to be at the coronation of the new monarch. In April and May, 1731, he and Nitschmann the Carpenter traveled to Copenhagen for the ceremony and to deepen contacts with congenial Danish officials. The new king, Christian VI, decorated the Saxon count with the Cross of the Order of the Knights of the Danebrog and offered him a post as councilor to the king. Although he declined the office, the trip proved important for another reason: Nitschmann and Zinzendorf met Anthony Ulrich, from the Danish West Indies, a servant of a Danish count. The results developed into the Moravian mission to St. Thomas and St. Croix and, later, Zinzendorf's first journey to the new world (1739). When he returned to Herrnhut and shortly before Leonhard Dober and Nitschmann the Carpenter left for the Caribbean (October, 1731), Herrnhut and the Count were put on the defensive.

Emperor Charles VI complained formally to Augustus the Strong that Zinzendorf enticed the Empire's citizens to emigrate to Saxony. The Elector ordered that no further émigrés be allowed to settle at Herrnhut, and appointed Georg Ernst von Gersdorf, a relative and prefect of Upper Lusatia, to investigate conditions on the Count's estate. The investigation, conducted January 19–22, 1732, came to positive conclusions about the conditions and theology of Herrnhut, thereby accepting Zinzendorf's view that Herrnhut's six hundred inhabitants were an *ecclesiola* in the Berthelsdorf Lutheran congregation. In this context, Zinzendorf finally resigned his Dresden court position and had the Ebersdorf press bind his *Dresden Socrates* as one volume and issue it under the title, *German Socrates*. The reissuing of the earlier *Socrates* with its expanded title and gesture to a wider audience could be read as a challenge to the established churches and the various governments.

The Elector's decision (October 16, 1732) was a surprise. He fined Herrnhut, ordered Zinzendorf to divest himself of the ownership of Berthelsdorf, and commanded him to leave Saxony. An appeal was filed, and Zinzendorf went into exile after signing over title to the estate to the Countess Erdmuth Dorothea. His first stop was Ebersdorf and then Tübingen. Zinzendorf wanted to offer the post of assistant pastor of Berthelsdorf (really to be the minister to Herrnhut, given Rothe's withdrawal from the Brethren) to a professor in Tübingen University's theology faculty, Friedrich Christoph Steinhofer. At the same time, he made positive impressions on the faculty — an impression that was reversed beginning in 1743. In mid-April the Tübingen faculty issued a favorable opinion about the arrangements at Herrnhut being acceptable within Lutheran understandings.

The situation changed dramatically on February 1, 1733: Augustus the Strong died. His successor, Augustus III, accepted the property transfer, required the Schwenkfelders at Herrnhut to leave gradually, and proposed toleration for the Herrnhuters and the Count contingent on their lawful and peaceful behavior. The Count returned to the estate on May 5, 1733. Four days later, Spangenberg joined the community.

For several years Spangenberg had been deepening his relationship with the Count and the Moravian Brethren. The Halle Fathers offered Spangenberg the position of superintendent of Halle's Orphans' House (September, 1732). His actual tenure lasted a scant five months. The fundamental cause for his departure was the continuing and mounting hostility between Halle and Zinzendorf and Herrnhut. The presenting cause was his sharing the Lord's Supper with exiled Zinzendorf when they were both visiting Ebersdorf and the Count was on his way to Tübingen.[22] Spangenberg's arrival and rise to leadership at Herrnhut proved a long-term blessing for the Moravians and their patron, but it precipitated a powerfully negative reaction: the Halle Fathers, infuriated by Spangenberg's conduct and departure, broke almost totally with Zinzendorf and moved into determined opposition. At the same time, many previously sympathetic German Lutheran clergy and church officials shut their church doors, pulpits and minds toward the Moravians and the Count.

Following his return from the brief banishment, Zinzendorf strengthened his ties to Tübingen by inviting the university's philosopher-theologian, Friedrich Christoph Oettinger (1702–1782), to conduct Bible studies at Herrnhut with him. Oettinger was favorably impressed and commented publicly that he had no doubts about Herrnhut's fidelity to Lutheran understandings of Scripture. Oettinger, however, was a weak reed on which to lean for theological support: he went on to be fascinated by Jewish mysticism, Boehme and Swedenborg.[23]

By January 1734 Zinzendorf decided to follow his *Trieb*, or driving call to be an ordained Lutheran minister. But how should the nearly thirty-four-year-old noble proceed? He was not about to enroll in a university theological program, and he assumed that he was fully versed in Christian, specifically Lutheran, theology. He also knew that it was virtually out of the question for him to gain the approval of the Dresden Consistory for ordination. If he could not work through the regular channels, then he would use those channels insofar as he could and circumvent them when necessary to achieve the ends he was convinced God wanted him to achieve. The centerpiece of his efforts became his gaining the acceptance of theological faculties that he was theologically sound to preach, teach, administer the sacraments, and labor on behalf of Christ in the world. Consistorial approval and formal call, as far as he was concerned, were matters of lesser importance.

When the widowed Abraham Ehrenfried Richter, a merchant in Swedish-ruled Stralsund, requested Herrnhut to send to him a devout tutor for his children, Zinzendorf saw the opportunity to travel to the region and obtain the needed theological approval by representatives of the theological faculty of the University of Greifswald.[24] Spangenberg persuaded him to call himself "Ludwig Freydeck." This was not exactly an alias because Freydeck was part of his title. The gesture to operating incognito, however, gave critics the impression of his being clumsily sly and deceitful. After he disclosed his identity to friends, he requested and gained a three-day examination by Gregorius Langemack and Carol Joachimus Sibeth, the faculty members the university appointed to examine candidates for ordination. They found him highly prepared and sound in doctrine, and that Herrnhut's practices were permissible within Lutheran understandings. The Count preached five times as part of his examination. His final *Rede* was based on Mark 14:8: "She did what she was able." He used the same passage for his *Abschiedsrede* (Farewell Discourse) on December 31, 1742 (OS), the evening after his argument with Muhlenberg and immediately before his departure from Philadelphia.[25]

On his return to Herrnhut (April 26), Zinzendorf informed Superintendent Löscher about the successful faculty examination and his eligibility for ordination. Löscher insisted that Zinzendorf do as all other candidates for ordination were required: subscribe to the full text of the Augsburg Confession. This he could not do; the condemnations included in numerous articles of the Confession were inimical to his understanding of Christian love, the unity Christ willed for believers, and the pressing need for an end to theological wrangling. In refusing to acquiesce to Löscher's demand, he ended any possibility that the Dresden Consistory would approve him for ordination.

Next, he presented an interesting proposal to Karl Alexander, Duke of Württemberg. The Catholic ruler of a mostly Lutheran state walked carefully in political-religious matters. Zinzendorf's Covenant envisioned the establishment of schools and the training of pastors, missionaries and catechists who would be leaders in the reform of the churches. The Count had expanded and connected these points to seeking a theological training institution with himself as its head, in a sense as its abbé. To head it, he reasoned, entailed his being ordained, and that Duke Karl Alexander would arrange for the ordination. The institution, Zinzendorf proposed, would be located in the dilapidated Protestant-owned St. Georg cloister in the Black Forest. He added that he would restore and furnish it at his own expense. The journey to Württemberg also reconnected him to the University of Tübingen. The Count resumed his efforts to retain Steinhofer for the Herrnhut community. The Dresden authorities would have to approve the appointment. Steinhofer was willing, but Dresden refused to give the necessary authorization. Instead, Count Heinrich appointed him as the court preacher at Ebersdorf. In July 1734, after Zinzendorf had returned to Herrnhut and before Karl Augustus rejected Zinzendorf's proposal on political grounds, Spangenberg arrived to wait for the Duke's decision. Spangenberg suggested that the Tübingen theological faculty examine Zinzendorf's Lutheranism with an eye to certifying him as acceptable for ordination, and raised the issue of the Count's idea that he would "assume" the duties of the office of a pastor. At this juncture, the Count, frustrated with the resistance he encountered from the ecclesiastical authorities, asserted to Löscher and others that he would soon consider himself an ordained minister and begin to function as such on the basis of his application of Stephanas in 1 Corinthians 16:14–18 to his own case.

The crucial portion of 16:15 reads in Greek: "*kai eis diakonian tois hagiois etaxav heautous*," which may be translated "who have ordered themselves for the ministry to the saints." I translate the German passage (emphasis added) in a manner that lends itself to his interpretation:

> Let all your things be done in love! I admonish you, however, dear brothers: you know the house of Stephanas, that they are the first fruits in Achaia and *have ordained themselves for the ministry of the saints*; so that you also should submit yourselves to such who help and work! I rejoice for the arrival of Stephanas and Fortunatus and Achaicus; because where I had need on your account, they have supplied it. They have enlivened my and your spirits. Acknowledge them and those like them![26]

Stephanas and his family carried on some sort of recognized, public ministry (*diakonia*) on behalf of the congregation and their service was praised by the Apostle. Paul also claimed to be set apart or commissioned for his ministry not by the authorities of the church in Jerusalem but by Christ.

The University Chancellor responded positively (September 19, 1734), and in November Zinzendorf contacted the Württemberg Ecclesiastical

Directory in Stuttgart, informing it that he planned to enter the ordained status on the basis of Stephanas and apparently after appearing before the Tübingen faculty. By confessional Lutheran standards, especially as expressed in the Augsburg Confession, Article 14, this was irregular and invalid.[27] Zinzendorf appealed neither to the Lutheran Confessions nor to Luther's writings.[28] Beyreuther observed that Zinzendorf had been developing his ecclesiology to the point where, to paraphrase Beyreuther, without being attached to a particular ecclesiastical office (*Amt*) in a territorial church (*Landeskirche*), he entered into the position of a pastor (*Pfarrerstand*) as a free preacher, and maintained the right to preach and administer the sacraments publicly in the chancel.[29]

The Directory responded, as quoted by Spangenberg:

> That they would praise the Lord for, and implore his blessing on the Count's rare and laudable decision, to devote himself entirely to the service of God and the souls of men, imploring him to glorify himself in it, crown such distinguished fidelity with much spiritual success, and preserve everything, in its progress and accomplishment as his work, to the praise and glory of his grace. [30]

The statement is scarcely a ringing endorsement of Zinzendorf's intention. He still lacked a "local call" to a congregational setting, and his interpretation of 1 Corinthians 16:14ff was strained. In any event, on December 18, 1734, he appeared before the already favorably disposed Tübingen theological faculty and delivered an explanation of his theological position in which he said:

> I reserve to myself liberty of conscience; it agrees with my internal call to the ministry.... I love and honor the church, and shall frequently seek her counsels. I will continue as heretofore, to win souls for my precious Saviour, to gather his sheep, bid guests, and hire servants for him. More especially I shall continue, if the Lord please, to devote myself to the service of that congregation whose servant I became in 1727. Agreeably to her orders, under her protection, enjoying her care, and influenced by her spirit, I shall go to distant nations, who are ignorant of Jesus and redemption in his blood. I shall endeavor to imitate the labors of my brethren, who have the honor of being the first messengers to the heathen. I will prove all things by the only criterion of evangelical doctrine, the Holy Scriptures. Among the brethren at Herrnhut and elsewhere I shall endeavor to maintain their ancient church discipline. The love of Christ shall constrain me, and his cross refresh me. I will cheerfully be subject to the higher powers, and a sincere friend to my enemies.... I am poor and needy, yet the Lord thinketh upon me. He shall deliver the poor and needy.[31]

On December 19, 1734 the faculty certified the soundness of his Lutheran theology, stating:

> For though a particular call and ordination to the pastoral office and its functions is requisite, yet we cannot see how bounds are to be set to the course of the gospel; and why able and suitable individuals, especially with the consent and at the desire of the church, should not preach occasionally in public, since such a prohibition would run contrary to the customs of our church.[32]

The faculty statement, like that of the Stuttgart Directory, is limited. The faculty did not sanction his entering into the full ministry of Word and Sacraments but allowed for occasional preaching. Nor did the faculty deal with the question as to the identity of the church that desired and consented him to serve it in that manner. The Stuttgart Directory might not have wanted to be put in the position of ordaining a person who was not acceptable to his home consistory and the subject of another state. The university was not empowered to ordain anyone, and the Duke recognized that Zinzendorf was so controversial, it would be better to stay out of the fray that would certainly ensue. The Count, however, was satisfied that he was certified as doctrinally pure by representatives of two university faculties, had received the tacit consent (or at least no obvious opposition) of a consistory or directory, and was able to strengthen his developing self-understanding that like Paul, he was a missionary-apostle commissioned by Christ to travel the world bringing the news of salvation to those who could be awakened to the Gospel. He would not be under the discipline of any ecclesiastical authority. Zinzendorf loved and honored the church, but reserved his liberty of conscience on the basis of his inward call to ministry. His statement was hedged further; he would "frequently seek her counsels," but that did not mean yield to human authorities when those authorities insisted on obedience.

Later on December 19 he was permitted to preach in Tübingen's cathedral, as the faculty statement indicated, and then in the city's St. Thomas Church. As far as he and his supporters were concerned, he was an ordained Lutheran minister of Word and Sacraments. Yet there was no formal customary human rite of an ordination ceremony. Others, when they learned of his functioning as an ordained minister, were outraged. To them he appeared as a schismatical disturber of the peace and health of the church, a throwback to the sixteenth century Schwärmer (the bane of the Lutheran Reformation) and companion of other, self-serving charismatics and illuminati. On January 1, 1735 Zinzendorf returned to Berthelsdorf. Events in 1735 united the opposition and animosity toward Zinzendorf and the Moravians crossed borders and the Atlantic.

Two other 1734 journeys had major results. The first was undertaken by the Moravian leader who longed to be a missionary in the new world, Georg Böhnisch. He traveled with a small group of Schwenkfelder exiles to Pennsylvania, becoming thereby the first of the Unity to settle in the "richest poor man's land." The second journey was by the now-invaluable Spangenberg. He arrived in England on December 17, 1734, two days before Zinzendorf assumed the office of the ministry of Word and Sacraments. Christian Ernst zu Stolberg-Wernigerode, the Count's cousin, already in England, warned Ziegenhagen against Spangenberg and stressed that discord accompanied Zinzendorf. Christian Ernst was part of the Halle-Wernigerode-Münchausen network that opposed Zinzendorf and which independently befriended and supported Muhlenberg's theological studies and ministry. He became one of Muhlenberg's patrons and correspondents. Spangenberg had been instructed by Zinzendorf to negotiate with Oglethorpe to obtain places on the general's ships en route to Georgia. The Count sensed that Augustus III would reconsider his reconsideration of Augustus II's strictures against himself and the Herrnhuters. Zinzendorf wanted to provide a safe haven for the Brethren in the new world.

Georgia's trustees included wealthy and influential London merchants, and Spangenberg set about to cultivate their favor for the sake of the potential émigrés. He encountered some seemingly residual undertones and leaders of the supposedly defunct French Prophets and those touched by Philadelphiaism. Some years later a resurgence of these movements would surface in Moravian and British circles associated with the Fetter Lane Society. Almost always a courteous person who calmed stormy situations, Spangenberg contacted and impressed Ziegenhagen favorably in spite of Christian Ernst's caveats. Two days after Christmas (OS), Ziegenhagen introduced Spangenberg to Oglethorpe and the Court Chaplain acted as translator for most of the interview.[33] Oglethorpe became convinced that the Moravians were an ancient Christian church and ought be accommodated in the colony. While this position led to the inclusion of the Moravians as passengers, Oglethorpe had to overcome the suspicions some trustees harbored about Zinzendorf and the Herrnhuters.

Ziegenhagen was in a curious position. Zinzendorf's cousin, Christian Ernst, actively promoted opposition against the Count. Halle sought to undermine the passage of the Moravians to Georgia, convinced that they and Zinzendorf would only increase the confusion in an already confusing place and that the limited funds from the London merchant-philanthropists might be siphoned away from Halle's projects, such as the resettlement and support of the Salzburg Lutherans, to be applied to the Herrnhuters. Georgia director, Viscount Perceval, Earl of Egmont, wrote that the Moravians were "a lot of enthusiasts... under the protection of a Baron Sindersdorf, himself an enthusiast, who, though a layman, preaches."[34] On the other hand, Ziegenhagen genuinely liked Spangenberg and felt that his Halle colleagues could have handled the situation more diplomatically. At this point, Ziegenhagen seemed to have a more kindly view of Zinzendorf than others in Europe. That perspective was to change.

Spangenberg decided to accompany the fourteen settlers to Georgia. Ziegenhagen suggested that the Brethren settle forty to fifty miles from the Salzburgers. The trustees donated some land for the Moravian settlement. Moving quickly, Spangenberg and the Moravians left England before the end of January, 1735. When, shortly afterward, Ziegenhagen learned a fuller account of Spangenberg's departure from Halle and his closeness to Zinzendorf, he grew cooler toward the now America-bound young leader. In April, 1735, the trustees agreed to settle fifty-five more Brethren in Georgia. On board the same ship was the recently consecrated Moravian bishop, David Nitschmann, and the Anglican priest who longed for the assurance of God's grace, John Wesley.

Nitschmann's consecration raised again the issue of Moravian identity. Many Moravians, often in hiding or connected to Lutheran and Reformed churches, were determined to maintain their ancient customs, languages, and distinctive sense of community. The Count's providing a sanctuary was appreciated, but his vision for the *Jednota Bratrská* was different than theirs. The Brethren in the Polish, Hungarian, Czech and Prussian diaspora were eager to retain the continuity of their historic episcopate as a definite sign of their identity.[35] Herrnhut was neither the totality of the Unity nor was Zinzendorf the only leader. Being part of Lutheran and Reformed congregations was, for many, temporary, even if they received ordination in such a church. The Reformed in Poland and Prussia handled Moravian matters differently than the Lutherans. The latter expected the Brethren to become Lutherans and to be integrated into the Lutheran congregations. The Reformed were willing to establish Reformed-Moravian congregations, and therefore avoided the questions of schism and violation of the Peace of Westphalia. These congregations would be served by Moravian pastors who also functioned within the Reformed context. In this manner Christian Sitkovius, one of two consecrated Moravian bishops (also called "Seniors"), served a Czech Reformed-Moravian congregation in Thorn, Poland. The other bishop, Daniel Ernst Jablonsky (1660–1741) was Senior in Poland during the reign of Augustus the Strong. At the same time Jablonsky was the court preacher to the Reformed Prussian king, Friedrich Wilhelm I. From a Reformed perspective, Jablonsky could function as a Moravian bishop and as a Reformed minister.

In 1734, Sitkovius inquired if Zinzendorf thought it fitting for the Moravian Seniors to consecrate one of the Brethren at Herrnhut as a bishop. Zinzendorf agreed, asking that it be done quietly and for mission-ary purposes. By March 13, 1735, Sitkovius was too frail to travel to Berlin for the consecration, so he sent his written consent. On that day, after a theological examination, Jablonsky consecrated David Nitschmann the Carpenter as a bishop of the Unity. King Friedrich Wilhelm urged the Count to be consecrated as a bishop for Moravians. Zinzendorf de-clined, fearing the step would be considered schismatic.

By now the word was out that Zinzendorf was "ordained." The Swedes and others were displeased by what they understood was a violation of Lutheran standards. In May, 1735 the Count traveled to Sweden to request from the king a certification from the Swedish church that he was a thoroughly sound Lutheran. Such a document might be used as a tacit recognition of his ministerial status. The ruler informed the Count that there was no need for such a certificate, and Zinzendorf returned to Herrnhut (May 28). Two weeks later, he and his associates were shocked by a Swedish royal rescript against Zinzendorf. The Swedish royal court saw the Count as schismatic, trouble-making and unorthodox. In response, he wrote the king a lengthy open letter detailing his adherence to the Augsburg Confession. Attacks intensified from several quarters. As he left Europe (July 29, 1735), Nitschmann ordained Johann Georg Waiblinger, a citizen of Swedish-controlled Schleswig, to be pastor-elect of the recently organized Moravian community in Pilgerruh, Schleswig. Waiblinger's ordination without benefit of referral to the official church was taken as an act against the official church. And Zinzendorf's neighbor, Baron Huldenberg, lodged a complaint with the government about Zinzendorf and the Herrnhuters enticing Huldenberg's tenants and servants to become virtual vassals of the Count through Herrnhut's religious warmth. Tensions with the government and state churches heightened as more Moravian missionaries were sent to the Danish West Indies, Georgia, Russia and Surinam. Zinzendorf reacted by undertaking a walking tour or "witnessing journey" through southern Germany and into Switzerland. This appears to be in partial fulfillment or perhaps a trial of one of the Covenant's goals: reforming preaching and witnessing through itinerancy. Plainly, the established authorities suspected his intentions and activities.

Criticism mounted in Scandinavia and Germany. On January 1, 1736 Zinzendorf, knowing that the Danes were among many who voiced objections about his claim to be ordained, wrote the Danish monarch, Christian VI. He asked for what amounted to an endorsement of his status as a Lutheran pastor. Failing that, Zinzendorf offered to return the Cross of the Order of the Knights of the Danebrog. The response was ominous: Christian VI requested that the decoration be returned because Zinzendorf's retention of the Order might convey the impression that the king favored the Count's controversial innovations and ideas. It took him six months to comply.

In those months, the situation deteriorated rapidly. He spent most of January in Herrnhut, strengthening the community's structure and advocating that they avoid any appearances of schism or separation from the Lutheran church. Buoyed by the apparent reception of his views by the Herrnhuters, he undertook another mission. He and the Countess traveled to Holland to discuss the possibility of sending more missionaries to Dutch overseas territories and to set up a Moravian settlement in Holland. When the couple stopped at Cassel on their return trip on April 21, they were informed that on March 20 Augustus III had determined that Huldenberg's complaint was justified and that the Count had violated the terms that lifted the first banishment. Accordingly, the Elector-King ordered Zinzendorf banished again from his Saxon homeland, and that another commission make an investigatory visit to Herrnhut. He departed for Ebersdorf and she for Herrnhut.

The second Saxon investigation took place from May 9–18 with Superintendent Löscher among the examiners. As had the earlier commission, these examiners determined that Herrnhut's practices were within the norms of the Augsburg Confession, and that the Countess should be unmolested by the authorities. Löscher even praised the Herrnhuters but he and the government stopped short of lifting the ban on the Count. In July, Augustus III issued the *Konventikilpatent*. Through it, conventicles were forbidden in Lutheran congregations, but Herrnhut's status was left unmentioned and unclear.

In the ensuing months the Count became the Pilgrim Count. Negotiations with the financially strapped counts Ysenberg led to the establishment of the Moravian settlement at the Ronneburg castle in Wetteravia. Zinzendorf used the nearly ruined castle as the center from which he would go and to which he would return. His plans led to the development of a larger-than-Herrnhut community called Herrnhaag. In the same period, he leased property at nearby Marienborn. From an organizational perspective, Ronneburg was the seat of the *Pilgergemeine*, the Pilgrim Congregation. This was not so much a congregation as it was an "itinerant executive conference" whose personnel changed and through which missionaries were trained.[36]

Energized by rejection and opportunity, the Pastor-Count went on a wide-ranging missionary journey through the Baltic states. During his travels, he contacted the Prussian king, Friedrich Wilhelm, suggesting that the Brethren establish an orphanage in Prussia. Friedrich invited Zinzendorf to meet with him and his court in October, 1736. The meeting took an unexpected turn; the king contacted Jablonsky to establish a panel to examine Zinzendorf's doctrinal stance with a view of consecrating him as a Lutheran bishop for the Moravians. The examination did not occur until April, 1737. In the interim, Zinzendorf's situation both improved and worsened.

The Herrnhuters and Zinzendorf generally were accepted in religious circles in Frankfurt am Main, but residents near Ronneburg were increasingly troubled over their presence and activities. The exiled Count continued to travel as new settlements were founded in German states and Holland. From December 6–9, 1736 at a conference of leading Moravians held at Marienborn, discussion centered on the Moravian episcopate, the ways to strengthen the new settlements, establish new ones, and support the missionaries. The conference is traditionally regarded as the first synod of the Renewed Moravian Church.[37] Zinzendorf and others of the *Pilgergemeine* moved on to Amsterdam and then to England.

This English visit, January–April, 1737, had mixed results. Zinzendorf offended Ziegenhagen by not notifying the Court Chaplain of his arrival and not paying a timely courtesy call on him. Instead of contacting Ziegenhagen immediately, the Count was introduced to Oglethorpe (January 9) and, through Charles Wesley, to the man nominated to be the next archbishop of Canterbury, John Potter (d. October, 1747).[38] Potter was receptive to Zinzendorf and his version of the Moravian tradition. He seems to have known of earlier contacts with the Brethren.[39] Potter and Oglethorpe began the process by which the British parliament later recognized the Moravian Brethren as an ancient episcopal church and considered their clerical orders valid by Anglican standards (1749). In turn, Zinzendorf made Oglethorpe and Potter members of the revived

Order of the Mustard Seed. Potter encouraged Zinzendorf to be consecrated a bishop for the Moravians.

But Edmund Gibson (d. September, 1748), the bishop of London and prelate who had jurisdiction over religious affairs in British North America, opposed the Moravians in England, was suspicious of their influences in the Americas, and hostile toward Zinzendorf. Gibson wanted the Moravians to register as a foreign religious society and not seek to gain any Britishers as members. He opposed the Wesleys and Whitefield out of his concern for the fragmentation of the Anglican church through the enthusiasms and tactics of the Evangelical movement. The Count held services and meetings in his own lodgings, developed relationships with German expatriates, and met with sympathetic English evangelicals and Quakers. In 1737 the Moravians were marginally involved in British religious affairs. By the next year, however, a "Moravian crisis" took shape on the English side of the channel as well as on European and American shores.

When Ziegenhagen and Zinzendorf finally met, the Count offered to preach, a request that Ziegenhagen adroitly neither fulfilled nor denied. Zinzendorf inquired about the German settlers in Pennsylvania. Ziegenhagen told him about the United Congregations and Halle's decision not to pursue securing a pastor for the setting. The Chaplain probably reflected on the poor quality of German clergy, the presence of defrocked and imposter-pastors, the hodge-podge of groups who gravitated toward Penn's Holy Experiment. They may well have touched on the state of the Indians and the possibilities among them for the spread of the Gospel. After fewer than seven weeks in England, the Count was notified that his examination in Berlin had been scheduled, so he left Britain.

Zinzendorf went first to the Brethren in Amsterdam and Frankfurt. The affairs in the Heerndyk community appeared to be in good order, but the members of the Dutch Reformed classis of Amsterdam were becoming steadily more outspoken in opposing the Brethren, their seemingly schismatic settlements, and the Count. The classis was not about to recognize the Brethren as an *ecclesiola* in their *ecclesia*. Leading members of the classis were collecting complaints, conducting interrogations of the Brethren, and studying the Count's publications. The Frankfurt situation had changed from initial cordiality to active wariness. In response, Zinzendorf rapidly penned yet another confession of faith before hurrying to Berlin.

On April 16, 1737 the Lutheran deans in Berlin who conducted the theological examination concluded, as did all the previous examiners, that Zinzendorf was a theologically sound Lutheran. But they raised legal and canonical questions: would consecrating this Lutheran as a bishop for the Moravian Brethren in effect recognize the Brethren as a separate church next to the Lutheran, Reformed and Roman Catholic churches in Prussia? The Great Elector referred the matter to his court preacher, Jablonsky. In turn, he requested an opinion from the civil court. As might be expected, the response was that the anticipated consecration would not give the Brethren a separate status. Jablonsky's moving ahead with the rite indicates that he was persuaded that since a Moravian bishop (himself) could be a Reformed pastor, then, canonically, a Lutheran minister could be a Moravian bishop. But whose canon law? The Prussian Lutheran church's? Hannover's? Saxony's? The Anglicans? On May 20, 1737, in Jablonsky's residence, Moravian bishops Jablonsky and Nitschmann, with written certification from Sitkovius approving the event, consecrated Zinzendorf a bishop for the Unity.

While Zinzendorf carried on his ministry, his field marshal stepfather and others attempted to negotiate an amnesty that would allow the Count to return to Saxony and Berthelsdorf. During the course of the negotiations (June–December, 1737), he was able to be at home. Augustus III insisted, however, that he subscribe to the complete Unaltered Augsburg Confession, the same condition Löscher had imposed. Again, he refused, and again became the *Pilgergraf* (Pilgrim Count). One of his last acts before departing Herrnhut was his first episcopal act: he ordained the Lutheran, Peter Böhler (1712–1775), to be a minister-missionary to Georgia.

John Wesley returned from Georgia on January 29, 1738 (OS), and Whitefield had departed for Georgia the previous day. Böhler and several Herrnhut companions arrived in London on February 7, and met Wesley the same day. Over the next several weeks, the Brethren spoke with both Wesley brothers and members of the Oxford Holy Club. Böhler took an active role in organizing some Germans living in and around London into Herrnhut-like bands. English evangelicals, including the Wesleys, often joined them for prayer and edification. James Hutton (1715–1795), later publisher of Whitefield's journals, started an evangelical group that met in a room in Nettleton Court on Aldersgate Street, and Böhler arranged for his Germans to gather in rooms in Fetter Lane. John Wesley admitted that Böhler showed him more about the Savior's love and God's grace than he had experienced previously. Böhler left for

Georgia on May 13 to meet Whitefield and to move the foundering Moravian remnant to Pennsylvania. On May 24, while listening to Luther's Preface to Romans at the Aldersgate meeting, John Wesley's heart was "strangely warmed." Glowing with that warmth toward his Moravian friends, Wesley and several companions journeyed to Germany to meet the Count and observe the Unity and other religious communities.

They arrived in the United Provinces, met von Watteville, and on July 4 the Count and the Anglican priest met at Marienborn. Wesley, impressed by the faith among the Moravians, also had a positive response to Zinzendorf. The Count considered the troubled Anglican priest to be one of his followers. In the course of his travels, Wesley stayed in Herrnhut, Berlin, Jena and Halle. He retracted his initial enthusiastic reactions when he began to doubt the Count's and the Brethren's views on justification and sanctification. Several years later, he commented that Zinzendorf seemed so dominant among the Brethren that the Brethren seemed more like shadows than partners in the community.[40] His reservations about the Count and aspects of Moravian theology grew more pointed through 1738–1741, ending in a rupture of the relationship between the Methodists and the Moravians and a harsh confrontation between Wesley and Zinzendorf accompanied by mutually acrimonious pamphlets and treatises.

From January to April, 1738, in addition to his other activities, Episcopus Zinzendorf delivered numerous *Reden* (discourses) in Berlin. None of these was a sermon from the pulpit of a Lutheran or Reformed church; he was not welcomed by the clergy of either recognized Protestant church. Characteristically, criticism and polemics energized him. As the attacks directed against him and the Brethren proliferated, his vision of Christian unity and his role expanded. He started to plan a voyage to the Danish West Indies and British North America. The April rescript by Augustus III renewing his exile coupled with the intended trip to the new world led the bishop and the leaders of the Unity to expand activities and to strengthen their settlements. He arrived in Amsterdam, full of vigor and confidence, but was delayed in finding a ship to the Caribbean. While he waited, his foes in the Amsterdam classis struck.

On October 30, 1738 several leading clergy issued a *Hirtenbrief* or open pastoral letter to Dutch Reformed clergy and congregations.[41] Although the *Hirtenbrief* was not approved by the whole classis, it functioned as the classis' severe denunciation of the Count and the Herrnhut-related Brethren. The authors, led by Dr. Gerardus Kuhlenkamp, had conducted the interviews and debates with Moravian laity and catechists. The *Hirtenbrief* is a long, detailed assault. It warned almost up to the point of prohibiting the Brethren and the Count from preaching and teaching in Dutch Reformed congregations. Along with the warning were admonitions to governmental officials to curtail the activities of the Brethren because they were accused of being schismatics. While the document's rhetoric was standard fare using expressions such as wolves in sheep's clothing, destructive foxes destroying the Lord's vineyard and poisonous leaven in the loaf, it was effective. The faithful were warned not to listen to their smooth talk. The Herrnhuters must not be linked to the ancient and honorable descendants of Jan Hus and the Bohemian Brethren. They had no clear doctrines or confession of faith and shared nothing with the apostolic church. The Count's confession of faith to the Swedish king was ridiculed as a garden without walls and a house without doors or roof. He was accused of agreeing with anything as long as he could draw the gullible into his orbit. Translated into German, it was widely circulated in Germany and soon crossed the Atlantic. The *Hirtenbrief* summed up the major criticisms that Halle and others had been saying about Zinzendorf and the Brethren. Zinzendorf attempted a quick response and von Watteville was more detailed in his rejoinder, but the damage was done. The word was out in Europe and America: steer clear of the Count and the Moravians, neither listen to nor trust them.

Zinzendorf embarked for the West Indies in the closing days of 1738, arriving in mid-February, 1739. He dealt effectively with several major problems related to the local Danish authorities' denial of the Moravian clergy's legal status. Could they perform legal marriages without a document permitting them to do so from the state church? Who had ordained them and were their ordinations valid? The issue of proper credentials would be raised repeatedly in Pennsylvania. The Count-Bishop shortened his visit to the Americas because he heard reports of disorders in the Fetter Lane Society and the drift in England and Europe of Brethren seeking independent status and not being *ecclesiolae* in the legally sanctioned churches. Wesley was becoming vocally disenchanted with the Brethren, their lack of structure, and with Zinzendorf personally.

Favorable seas and winds brought him to England in late April 1739. Inspirationalists akin to the French Prophets and controversies in the Fetter Lane Society threatened to rend the community. Wesley was moving into opposition. The Moravians attracted Britishers in England, Scotland and Ireland, thereby raising questions of their relationship to the Church of England. Should they register as "dissenters"? If they did, would that have a negative impact on the Brethren in Scandinavia, the

German states and Holland? Should the Brethren in Britain seek, instead, some affiliation within the Reformed and Lutheran communities?

The inspirationalists active in the Fetter Lane Society denied the efficacy of the sacraments, expressed negative views on Biblical authority and claimed that a visible church was not necessary. Emotional outbursts occurred during the meetings. Philip Heinrich Molther (1714–1780) arrived in London to calm the situation. His view of what came to be called "the Stillness" of waiting for the Spirit to lead the community was rejected by Wesley. In December, 1739 Wesley broke with the Fetter Lane Society and established a society in an old foundry. The Foundry Society soon drew many English away from Fetter Lane. News about the arguments and problems in London spread to Pennsylvania where Whitefield was arguing with the Brethren over predestination. Again, Evangelicals in America who were engaged in the Great Awakening were aware of the *Hirtenbrief*, anti-Zinzendorf treatises, Whitefield's criticisms and Wesley's growing breach with Zinzendorf and the Brethren.

By June 1 the Pilgrim-Count was back in Marienborn. A series of conferences or synods between June 1739 and December 1740 among the leaders helped to shape the Unity's future and renewal. During this time, Leonhard Dober proposed to resign as Chief Elder and Zinzendorf sought to lay aside his episcopal office. He felt that too much of his time and energy was being consumed in administrative tasks. The synods also moved toward understanding the Unity as a separate ecclesiastical body wherever that could be safely maintained and as leaven-like movements or a diaspora within the state churches. While the Count was in proximity to the decision-making process, the movement toward separate status was more latent than active. Between January and May, 1740, the Count and members of his family undertook a mission to Switzerland and established contact with Calvinists in Geneva. The December, 1740 Gotha Synod attempted to establish some doctrinal positions to counter the sometimes extreme accusations of Halle, Wesley, the Reformed, and the Lutherans. His next step was to complete his abbreviated journey by traveling to British North America. In June, 1741 he temporarily laid aside his episcopal office, and another synod at Marienborn accepted his decision and Dober's resignation. The Brethren were faced with the issue of ascertaining who would be the head of the *Gemeine*.

Shortly before he left Holland, he made two presentations. First, on August 16 he preached at the monthly Brethren *Gemeintag* or Unity day. One citation, Revelation 3:10, concerned the congregation in Philadelphia. In the sermon he shared his understanding of a true prophet as someone who forgets his own welfare, goes into the world with the Savior's testimony, and does not hold back on expressing that message even if others find it offensive and opposition is raised. He continued that the prophet proclaims the word about the Lamb, cross and blood wisely so that the listeners will understand and respond. His pastorate, like that of all true prophets, was for the whole world. He then became specific about his relationship to the Brethren and his mission. Is he warning the Unity about separatist tendencies and moving away from the Brethren as his ministerial base? In any event, he expressed his understanding of the *Kirche* and his mission.

> I have met many people who thought that we Brothers and Sisters, we who live in the world, were Moravian Brothers, as if we comprised the Moravian Church. I could not correct this idea but had to remain silent about it, although unhappily....Those who were with us from the beginning know that we [that is, the Count] proclaimed the Gospel even before we knew that there was a Moravian Church, before we read a book that told about such things, before we saw a single person....There is at all times a house of God, an invisible one....The Savior has had his own people at all times. At times it had to be single prophets and witnesses, at other times whole societies....Claudius of Turin had the Waldensians close at hand for the testimony he bore. Luther had the Moravian Bohemian Brethren. These were whole *Religionen* which helped the witnesses....We had to be content with the places given to us. Just so, in the beginning we were happy that the Savior sent us the Moravian Brothers until we clearly saw their great attachment to their old church, beyond our expectation and hope, and that they either had to become separatists or we had to yield to them....You have the witness of three hundred years that you are servants of God. Then they [the Moravians] called some of us into their congregations so that various individuals served among them as God's servants, as others service in the Lutheran or in another church with whose principles he is in harmony....The Herrnhut *Gemeine* is a pure Lutheran *Gemeine*, as the one at Herrnhaag is mostly Reformed in its structure and its residents....But basically and in accordance with the main concern, people should not think that we [Zinzendorf] could ever be bound to one sect in the world. Precisely for this reason, we are able to accept people from all kinds of *Religionen* into our *Gemeine* without requiring them to change their denominational form. The Brothers and Sisters believe the following, and before the Lord I say this as a truth of which my whole heart is convinced, "the real testimony of Jesus Christ is not contrived and does not include all sorts of statements which can

teach human wisdom. Rather we absolutely remain with the preaching of the Lamb's death and merits. Testimony is limited to witnessing and writing according to the spirit and style of the Scriptures without worrying about or fearing the consequences….It proclaims the truth of the divinity of the Lamb and all the results of his humiliation in general and in particular. Thus indeed neither death nor the devil can harm us all."[42]

Second, as he left Holland, he issued what has been called the Heerndyk Statement:

> I have been commissioned by the Lord God to spread the word of Jesus' blood and death, without concern as to what happens to me as a result. This has been my calling even before I knew of the Moravian Brethren. I have been and still am, associated with the Moravian Brethren, who have taken our Gospel of Jesus Christ into their hearts and called me and other Brethren to serve their fellowship. Yet I do not separate myself thereby from the Lutheran Church, for a witness of Jesus can remain in this church. Meanwhile, I cannot restrict myself as a witness to one church, for all the earth is the Lord's, and all souls are his. I am a debtor to all.[43]

Zinzendorf made several points. First, as did the Apostle Paul, he insisted that his commission to proclaim the Gospel came from God and not through any human agency or institution. Given his disagreement with the Dresden Consistory, refusal to subscribe to the complete Augsburg Confession, view of his Stephanas-style ordination, and entry into the ministry of Word and Sacraments, he reasserts his claim to ministerial legitimacy. Second, his calling from God to "spread the word" antedated and is independent of his relationship with the Moravian Brethren. They did not authorize his ministry (God did) nor is his ministry linked to any office he may have held or will hold among the Brethren. Third, the Moravians have taken into their hearts Zinzendorf's understanding of the Gospel. He did not learn it from them; they learned it from him. Fourth, only in the sense that the Brethren have requested him and others to serve their fellowship can the term "call" be used. He does not rely on their sanction or anyone else's, but solely on God's summons. Fifth, he still regarded himself as a member of the Lutheran church. That was his genuine ecclesial base. The sub-text is that he insists that he is a full-fledged Lutheran pastor and that he will exercise ministerial functions within that church. Finally, God's communion of believers and consequently Zinzendorf's ministerial functions cannot be restricted to merely one church body. The concept of one, holy, catholic and apostolic church called, gathered, enlightened, and in the process of being sanctified by the Spirit will grow more prominent as he takes up his work in America. Unlike his venture into the Danish West Indies as a Moravian bishop, his sojourn in British North America was intended to relate to the Lutherans and diaspora Brethren.

In late August or early September, Zinzendorf and a group of others, including the sixteen-year-old Countess Benigna, arrived in England. Now Pastor Zinzendorf sought to have an interview with Archbishop Potter and presented to him a copy of his recently printed edition of the Berlin *Reden*. The work was being circulated in Europe — and criticized heavily by those who pounced on whatever the Count had to say or write. In order to prevent a further breach between Wesley and Zinzendorf, Hutton arranged for Zinzendorf and Wesley to meet on the afternoon of September 3, 1741 in the Gray's Inn Walk or garden. This meeting turned out to be a rehearsal for the session with Muhlenberg. Wesley wrote a Latin version of the wrangle.[44] According to Wesley, Zinzendorf opened with an attack on Wesley for changing his "religion," that is, for shifting into a series of central disagreements with Zinzendorf. Zinzendorf's Lutheran position on justification and continual human sinfulness and Wesley's understanding of perfection were at odds. The Count was not about to yield a single point to the young English cleric. Zinzendorf accused Wesley of wanting to wreck the Brethren's mission in Britain and of sowing discord at Fetter Lane. Zinzendorf recognized the potential for legalistic works righteousness in Wesley's position and the latter saw the former as verging into antinomianism. From the Gray's Inn Walk onward, a war of words was fought in print and open debate. The Moravian account of the encounter is muted or even unmentioned.[45] Methodists, however, recall it not only with praise for Wesley but describe the Count as hostile, arrogant, unreasonable, evasive — and shocked that Wesley repudiated him.[46]

The London Conference (September 11–23) struggled and prayed about the next Chief Elder. The answer came on September 18 through prayer and the lot: Jesus is the Chief Elder. The announcement was postponed for the European settlements until November 13, and not made effective for the Americas until 1748. On September 28 Zinzendorf, Benigna and others left England for British North America. The door for new beginnings was open, and he was determined not to yield to anyone but God.

Endnotes to Chapter Four

1 The coat of arms is in the Unity Archives at Herrnhut and was reproduced and printed in calendar form for the tercentennial of Zinzendorf's birth (2000) with notes as *Kostbarkeiten.*

2 The descriptions of Zinzendorf's family are drawn from Weinlick, Snyder, Hamilton and Hamilton, Zeiser, and Freeman.

3 Sebastian Andreas Fabricius, director of the Bible House, wrote Muhlenberg to keep him abreast of news from Halle (e.g., *Journals*, Vol. 2, 31).

4 Georg Ludwig had a son (Friedrich Christian) and daughter (Susanne Louise) by his first wife.

5 Weinlick, *Zinzendorf*, p. 19.

6 Weinlick, *Zinzendorf*, p. 19.

7 Born in Bern, in the same year as Zinzendorf, he also entered and left the Paedagogium in the same years as the Count. After working with his father, he reconnected with Zinzendorf in 1722. In 1727 he became the Renewer's adjunct at Herrnhut, was ordained in 1740, and, in 1744, was consecrated as the bishop for the Reformed tropus. A significant part of his ministry before formal ordination was as the *Vorsteher*, roughly "business manager," of various Moravian communities. His adopted son, Johannes (1718–1788), enrolled at the University of Jena with Zinzendorf's son, Christian Renatus. In 1746 Johannes married the Count's daughter, Benigna (1725–1789).

8 See A. Salomon. The German version is in *Hauptschriften, Ergänzungsbände*, Vol. 10. The collection does not contain all the correspondence, but has six of the Cardinal's notes and letters to Zinzendorf and twenty-seven by the Count to de Noailles.

9 See Cheetham, pp. 223–233.

10 An aristocratic peer, he was appointed archbishop of Paris by Louis XIV. He was created a cardinal in 1700. Critics as well as admirers have considered him as pious but lacking in discernment in choosing his confidents. See Herberman, Vol. 11, pp. 85–86.

11 See McManners, Vol. 1, pp. 647–680.

12 In 1697, before he became a cardinal, Archbishop de Noailles attempted to stop the appointment of children to the rank by stipulating that the person must be at least fifteen years old and under clerical supervision for at least six months prior to receiving the tonsure. Over time the title was applied even to parish priests.

13 Christian Ernst (born and died in 1724) and Christian Renatus (1727–1752).

14 Weinlick, *Zinzendorf*, p. 47.

15 He was said to have the strength to bend iron bars, and to have fathered over 320 children.

16 Hamilton and Hamilton, p. 24.

17 The *Ratio Disciplinae Ordinisque Ecclesiastici in Unitate Fratrum Bohemorum* (*Řád církvení Jednoty Bratři českých*) was the basic church order that delineated the Essentials, Ministerials and Incidentals of the Unity. Edited by Comenius in the mid-seventeenth century, it evidenced the desire of the Unity to achieve substantial consensus among the leaders in the context of communal discipline and good order. See Říčan, pp. 350–388 and Hamilton and Hamilton, pp. 32–33.

18 See Weinlick, pp. 79–82.

19 David the Father had also been a carpenter. There also were three Johanns and another Anna in addition to a Georg, Melchior and Rosina.

20 See *Hauptschriften*, Vol. 14, *"Antizinzendorfiana aus der Anfangszeit 1729–1735,"* part 1. Note Carl Regent, S.J.'s 1729 treatise against the "new sect" in Silesia, the so-called *Schefferianer* (Schaefferites, that is, Melchior Schaeffer) and *Zinzendorffianer* who publish their catechism and other works at Herrnhut. The same volume contains the extensive and detailed 1743 attack by an anonymous author on the Herrnhuter Brethren who have sent their missionaries through a spate of territories including Lapland, among the Hottentots and in Pennsylvania. See also Vols. 6, 15 and 16.

21 Hamilton and Hamilton, p. 43.

22 Suspended from office by the Fathers on February 27, he was dismissed by royal decree on April 2, 1733.

23 See Erb, *Pietists*, pp. 18–19 and 277–287.

24 Richter became a Moravian missionary to Christian slaves in Algiers. See Weinlick, p. 118.

25 See Weinlick, p. 117–118. The last of five *Reden* inspired Langemack to resume an active ministry.

26 The modern German version uses *"bereitgestellt"* (made available), while the more traditional text, *"verordnet,"* may be taken as "be in an ordered office."

27 The German and Latin texts for Article XIV agree closely.

28 "Apology" of the Augsburg Confession, Article XIX might be stretched to provide room for interpretation if bishops rage against sound canonical order. Zinzendorf could have appealed to Luther's "That a Christian Assembly or Congregation has the Right and Power to Judge All Teaching and to Call, Appoint, and Dismiss Teachers, Established and Proven by Scripture," (1523). Luther, an ordained priest and never consecrated as a bishop, actually functioned in an episcopal manner even before the presentation of the Augsburg Confession (1530). He ordained Georg Röher in 1525, conducted a disciplinary visitation of congregations in 1528, assigned and sometimes attempted to remove men as pastors in congregations. After 1535 he often presided over the process leading to the ordination of candidates and was the ordainer as well as the writer of the ordination liturgy. See *Luther's Works*, Vol. 53, pp. 122–126.

29 Beyreuther, pp. 73–74.

30 Spangenberg, p. 182; also see Weinlick, p. 119.

31 Weinlick, pp. 119–120.

32 Spangenberg, p. 182.

33 During the conversation, Spangenberg switched to Latin when he sensed that Ziegenhagen was spicing the translation with anti-Zinzendorf comments.

34 Podmore, *Moravian Church*, p. 15.

35 See Říčan, pp. 382–386.

36 Weinlick, pp. 129–131.

37 Weinlick, pp. 134–135.

38 Potter had been Regius Professor of Divinity at Oxford and a recognized authority of the Greek patristic theologians. He was bishop of Oxford prior to his election as archbishop of Canterbury. Potter was suspected of sympathizing with Arianizing Unitarians in the Anglican church.

39 Amos Comenius (1592–1670) spent nine months in England (1641–1642). Jablonsky spent three years at Oxford and also corresponded with English bishops as well as becoming a member of the Society for the Propagation of Christian Knowledge. Potter had been nominated for the archepiscopal post on the same day that Charles Wesley introduced Zinzendorf to him.

40 Wesley, *Journals* for July and August, 1738.

41 See *"Antizinzendorfiana,"* pp. 285–339 for a German rendering of the Dutch original.

42 Weber and Atwood, pp. 4–7 (quote taken from a prepublication text).

43 Weinlick, p. 152.

44 Wesley. The translation appears as footnotes on pp. 211–215. Wesley referred to the conversation in other writings.

45 Spangenberg omits it in his biography of Zinzendorf.

46 Tyerman, pp. 336–341.

Chapter Five

MUHLENBERG PRIOR TO HIS ARRIVAL IN THE COLONIES

From his birth (September 6, 1711) to his death (October 7, 1787), Heinrich Melchior Muhlenberg left journals, reports, letters, records, an autobiography (*Selbstbiographie*), and persons as witnesses. Nevertheless, if the external record is ample, the internal requires scrutiny. Moravians, when they recall him, seem to regard him as a carping critic.[1] Traditionally, American Lutherans regard him as the patriarch and many revere him as the patron saint of the Lutheran church on the continent. Revisionists caricature him as a patron-pleasing, credential-touting, subservient-stubborn German whose scant creativity matched his shallow theology.[2] He is, however, more complex. Muhlenberg's *Lebenslauf* or life-journey to Philadelphia provides insight on his impact in the controversy and later on his influence in American religious life.

An initial question opens a way to understand him: "Where was he?" With regard to space and time, he was largely in the German states from his birth to his last glimpse of Europe, July 24, 1742. The Hannover he left and the Britain to which he headed were in the midst of the War of the Austrian Succession.

His nine week orientation with Ziegenhagen in England (April 17 – July 9, 1742) was critical for his future ministry. Ziegenhagen gave him a vigorous, if condensed, introduction to the English language, further theological education, and practice in preaching in English. Muhlenberg spent the rest of his life in the colonies that became the United States. Politically, he lived all but his last decade as a subject of one or another prince from the House of Hannover. Muhlenberg died two months before his son, Frederick Augustus, then chairing Pennsylvania's special convention, declared that the state had ratified the new national constitution.

Yet, where was he as a writer? When he wrote his journals, reports, letters and *Selbstbiographie,* he was on stage presenting himself to at least four audiences, and he shaped his rhetoric accordingly. He consciously excluded as well as included materials and observations in light of audience expectations and sensitivities, e.g., his views about the colonials who revolted against the House of Hannover. The extant writings are intended to be public and are not of the same quality one expects if a person is sorting through her or his intentions and deeds.

First, he was his own audience. The writings have a diary-like quality intended to promote self-reflection and spiritual growth through the process of writing and later reading the entries. Here he stood in the tradition of Augustine's *Confessions*. While the *Journals* and *Selbstbiographie* reflect sincere expressions of personal humility before and devotion to God, Muhlenberg omitted important spiritual points usual in such literature. A case in point is the absence of when and how he felt God calling him to the ordained ministry. Yet he followed, with his family's consent and encouragement, a determined course of preparation for the ministry. He pursued that goal at the same time he confessed to having his aspirations to godliness "smothered" and that he took little heed to the cultivation of his soul.[3] He seems to have been unaffected by Enlightenment criticisms of revealed religion, Scripture and the Church. While Muhlenberg struggled through delays to his obtaining an education occasioned by his father's untimely death and persistent financial hardships, he moved steadily through a regular theological education on the way to ordination. His road to ordination contrasts sharply with Zinzendorf's.

God was another audience. Augustine shaped his *Confessions* as an extended prayer to God with humans as a secondary audience. We overhear Augustine speak to God. Zinzendorf did not hesitate to speak of himself and to God especially in his poetry and hymns. Muhlenberg made occasional asides to God rather than focusing on God as the major reader-listener. He was conscious, however, that the Lord was always present in the events described, listening to the prayers raised in dire circumstances. Still, his extant writings do not reflect the intense spiritual soul-searching or heart-warming exaltations that other Pietists and contemporary evangelicals shared with God and their readers. If Muhlenberg often mentioned his prayer life and meditations, he kept their contents between God and himself. He did not hesitate, however, to speak his mind to others when he warned that God overheard and would act upon their cursing, brawling, and frivolities. God is in everyone's audience and would soon step on to the center stage of life. Muhlenberg felt and acted in the confidence that God was constantly, reliably present, observing his attempts to witness faithfully and forcefully to the Law and the Gospel as sailors, sinners and Zinzendorf were to discover.

The third was the immediate and most important human audience. Its members were his German patrons and the Halle authorities. At critical junctures in his life, Muhlenberg was encouraged and supported by teachers, pastors and, especially, wealthy aristocrats. The latter made possible the completion of his studies and the ecclesiastical call necessary for a ordination. Muhlenberg experienced the gracious willingness of brothers and sisters in the faith to nurture devout, potential leaders. Given the rhetoric of his time, his references to friends and sponsors are far from obsequious; they disclose a network of individuals and families who were ready to aid him and to whom he would return thanks, service, and correspondence. They formed part of his understanding that he, they and other "children of God" were part of God's soteriological enterprise of extending the Gospel's reach. Pietist connections within the official Lutheran churches kindled spiritual warmth within the ecclesiastical structures. Those persons and connections also generated debate and dissension.

Most of his patrons were closely associated with the institutionalized Pietism headquartered in Halle. The Halle Fathers required their missionaries to send to them journals and regular reports about their activities. Muhlenberg continued the practice from his arrival in North America until he died. He also used the reports and correspondence as a means to make requests for further support for funds and additional personnel. On their part, the Fathers excerpted portions from the missionaries' writings, circulating these as part of the *Hallesche Nachrichten*. Through the *Nachrichten*, the Fathers kept European Pietists informed and inspired about the progress God was making through their representatives on the mission fields. The Pietist readers were also encouraged to continue and increase their spiritual and financial support of the Halle *Stiftungen*.

Through the written records sent from America and elsewhere, the Superiors, as Muhlenberg also termed them, kept the missionaries connected to the source of their spiritual formation. Self-conscious about their German audiences, men like Muhlenberg cast their reports in terms that linked them and their readers across thousands of miles. They shared spiritual bonds and a common religious language. Muhlenberg adjusted but did not forsake his Pietist expressions when addressing American audiences, but he retained the language in his journals, reports and letters. An examination of the *Journals* shows that while he did not formally set forth the Hallesian steps in the plan of salvation, readers can see the outlines of the prescribed conversion process.

Muhlenberg also cast his communications in light of what he knew his Halle readers wanted to learn. In the encounter with Zinzendorf, therefore, references to Halle, Ziegenhagen, Zinzendorf's aunt and Pietism in general had a special bite and satisfaction for the readers when they read of how their man handled the Count. Muhlenberg's same awareness of his Halle audience is also clear in his reports about the sinful attitudes and activities he encountered in his travels, the accounts of troubled souls coming to accept God's grace and being reborn, and the colonists' indifference to religion. Modern readers might see Muhlenberg as a self-righteous prig, but, given the Lutheran-Halle emphasis on human corruption, repentance and *sola gratia* (grace alone), his style and conduct were to be expected. Occasional successes seemed to vindicate his and Halle's theological strategy of moving persons to *Bekehrung, Wiedergeburt* and sanctification. He also went to great lengths to present his position to the Halle authorities during the American rebellion. He had to walk carefully each day between being a Tory and being a "Patriot" in order to carry out his ministry. At the same time, he had to report to Halle Fathers — good subjects of the House of Hannover — that he neither supported nor sympathized with the rebellion.

Muhlenberg's contemporaries in America were the fourth audience. On the one hand, the *Journals* contain records of pastoral acts, minutes of meetings, texts of documents, names of deacons and elders, and accounts of controversies and their resolutions. These are official in the sense that he and others could return to them as a register of activities, supporting evidence in disputes and a chronology of events. Another purpose for the *Journals* was the reading of entries to small groups of pious ministers and laity. These readings were intended to edify the listeners as they heard about God's work among them. The *Journals* not only spread news; they served as a basis for the audience and reader to recollect God's providential care, the rigors of ministry and the advances made in applying the Law and Gospel in a raw land. If Ziegenhagen gave him an orientation through personal conversations and worship at St. James Chapel, Muhlenberg used his *Journals* to encourage his ministerial colleagues and congregants in carrying on the Lord's work.

The question, "Where was Muhlenberg?" reaches beyond the prefatory concerns to understanding the man who faced Zinzendorf. Considerations about his character and experiences prior to landing in the colonies are vital if we are to make sense of the controversy. Muhlenberg's native Einbeck was particularly grateful to Hannover's Elector Georg. In 1718 the already King George I ordered repairs to the parts of the city damaged in the closing years of the Thirty Years War. In the same year, the seven-year-old Muhlenberg entered the city's Latin school. He claimed his mother was the daughter of a superior officer in the Elector's army. His father, a cobbler-craftsman, was respected enough by his fellow citizens to be selected as a town councilman. Nicolas Muhlenberg apparently recognized his eldest son's abilities and prospects to move up in the social hierarchy. The twelve-year-old adolescent received catechetical instruction at the Neustadt church near his home and was admitted to Communion in 1724. Around the same time his father died suddenly. Muhlenberg reported that in this period he began "the first reproaches of conscience, awakening, and resolutions toward godliness."[4] These nascent movements of conscience, he wrote, were gradually smothered.

Forced by his father's death and the consequent need to support the family, he left the Latin school. Within two years, however, his family permitted him to spend his evenings taking lessons in arithmetic and on the organ (1726–29). The family also gave him leave, once he was twenty-one, to select his own evening activities. He chose to study Latin and Greek under the rector of the Latin school and eventually was admitted to the regular program. Resented at first by the younger boys, he studied hard and gained their respect. To supplement his income and pay his debts, he sang in the school's choir.

To this point, Muhlenberg can be seen as being recognized for above average academic ability, having an affinity for Latin, and possessing musical talent. He also showed enormous drive to move forward in being a "child of God" in the Pietist sense. Reflections on his spiritual life repeated the refrain of budding awareness of his sinful dispositions and God's grace, but he never specified worldly conceits of which he was culpable. Why he studied Latin and Greek remained unmentioned, yet both were expected of ministerial candidates.

In 1732, thinking he had a teaching position in the town of Clausthal, Muhlenberg left home. When the position did not materialize, he was both sorely disappointed and financially destitute. Providentially, he believed, Raphelius, master of a school in nearby Zellerfelde, offered him a post he could not refuse. Muhlenberg's chief responsibility was to continue his studies in preparation for the future. In return for lessons from his senior teachers, he taught the boys Luther's catechism, writing and arithmetic, and played the clavichord for school functions. He clearly enjoyed teaching and the relationships he formed with the students. His own studies centered on a thorough engagement with the Latin texts of Cicero, Julius Caesar, Virgil, Horace and Terence, the Greek New Testament, Hebrew and French. Raphelius urged him to enroll in a university, probably the newly established (1734) University of Göttingen. Not only was his lack of money an obstacle to his entry to the school, but he seemed too old. Younger persons were being given preference for the stipends from the cities pledged to support their native sons at Göttingen. Again, Providence intervened; no one younger than he applied for

Einbeck's municipal funds, and his mother provided the balance. In 1735, at the age of twenty-four, he enrolled at Göttingen.

Making due allowance for his confession of being spiritually indifferent and on the verge of associating with dissolute companions, his time at Göttingen was marked by two life-shaping experiences, and a third such experience occurred as he left his Fatherland. The first was his association with Joachim Oporin (1695–1753). The Reverend Doctor was Göttingen's first professor of Dogmatic and Moral Theology. Muhlenberg lived in Oporin's home and became his secretary. Under him, Muhlenberg learned his theology and ethics. More important, the older man guided the student's religious development through the Hallesian steps in the plan of salvation. So, as Muhlenberg wrote in the *Selbstbiographie*:

> In short, I was convinced that there was not a drop of blood in me that was not filled with many sins. So now, when I learned to know sins as sins, there followed there from sadness, remorse, suffering, hatred of these sins, shame, humiliation and contrition, hunger and thirst for the righteousness of Jesus Christ. In such a state, I was directed by the Rev. Dr. Oporin toward Jesus the Crucified, who was wounded for my transgressions and bruised because of my iniquities, the sinner's Friend who calls all the weary and heavy-laden to Him and refreshes them, the free and open Fountain, for sin and impurity; Christ, who declares the believing sinner just and receives him in grace, the Covenant God and Saviour who blots out transgressions for His own sake, the faithful and good Shepherd who pastures His sheep and leads them in the paths of righteousness for His Name's sake! These and other like promises, which are spirit and life, refreshed my heart. The wounds of Christ healed my wounds. The merit of His death gave me power for a new life. What I heard in the five courses in Dogmatics, Exegesis, Morals and Homiletics strengthened my new faith.[5]

This was his paradigmatic experience of *Bekehrung* and *Wiedergeburt*. Muhlenberg used the power for a new life gained under the tutelage of an honored teacher and supplemented by formal theological instruction to spur his life and ministry. Oporin always held a cherished place in Muhlenberg's estimation.

The second experience was potentially calamitous. While the situation itself is instructive about the attitude of Orthodoxist clergy toward Pietists, Muhlenberg's reflections on and expressions about it in the *Selbstbiographie* indicate the ways in which he dealt with controversies and his self-understanding throughout his ministry. Shortly after his conversion-rebirth, he and two of the university's theological students began tutoring and catechizing local poor children. The effort was an outgrowth of the Hallesian view of good works and *Inneremission* (domestic social ministry). Muhlenberg taught them the Small Catechism, arithmetic and writing. The trio of teachers acted without notifying the local pastors and congregational leaders of the parishes to which the children belonged. Those pastors and leaders concluded that the independent project smacked of divisive sectarian impulses endemic to Pietism. They lodged a formal complaint against the student-teachers with the authorities in Hannover. For the first and probably last time in his life, Muhlenberg operated without the semblance of due authorization and outside the duly constituted organizational structures. He reported on the resolution of the affair:

> But since we had no understanding of the law, the good God sent us an experienced advocate, who was a chancellor in the court of a high-born count there. This man took hold of the matter as a lover of truth and brought it to the point where the high provincial government made a decree and placed it under the supervision of the theological faculty. This also had the effect of provoking good benefactors to gather the expenses needed for the rental of classrooms, heat, and the other necessities. This little institution served the purpose of keeping many beggar-children from the streets and idle ways and instructing them in the doctrine of the faith. So, too, the young students had opportunity to practice catechization.[6]

Muhlenberg realized that with timely assistance, persistence and effective use of the relevant authorities, he could achieve even more than he expected while preserving good order. Further, the results included establishing an arrangement, in this case the Poor School's supervision by the university's theological faculty, that could have the project continue in a responsible manner once the originators moved on. In addition, he experienced the generosity and support of persons who were eager to expand a low level project and who would become his patrons and partners in carrying forward God's work. Finally, he also realized that he could handle critics by working through due processes. This and two other incidents prior to his departure for America provided a pattern for his ministry and later reflections on the many controversies in which he was embroiled — and his meeting with Zinzendorf.

The complaint about the Poor School led to his being accepted as a student in the university's theological program. As one of its students, he was permitted to catechize and preach occasionally in the university's church. The noble Reuss family — Zinzendorf's in-laws — with several of its numerous counts, countesses and baronesses along with the High Sheriff von Münchhausen moved to make him a chaplain in the XI Count

Reuss' mansion and secured the money for his tuition and other expenses. Through a series of events that involved Halle-based missionaries, Muhlenberg was supported by his patrons to study under the Halle Fathers.

The Halle connection became tangible in May 1738. Upon his arrival at the Pietist center, Muhlenberg was quickly incorporated into the programs and institutions founded by the Franckes and their colleagues. Taken into the network of pastors, professors and nobles related to Halle, he was assigned to teach in one school while pursuing his own courses. He served as a teacher of theology, Hebrew and Greek. His keen eye for detail, manner of improving conditions and experience in managing organizations were all honed for his later ministry, as he became the inspector or superintendent of the sick wards in the Halle clinic.

His intentions to be a missionary to India were changed when Count Heinrich, Zinzendorf's brother-in-law, proposed that he be called to the diaconate and superintendency of four departments of an orphan home at Grosshennersdorf in Upper Lusatia. The post carried with it responsibilities as the assistant pastor of St. Peter's church. The orphans' home-school was founded and supported by, among others, Henriette Sophie von Gersdorf — Zinzendorf's aunt and implacable critic. Muhlenberg successfully hurdled his interviews with her, preached a trial sermon, then received and accepted a call to the pastoral position with duties at Grosshennersdorf. He detailed the process in the *Selbstbiographie* at least partially to substantiate his credentials while contrasting the legitimacy of his authorization as an ordained pastor with the shaky claims of others — including Zinzendorf:

> After the acceptance of the call, which took place on August 12, 1739, I had to journey to Leipzig and be examined by the councillors of the Consistory, Dr. Deyling and Dr. Boerner, in Hebrew and Greek, the dogmas of Christ, conversion, regeneration, justification, and sanctification, and especially in the history of the symbolical books [Book of Concord]. Several days later I was ordained to the preaching office by the Rev. Dr. Deyling in the presence of the whole ministerium of Leipzig and provided with testimonies thereto.[7]

During the nearly three years he spent at Grosshennersdorf, Muhlenberg supervised four departments: the paedagogium for the sons of impoverished noble Silesian widows, a free school for thirty-two poor boys, a school for poor girls, and a charitable home for "old, decrepit, blind, lame, and deaf widows and those neglected in their youth."[8] He mentioned the arrival and inclusion of Bohemian refugee children, commenting that they were made welcome at Grosshennersdorf rather than to have them proceed to Herrnhut. Obviously expecting that the Baroness' descendants would read his account, he was also moved by honesty when he reflected that the "whole institution was under the finest laws and regulations." The experience he gained in teaching, organizing, and administering the complex departments provided him with further evidence that good order and steady leadership were essential for ministerial endeavors to succeed.

The Baroness' fiscal situation deteriorated. Creditors were closing in and staff, including Muhlenberg, had not received their salaries for months. She kept the departments going for over twenty years, but was finally forced to turn it over to one of her cousins. He sought to save the estate by reducing staff, expenses and enrollments. At the same time, Muhlenberg felt impelled to fulfill his prior intention to be a missionary. After some hesitation and declining further positions with the von Gersdorf and other families, he returned to Halle (July, 1741). On Muhlenberg's thirtieth birthday, Gotthilf Francke urged him to accept the invitation to be the pastor of the "poor folk" in the Province of Pennsylvania. Three United Congregations, as noted earlier, had petitioned the Fathers three times to send them a minister. The Father's inaction verged on rudeness, for they had not even acknowledged the last communication in 1739. As Muhlenberg later discovered, the same Halle authorities did not inform the congregations that they were dispatching him to serve the Lord's scattered Lutheran sheep in Penn's wilderness. The change of tactics was motivated largely by news that Count Zinzendorf was planning to be in Pennsylvania to work among the Lutherans in the United Congregations and elsewhere. Within Francke's invitation was the desire to stop Zinzendorf and the Moravians. And they wanted Muhlenberg to be the man to do that task.

Appropriate ecclesiastical bodies took the next steps. For his whole time in America, Muhlenberg was formally under the Halle-oriented German ecclesiastical jurisdiction of the Lutheran Consistory in Wernigerode. Because he was going to a British province, two other appropriate ecclesiastical bodies were involved: the German Court Chaplain at St. James, and Gibson, Bishop of London. Finally, Muhlenberg had to be called by and to accept the call proffered by the lay deacons and elders of one or more of the United Congregations. The SPCK also endorsed Muhlenberg and supported him occasionally in America. The procedure was intended to safeguard congregations and the ordained ministry from abuse and swindlers. It put a premium on deliberation, order and mutual responsibility. Given the American situation and the dangers of pretenders, renegades, schismatics and sectarians, the process aimed at minimizing such risks while drawing on a vision of the Church as a set of interpenetrating and mutually responsible communities and leaders.

Muhlenberg's third life-shaping experience unfolded as he prepared to leave his German homeland for England and America. Opposition to Pietism within and secessionist movements from the established Lutheran church generated anti-conventicle laws and clergy opposition. Those who held prayer and discussion meetings in their homes were seen as potential sectarians, while pastors who invited others to preach at worship were suspected of being schismatic or at least critical of other clergy. Local clergy groups and consistories attempted to halt the Pietist influences by intimidation and formal accusations. The presumed perpetrators were alleged to teach and preach heterodoxy and schism, suspected of being frauds and renegades, and to lack authorization and credentials to carry on the ministerial office.

In the course of winding up his affairs, bidding farewell to various patrons, and spending time with family and friends, Muhlenberg met for prayer and exhortation with his associates and relatives. Wherever he went, Pastor Muhlenberg informed the area superintendent and senior pastor of his presence and availability to be of service in congregations. This was standard procedure, and he maintained it punctiliously. The initial responses to his presence and overtures were decidedly negative. His first pastor and spiritual guide at the Neustadt church risked severe criticism but persisted in his invitation to Muhlenberg to preach. Rumors and complaints about Muhlenberg spread quickly. Some said that he was a disgraced minister who recently returned from America and was bilking people of funds for a spurious mission effort. This may have been an echo of the Schultz incident. Muhlenberg carefully recorded his intentions and activities in the *Journal* (February – March, 1742 entries). He detailed the voluntary and innocent nature of the gatherings in his family's home, the propriety of his preaching, the jealousy of other clergy, the falsity of the whispering campaign against him, and his exoneration and vindication by all authorities. He detailed instances in which he confronted authority figures in secular and church governments, showed himself to be an able debater and master of procedures, and gained the respect of those who finally understood the malice of persons who opposed Muhlenberg. Throughout his aggressive defense, he displayed his several credentials at key junctures to prove the validity of his ordination and authorization to go to America. Muhlenberg was feisty when he knew he was on solid ground, even to the point of arguing with his social and ecclesiastical "betters."[9]

If in the Göttingen incident he and his companions were extricated by a noble patron, Muhlenberg handled the departure confrontations himself, relying on his wits, credentials and careful presentations. He was well prepared to meet his critics in the Old World, and he would follow the same strategy in the New. By the time he met Zinzendorf, Muhlenberg was a veteran in arguing and winning his case.

The road to Pennsylvania led him from Germany through Holland to London. From mid-April to mid-July, 1742 he was the guest and student of Court Preacher Ziegenhagen. While at the St. James Chapel, Muhlenberg re-acquainted himself with Halle's Hebrew and Old Testament professor, Johann Michaelis. The latter had been in England since the previous year. For slightly more than two months Muhlenberg was introduced to the Church of England, British colonial procedures and the English language. In addition, he had the stimulation and joy of learning more theology from Ziegenhagen. He was especially impressed with the Court Preacher's exegesis of the Gospel of John on the new birth, Jesus the Shepherd, false shepherds and hirelings. He gained much from Ziegenhagen's discourses on Galatians and Michaelis' on Isaiah. These biblical portions and images were to recur throughout Muhlenberg's preaching and writing. For all practical purposes, the London interlude was the capstone to Muhlenberg's formal theological education and the last time he was a student. From that point forward, he was on his own. Throughout his later life, he looked back on the days before his departure with gratitude and nostalgia.

One further inquiry about Muhlenberg's stance, "Where was he with regard to Zinzendorf?" By the time he was twenty-one (1732), Muhlenberg certainly would have heard about the already thirty-two-year-old Count, the controversies surrounding him, the Herrnhut settlement, and the beginnings of the Moravian mission-diaspora. By 1732 Zinzendorf had published enough to become quite familiar to friend, foe and Muhlenberg.[10] Since Muhlenberg, a Hannoverian, was both geographically, politically and spiritually in Halle's orbit, he knew the antipathy between the Halle Fathers and the Lord of Berthelsdorf. While Muhlenberg was at Göttingen being criticized for acting in defiance of the law and gaining a regular theological education, news of Zinzendorf's approvals by the theological faculties at Stralsund and Tübingen (1734–35), assuming the pastoral office, and consecration as a Moravian bishop

(1737) elicited swift, negative responses from Göttingen, Halle, Württemberg, Wittenberg — and Muhlenberg. His opinions about the Count were sharpened by what he heard first hand at Halle from Zinzendorf's former teachers. News of Zinzendorf's being banished from Electoral Saxony and Upper Lusatia (1736) probably was greeted with feelings of vindication by the Fathers and Muhlenberg. Finally, his close contact with Baroness von Gersdorf added to Muhlenberg's store of stories, impressions and information about Zinzendorf's character and temper.

As he prepared to leave for America, Muhlenberg learned more pointedly that Halle's impetus for sending him to Pennsylvania was spurred by the Fathers' intention to thwart Zinzendorf. He wrote Gotthilf Francke from Grosshennersdorf: "My lordships [Count Edmund Henckel (1687–1752) and Heinrich, XXIV Count Reuss] wanted to assure me that Count Zinzendorf with a retinue of twenty persons had already preceded me and gone to Pennsylvania, which in their opinion would be a tough test for me. All of this and much more has driven me to prayer and has also sometimes made me uneasy."[11] Before he left his Hannoverian Fatherland and Europe, Muhlenberg knew where his most formidable adversary was and knew how to goad him into making the rash public statements that the Halle-sent missionary would report to his German and American audiences through letters and journals.

In May, 1742 Ziegenhagen gave Muhlenberg three documents. The first was a letter to the German Lutheran pastor with the Salzburg Lutheran refugees at Ebenezer, Georgia, Johann Martin Bolzius. It instructed him to travel to Pennsylvania with Muhlenberg to help in his mission. The Court Chaplain may also have given the new missionary the name of a Philadelphia contact or perhaps Muhlenberg was informed about him later. The individual was Johann David Zwifler (or Zweifler, d. 1749). He was associated with the Moravians but apparently was alienated from Zinzendorf. The second, dated May 12 (OS) was an open letter, "Reliable Testimony Concerning the Call of Pastor Muhlenberg to America."[12] It began with a summary of the requests made by the three Pennsylvania congregations for a pastor. Ziegenhagen simply passed over the delay in responding and Halle Fathers' failure to answer their 1739 plea for a pastor. Gotthilf Francke was mentioned prominently and often in the Testimony. The Court Preacher gave the reader-listeners a glowing account of Muhlenberg's experiences as a pastor, teacher and administrator, stating further that he "accepted the call issued to him" by the congregations — although they had not taken that step and did not know that he was coming to them. The Testimony's initial point is:

> [H]e is a man who has a good report and until now has been found to be both correct in doctrine as well as blameless in life. Furthermore and especially we herewith declare and announce that he is the rightfully called teacher and pastor of the aforementioned congregations; he has the right and the authority to teach the pure and genuine word of God publicly and privately among them, to administer the holy sacraments, baptism and the Lord's Supper; to proclaim to the penitent the forgiveness of sins in the name of God and Jesus Christ, but also to announce God's righteous wrath and punishment to the impenitent if they persist in their self-security and godlessness; to arrange for catechetical examinations for adults and young people; and he is authorized to carry out freely and unhindered everything else which belongs to the office of an evangelical teacher and to the salutary discharge of the same. For that reason he is also to be acknowledged, loved, and received as a servant of God upon his — God grant it — safe arrival among them.
>
> They will treasure his office and conduct of the same and thank God for it from the heart; and, that the same may become and be fruitful and blessed for all, they will do all they can gladly and with pleasure.[13]

The final document, dated May 18 (OS) and addressed to the elders and lay deacons of the three congregations, covers much of the same ground as the Testimony, giving more detail about Muhlenberg's ministerial experience and the love his German constituents had for him. Anticipating objections and objectors, Ziegenhagen wrote:

> His heart is entirely and favorably inclined toward you, and all that he desires is to bring forth fruit in adults and young people among you. Therefore I beg you from the bottom of my heart and in the name of God and Jesus Christ, remember how long you have been without an upright shepherd and teacher; remember how difficult it was before one was found who out of love for you overcame everything which might have held him back and dedicated himself to what is of help and service to you. Love him all the more. Be of one mind with him, let there not be separations and divisions among you but agree with one another from now on in Christian brotherly love. Acknowledge that his arrival among you is an important kindness and gracious visitation of God for you. For that reason agree among yourselves and help with combined energy so that he may not only carry out his ministry unhindered and in an orderly manner but also and especially in a blessed way. He who despises him does not only despise him but also him who has sent him and in whose name he comes to you. See to it that no one among you burdens himself with guilt so that what is intended by God for your salvation may not turn out to be for you and your children's great harm.

Do not allow anyone to make trouble for him or to oppose his ministry maliciously but be his helpers and coworkers.[14]

Muhlenberg had his papers in order when he boarded the *Georgia Packet*: matriculation and certificate from the University of Göttingen, ordination papers from the Leipzig Consistory, and the documents from Ziegenhagen. He was a bold and shrewd debater, experienced administrator and determined Halle man. He also knew that he had to neutralize, if not discredit, Zinzendorf as soon as possible. Yet there were facts he did not know. He did not know that Zinzendorf had been called to be the pastor of the Philadelphia congregation, that the other congregations were being served by other men, and that no one knew he was coming. Nor did he or Halle have any idea about the conditions of colonial life and faith — or lack of faith. As the *Georgia Packet* moved across the Atlantic, the momentum for controversy increased rapidly.

Endnotes to Chapter Five

1 See Reichel.

2 See Bodling.

3 *Journals*, Vol. 1, pp. 1–4.

4 *Journals*, Vol. 1, p. 1. Actually from the *"Selbstbiographie."*

5 *Journals*, Vol. 1, pp. 3–4.

6 *Journals*, Vol. 1, p. 4.

7 *Journals*, Vol. 1, p. 5.

8 *Journals*, Vol. 1, p. 6

9 Muhlenberg may have written a 1741 anonymous tract entered against anti-Pietist Balthasar Mentzer, the Court Preacher and Consistory member for Braunschweig-Lüneberg. See *Correspondence*, p. 18, note 16. Perhaps rumors of his supposed authorship accounted for reactions to him.

10 See *Journals*, Vol. 1, pp. 77–78.

11 *Correspondence*, Letter 4, p. 10.

12 *Correspondence*, Letter 8, pp. 24–26.

13 *Correspondence*, Letter 8, pp. 24–26.

14 *Correspondence*, Letter 9, p. 28.

Chapter Six
ZINZENDORF IN PENNSYLVANIA

Philadelphia was Zinzendorf's vision:

> And to the angel of the church in Philadelphia write; These things saith he that is holy, he that is true, he that hath the key of David, he that openeth, and no man shutteth; and shutteth, and no man openeth; I know thy works: behold, I have set before thee an open door, and no man can shut it: for thou hast a little strength, and hast kept my word, and hast not denied my name.[1]

Leade's Philadelphia and other radical movements had some influence on Zinzendorf, yet more important was the opportunity to shape the Christian community anew. Already at Herrnhut, Herrnhaag and Marienborn, Zinzendorf explored theological insights and images that could startle his contemporaries, e.g., Jesus the Brother-Husband-Father-Creator; the Spirit as the Mother; the centrality of Jesus' blood, wounds and flesh; and the need to make the invisible Church (*Kirche*) into a visible reality through *Gemeinen* (communities of faithful disciples) regardless of their ecclesiastical organizations (*Religionen*). God was opening the door through which Zinzendorf — God's prophet to the world — would go. That there would be hypocrites, liars, slanderers and perverters of God's truth, he knew right well. The clamor raised by his enemies in the old world was growing louder and more strident. He was to meet their North American counterparts on arrival. Nevertheless, he was confident that God would vindicate him. The perseverance and determination demanded of prophets would help usher in the New Jerusalem.

While his mission was expressed in his "Pennsylvania Plan," it reflected the 1723 Covenant of the Four Brethren.[2] Schools were to be established, itinerant evangelists sent to awaken unbelievers and to re-awaken lethargic believers, existing congregations would be reformed, and works of mercy accomplished. In addition, the new world called for missions to the Indians. Settlements such as Nazareth and the work in the Lehigh Valley (the future Bethlehem) would attract and inspire non-Moravians to revive their own ecclesial bodies. To that end as well as to give a faithful witness to Christ in expanding America, he would devote considerable effort and exercise virtually unchecked authority over the spiritual and moral discipline and temporal affairs of those settlements. Unlike his experiences in Europe, he met with no resistance from Brethren who wanted a separate Moravian church.

The Pennsylvania Plan was driven by his vision for a genuine Christian community that he called the "Church of God in the Spirit." Given his expanded concern for the unity and peace of the Church, he sought to end the bickering and continual fracturing among the German Protestants. He wanted a broad Christian community in which the *Religionen* kept their separate identities yet shared the essentials of the faith, reached the unconverted, and grew in devotion and discipleship. For the sake of the vision, he willingly laid aside his Moravian offices and duties, and assumed the office of prophet-apostle-servant of God in British North America. He and the Bethlehem Brethren soon called him "Johanan," that is John the Baptist. He was announcing the coming of the kingdom and the near-arrival of the Lord, summoning believers and unbelievers alike into a heartfelt and humble relationship with the Savior, and willing to speak hard words and set himself to endure the hostility of hypocrites and slanderers. In his Heerendyk sermon and statement, he identified Lutheranism as his base, so Pennsylvania's German Lutheran congregations were his particular areas of responsibility.

Even before he reached New York, the Count heard about the dire religious situation among the German settlers from Böhler, Spangenberg and others. Ziegenhagen described the plight of the United Congregations, commenting that the Halle Fathers had no intentions of sending a pastor to serve them. The Brethren had already started their activities and had positive as well as negative responses in the colony's urban and rural areas. The nearly dozen German religious groups were apprehensive about the Brethren and Zinzendorf in particular.[3] They suspected he wanted to draw them into his orbit and to impose his will on them. The Reformed had other concerns. In the aftermath of Zinzendorf's quick trip to the Danish West Indies, the Amsterdam Classis sent its New York ministers a covering letter with the *Hirtenbrief*, urging them to "watch against their [Zinzendorf's and the Brethren's] errors."[4]

Nevertheless, Spangenberg and Böhler also reported on the massive awakening occurring in British North America and the crowds that listened to Whitefield in Philadelphia. They told the Count of an arrangement that might be the start of his Church of God in the Spirit. The Separatist, Johann Adam Gruber, probably encouraged by Spangenberg, proposed in 1737 that persons from the different German groups gather on Sundays for prayer and mutual edification.[5] Spangenberg sent a copy of the proposal to Zinzendorf, commenting that this could be the Count's call to minister in Pennsylvania. By 1738 the resulting Association of the Skippack Brethren began meeting at the farm of Christoph Wiegner (1714–1777), a Schwenkfelder given refuge at Herrnhut until

90

Augustus III's expulsion decree. Among the Association's leaders were Johann Bechtel and Heinrich Antes (1701–1755).

Following his arrival in New York (November 18/29, 1741), Zinzendorf and several in his group stayed on Long Island and Staten Island with persons he met in the West Indies. From November 25–29/December 6–10 the company made its way through New Jersey, arriving in Philadelphia on November 29/December 10. While in New Jersey, Zinzendorf met and conversed in Latin with Whitefield's fiery colleague, Gilbert Tennent. Tennent soon thereafter lambasted the Count for theological errors and began a scandal-mongering war of words, accusing the Count of keeping a mistress (Countess Benigna, actually his daughter). Zinzendorf responded by inviting others to listen to what he said and to watch what he did. Accordingly, he wrote to Pennsylvania's Governor Thomas that he, Dominie de Thürnstein, would arrive in Philadelphia in order to minister to the German Lutherans there and in the area. Whether or not he wanted to repeat the pretense that he employed in Stralsund by using one of his name-titles, the Pennsylvania Gazette reported (December 3, 1741) that "Sunday night last, Count Zinzendorf arrived here from New York, attended by some of the Moravian Brethren, who are, with a considerable Number more expected in the Spring, to be settled at Nazareth on the Forks of the Delaware."[6] He invited the governor to send observers who understood German to attend events that he planned to conduct publicly and in his rented house. Thomas responded with a letter of welcome, noting that he did not need to dispatch such witnesses. For a time there was no need for observers: pulpits and meetings were closed to the Count. Many who knew of him avoided or spoke against him, while the "Pennsylvania Religion" of indifference was disheartening, especially in light of his expectations. He concluded that the so-called awakening was only an emotional and spiritual firecracker.[7] In February, 1742, through an open letter, he lashed out with Laodicean vigor at those who shunned him for his first two months in the colony.[8]

Benezet welcomed him into his home, and several days later the entourage moved into a three story rented house near Sassafras (now Race) and Second Streets. Zinzendorf planned to alternate living there and in Germantown, interspersing trips to Indian country and to Bethlehem. On December 8/19 he and others made their way to the Lehigh Valley. They celebrated Christmas Eve New Style in order to maintain solidarity with their brothers and sisters in Europe. During worship that night, he named the settlement "Bethlehem." It is possible that Antes and Zinzendorf were in contact with each other on the journey to Bethlehem. The Count approved Antes' and others' plan to convene a meeting for persons from the different German groups. On December 15/26 Antes sent out a circular letter, asking members of the Skippack Association and others to attend a *Generalkonferenz der verschiedener Religiousparteien deutcher Nation* (general conference of the different religious groups of the German nation) in Germantown on January 1–2/12–13. This was the first of seven conferences or Pennsylvania Synods that Zinzendorf attended.

Zinzendorf was not idle during the intervening two weeks. On December 16/27 he spoke for the first time to a gathering of Germans in Oley (near Reading). Bechtel provided Dominie de Thürnstein with a pulpit, and he preached his first American sermon at the Reformed church in Germantown on December 17/28. The text was 1 Timothy 3:16 and he centered on the "great mystery of God," Jesus' incarnation. Some who listened and a large number who heard about the sermon were offended by his comments. Using the Herrnhaag themes of the Lamb and Jesus' blood and wounds, he criticized those who claimed to be Christians and thought they knew and understood the mysteries of God; they were only deceiving themselves and those who followed them. He insisted on the new birth through thorough humility. The true *Gemeine*, he continued, is not in any institutionalized *Religion* or sect but in the invisible *Kirche*.[9] A number of Separatists, Dunkers and Mennonites, and those from groups claiming special revelations, concluded that he was attacking them.

The first of the Pennsylvania Synods met in Germantown on January 1–2/12–13. Antes restated the purpose announced in the invitation: "not to wrangle with each other over opinions, but rather to treat in love concerning the most important articles of faith, in order to ascertain how nearly we can approach each other in the fundamentals, and in other matters of opinion which do not subvert the ground of salvation to bear with one another in love."[10] As soon as Antes finished, a Separatist read a written statement denouncing the first sermon and the preacher. Spangenberg wrote that the Count responded with such gentle and reasonable words, that he rose in their collective esteem and was elected as the syndic or chair at the second synod (January 14–15/25–26). Less friendly reports claimed that the criticisms came from most of the persons at the meeting, and Zinzendorf, interrupting rudely, tried to argue his detractors into submission. Those who were wary of him regarded him as arrogant and patronizing.[11] Both types of reactions fit earlier responses to the Count. So too was his becoming the synods' leader.

Zinzendorf hoped that the synods would advance his vision for the Church of God in the Spirit. He claimed that he would not force any structure or theology on the members. At the fourth synod (March 10–12/21–23), however, he made the case for Lutheran teachings, catechism, worship and congregational polity. As one synod led to another, the membership as reckoned by groups diminished until by the sixth conference virtually the only persons attending were Reformed, Lutheran and Moravian. The immediate aftermath of the synods was confusion, frustration and anger. Except for the Brethren and persons scattered in several groups, suspicion and animosity toward the Renewer and the Unity spread. Synods in which some Lutherans and Reformed participated continued to meet after the Count returned to Europe, but eventually were abandoned as the churches went their separate ways.

After the close of the third synod (February 10–12/21–23) at Oley, Bishop Nitschmann, Zinzendorf (called *Episcopus emeritus*) and Anton Seyffert, Sr. (1712–1785) ordained four persons as "priests," that is presbyters, for ministry in the Reformed and Lutheran churches.[12] Two Lutherans, Johann Pyrlaeus (1713–1785) and Gottlieb Büttner (1716–1745) were ordained for the ministry of Word and Sacraments in the Lutheran church. It would be another matter for them to serve in those bodies. On the same day, Zinzendorf and other Brethren went to Tulpehocken where Zinzendorf preached. The congregation asked him to furnish a pastor. He soon had Büttner in that hot spot. Subsequently, Büttner was reassigned as a missionary in Indian territory, and Philip Meurer (1708–1760) was the second Zinzendorf appointee. The earlier struggle with Stöver was rekindled and the congregation divided into two factions. Zinzendorf probably cited the Tulpehocken setting when he told Muhlenberg that he had "deposed" Stöver. While in the area, the Count preached in the United Congregations at New Hannover and Providence.

Zinzendorf and the others who shared the Race Street house invited any who were interested to join them for prayer and mutual edification. Among those who accepted the invitation were Lutherans from the Arch Street congregation. They invited him to preach on January 10/21 just as he was finishing a sermon series for the Reformed in Germantown and preparing for the second synod (January 14–15/25–26). In order to forestall objections from Böhm, he wrote the Reformed pastor, inquiring if Böhm had any authority to protest Zinzendorf's preaching according to the Lutheran officials' request. Clearly, Böhm had no such authority. The congregation and the guest pastor seemed to get along well, although all of the former knew the latter was a controversial figure. Soon the lay members of the council proposed that he accept the call to be their pastor. Zinzendorf demurred, requesting that they all pray about and consider the matter carefully before proceeding. Following his ordination, Pyrlaeus was appointed the Pastor-Count's assistant and authorized to preach when Zinzendorf was elsewhere.

Perhaps because the liturgical seasons moved from Epiphany through Lent and then Holy Week, Zinzendorf's sermons, all grounded in the appointed texts for the day, stressed sin's damnable effects, repentance, justification by grace through the Lamb's suffering, and the necessity of a heart relationship with the Savior. There were frank criticisms of institutionalized churches and their worldly, dead-souled clergy, and the arrogance and ignorance of those who mocked and rejected the Lord's prophets past and present. While these topics and the manner in which they were handled could be anticipated from preachers such as Zinzendorf, he seems to be responding to the increasing objections and criticisms raised against him and the Brethren. Nasty articles and letters in Philadelphia's German language press, hostile refutations of the Count's February and March attempts to respond, denunciations by Presbyterians led by Tennent, frustrations over the progress or — more accurately — regress of the synods becoming a manifestation of the Church of God in the Spirit, reports from Europe about the mounting assaults against and often salacious tales about him and the Brethren, and word concerning the Wesleys' and Whitefield's harsh treatises opposing his theology and the Moravian mission in Britain, all saddened, disturbed and provoked Pastor Thürnstein. Added to those burdens were reports that the Brethren who favored a separate status for the Unity rather than being *ecclesiolae* in the official churches were making progress in England and Prussia. Spangenberg wrote that the Count's "external conduct at this time was singular in every respect, and uncommon for a person of his rank."[13] That may be overly generous.

Characteristically, when attacked, the Count not only responded in kind but he became more determined, yet he seemed unable to focus his efforts. He wanted to do many things immediately and was constantly on the move, spreading his physical and emotional energies widely. He ran five synods; started a school for girls and another for boys; preached nearly daily and often more than once a day; traveled to Bethlehem and Nazareth where he not only sought to fill in his vision for the future on the other side of the open door but engaged in the community's administrative details; wrote tracts, letters, catechisms, hymns and poems; and sought to settle disputes such as that at Tulpehocken — all before May 8/19, 1742. On that day, he accepted the call to be the pastor of the Philadelphia German Lutheran congregation.

Zinzendorf had already given notice about his special ministerial calling in his statements to the Tübingen faculty, Stuttgart Directory and Heerndyk Brethren and in various publications. He was called to be a *Freiprediger*, a prophet-apostle to the world with a particular emphasis on the renewal and reform of the Christian community seeking reconciliation among the various *Religionen*. He could not be "localized" in the sense of either denominational regulations or the day-to-day pastoring of a single flock. He and the Philadelphia congregation knew that hypocrites and opponents would level accusations, slanders and criticisms at him. Such charges might reflect adversely on the congregation and could generate problems among members. Because of his prophet-apostle vocation, there would necessarily be periods during which he would be absent from the Arch Street community. An available and duly qualified adjunct would care for the flock in those circumstances. Given those conditions, the lay deacons and elders extended the local call and he accepted it with the stipulations that Pyrlaeus was to be the adjunct pastor and that Zinzendorf would receive no remuneration for his ministry from them. The call, probably drafted substantially by Zinzendorf, also termed him the superintendent and inspector of Pennsylvania's German Lutheran congregations and pastors, thereby bestowing on him, he presumed, episcopal authority in Lutheran circles. For some unstated reason, neither the laymen on the council nor Zinzendorf attested to or signed the document. In that sense *alles* was not *in Ordnung*, at least for those who challenged him.

Given the circumstances of war, suspicions about Moravian allegiances, his own status in the colony and the Quaker egalitarian ethos, Zinzendorf decided to forego his noble titles through making a public statement before the colony's leaders. Originally, he intended to abandon his estates and standing in Saxony as well, but he withdrew from that position. After rehearsing a German version of his speech in Bethlehem and translating it into courtly Latin, he asked for a meeting in Governor Thomas' residence. On the Count's 42nd birthday NS (May 15 OS), and in the presence of supporters such as Benezet and Pyrlaeus, he claimed to disclaim whatever prerogatives might be given him and wanted to be known simply as Brother Louis Thürnstein.[14] The gesture did not really work for even the Brethren kept calling him "Count" and "Zinzendorf." It did provide critics with another opportunity to jab at him, asking who he really was and under which name he was operating.

The event in the governor's mansion might have been Zinzendorf's audition before some of Philadelphia's elite. Among the men present were eleven key political figures ranging from the attorney-general, city recorder (William Allen), several justices of the peace and attorneys, and the postmaster (Benjamin Franklin). They were wealthy and powerful. The coming election and the importance of the German vote could not have been far from their minds as they took the measure of the man who addressed them in stilted continental Latin. Would he be the leader who might influence the frugal Germans? Would he be amenable to their views on the city's and colony's future? How would he and those whom he influenced be part of the development of the outlying lands owned by Hamilton and others? By May all of them knew that the Count was one of the most controversial characters ever to come to town. His ornate, even bombastic, oration was scarcely the stuff that would inspire anyone, and when he retracted his renunciation of his Saxon lands and status, some had reason to think him unbalanced. So, Allen, Thomas and the others drifted toward the melee that marked the October, 1742 elections.

Also present was Eneas Ross, of the Anglican Christ Church. He was the "commissary" of the various religious groups in the city, apparently a position that meant he acted as the chair of a loose association of congregations. He probably reported the form and content of the meeting to his valued colleagues, the Reformed Böhm and the Swedes, Tranberg and Koch. Ross also knew about Zinzendorf from reports that reached him from London as well as from local news and gossip. Archbishop Potter was still too new in his position to wield much real authority. Bishop Gibson was increasingly critical of Moravian activities in Britain generally and London especially; Fetter Lane and the Foundry were in his episcopal care. Gibson knew, too, the invectives and more reasoned objections raised by the Wesleys and Whitefield against the Count. In all likelihood, Ross and other Anglicans were still recovering from the denunciations leveled against them by Whitefield, and Tennent was still attacking. Simply because they opposed the Count did not mean Ross had to support him. Was Zinzendorf aware of his audience and their concerns? Soon the same persons would meet another and quite different German.

Around the time he appeared at the Governor's residence or perhaps on the basis of receiving the local call to be the pastor of the Arch Street church, Zinzendorf proposed to the Swedish priests and their lay leaders

96

that they extend to him the right hand of fellowship and invite him to preach at Wicaco.[15] From the Count's perspective, such a step was brotherly and logical. He had had sound relationships with the Swedish crown and church officials, and the faculty at Stralsund had certified his Lutheranness. But the Swedes in America had already heard about the Count's claims to be ordained, his consecration as a Moravian bishop, Moravian settlements in the homeland being potentially schismatic, Nitschmann's ordination of Waiblinger, and the king's 1735 rescript against Zinzendorf and the Moravians. As Zinzendorf declaimed in Philadelphia, Paul Bryzelius (also Pryzelius), a former Lutheran theological candidate who now allied himself with the Brethren, was crossing the ocean as part of a company of over one hundred Brethren. Was this the start of a Moravian mission to the Swedish settlers? Olaf Malander, Tranberg's unordained assistant, showed signs of Moravian sympathies, and Tranberg was being challenged by laypersons in Christiana. He did not need further problems. And the memory of the Tollstadius affair still lived. The Swedish colonial priests and their lay leaders had already determined that no one who did not have the requisite written documents attesting to theological acceptability and proper ordination could be allowed to officiate or preach in one of their churches. It is not clear who made the decision to refuse Zinzendorf ministerial and pulpit fellowship, but Koch certainly had a hand in it and probably told the Count his proposal was rejected. Zinzendorf felt insulted and fixed blamed Koch for the refusal. The Swedes were to meet two more Germans before the end of the year, and one met their prerequisites.

Events moved at a rapid pace. Pastor Böhm still held services for the Reformed monthly, and lived outside of Philadelphia. Some members of the Reformed congregation approached Zinzendorf, asking him to hold services for them, too. Obviously and for theological as well as political reasons, Böhm had to react. He already was composing one of several publishable critiques of Zinzendorf and the Brethren. In Böhm's eyes, the so-called Lutheran Dominie was sheep-stealing or about to cause a schism in the Reformed congregation. On the Lutheran side, Stöver was continuing his efforts to undermine Zinzendorf at Tulpehocken and elsewhere.

While Brother Louis continued to preach at the Arch Street church, he was in conversation with Schwenkfelders, Baptists and sabbatarians, seeking some accommodation with them to salvage the synods and the vision of the Church of God in the Spirit, and preparing for the seventh synod to be held June 2–3/13–14.[16] Earlier in May the Brethren received news that a ship carrying co-religionists from Germany had arrived in Connecticut. While estimates of the numbers vary, up to 120 Moravians were on board, including Böhler. While on the Atlantic, the Bethlehem-bound immigrants formed a *Gemeine* for the journey. Moravian tradition calls it the First Sea Congregation. The travelers arrived at the Philadelphia dock on the Thursday afternoon, Ascension Day OS, May 27. They proceeded the short distance to the Arch Street church where Zinzendorf had just finished preaching. After being given temporary housing in Germantown and elsewhere in the city, they returned to Arch Street for Sunday worship, May 30/June 10. There is no record of the effect on the regular members of the congregation when scores of Moravians surged among them. The seventh synod opened two days later and accepted the Sea Congregation as members. The synod therefore was composed of a majority of Moravians with a number of Lutherans and Reformed and virtually no others. On the final day (June 3/14), Zinzendorf delivered the last talk in the Arch Street building. According to the *History of the Beginnings*, it "was a detailed one on the Fellowship of God in the Spirit in all the World, on the religious [denominations] in which the members are as it were united into one [John 17:21–23] and on the visible 'little limbs' [the Church] in which the members have a fellowship as close as the limbs of a body [1 Cor. 12:14 sq.]...."[17]

Did this begin the end of the Arch Street congregation's unity? Was it the event Muhlenberg described: "On one occasion, when [Zinzendorf] had preached to the Lutherans in a house which they rented jointly with the Reformed, a few buttons of the sheep's clothing flew open and the other side of his face was revealed, which made the sheep suspicious and scattered them."[18] Muhlenberg indicates that a secession of some elders and others took place at that time, but Moravian sources do not indicate so. In any event, murmuring against the Brethren and von Thürnstein became evident. Did some members of the Lutheran congregation, including most of the lay council members, feel that they were losing the congregation that they had sacrificed to sustain for the last decade? Did they review the criticisms that held the Count was really seeking to Moravianize Lutheran and Reformed congregations? He had been their pastor for less than a month and preached fervently, but where was he guiding the congregation? While the members of the Sea Congregation soon left for Bethlehem, how many more Moravians would come, and would they all leave or would some stay to change the congregation? How committed was the flamboyant von Thürnstein to them? They had gotten along well with Böhm and their Reformed co-tenants.

Was that relationship going to become acrimonious? Times were hard, the French blockade was taking its toll, and a yellow fever epidemic threatened to be revived. They needed pastoral ministry beyond what the prophet-apostle promised to provide.

At that juncture, Zinzendorf joined the Sea Congregation on its trek to Bethlehem, leaving Philadelphia on June 6/17, stopping along the nearly 85 miles to confer with associates, and arriving in Bethlehem on June 13/24, staying there until July 13/24. His adjunct, Pyrlaeus, went with him, so that Böhler returned soon after to act as pastor for several weeks.[19] How Arch Street members received that is not known. Pastor Pyrlaeus had happy reasons to be in Bethlehem; on June 29/July 10, "the following brethren and sisters were married: David Bruce and Judith Benezet, Joh. Christoph Pyrlaeus and Susanna Benezet, Johann Böhner and Hanna Hummel, Christian Fröhlich and Esther Robins."[20] Were there rumors about problems in Philadelphia or was it simply time for Pyrlaeus to go back? The *Bethlehem Diary* notes, "Bro. Pyrlaeus and his wife and Sr. Molther must return to Philadelphia this week, if possible this Thursday."[21] The newly wedded Pyrlaeuses left for Philadelphia on Wednesday, July 7/18, while the Count and the Brethren attended to the harvest and internal Bethlehem affairs. The groom probably preached on the Fourth Sunday after Trinity, July 11/22, not knowing that it would be the last time he would do so unmolested.

We have no record of the sermon or the dynamics within the Lutheran congregation or between the Lutheran and Reformed congregations. During the week, however, members of both congregations and Pastor Böhm decided to padlock the building's door. Later, the Zinzendorf faction insisted that Böhm gave the order, and he may have. Muhlenberg reported that a Lutheran deacon put the lock in place. When Pyrlaeus and those who sought to worship at the appointed time arrived on July 18/29, he had the lock broken and entered. The service proceeded to the point of the sermon, when a disturbance interrupted the preacher. Reports about the ensuing fracas vary, but Pyrlaeus was forcibly ejected and pummeled. He returned to his residence and concluded the service. Spangenberg claimed that the violence was incited by unnamed "others":

> Some wicked people who called themselves Reformed, burst tumultuously into the church one Sunday, when the Lutheran congregation were holding their divine service, tore Pyrlaeus out of the pulpit, dragged him out of the church, and kicked him; they then took entire possession of the church, although, according to the agreement made

with the Lutherans, they were to have it only every fourth Sunday for themselves and their divine service. This contract had not been infringed upon by the Lutherans; but the people, as it was pretty well ascertained, were incited to it by others. [22]

Pyrlaeus reported:

> A mob of angry Reformed members, some drunk, dragged me out of the pulpit with much clamor and profanity and dragged me into the street, themselves taking possession of the building. The Lutheran and some other devout people, having gathered around me to protect me from further insult and injury, now went with me to my lodgings, where I delivered the sermon, and here we met frequently afterward, undisturbed.[23]

Muhlenberg connected the incident with the Count's unbuttoned sheep's mask, indicating that a disruption in the leadership had occurred at that point:

> One had taken the church record book, another the alms bag, a third the alms chest, a fourth the chalice, a fifth the key, and so on. Afterwards a Lutheran deacon, Thomas Mayor, had put a lock on the church house. On the Sunday reserved for the Lutherans, the Count sent to the church his adjunct, Mr. Pirlaeus, and the people he had enticed away from the Lutherans. When they found the lock there, they broke it off with a piece of iron, went in, began to sing, and Mr. Pirlaeus was about to preach. The Lutherans and the Reformed also gathered outside the door and saw that the lock had been broken off. A Lutheran elder thereupon went in and exhorted Mr. Pirlaeus to leave. When he repeatedly refused, and accused the elder of not being a Lutheran and told him that he was going astray, the Reformed people rushed in and dragged the adjunct out. During all this rough work on a Sunday they trampled, pushed and knocked each other about, and the women began to scream; in short there was a tumult.[24]

Thirty-four members, including several elders, of the Lutheran congregation, followed Pyrlaeus. By December 30, all but one elder had returned to the Arch Street congregation.

What did the Count do? A passing reference to a letter written to the Philadelphia congregation on July 13/24 indicates that he may have had a sign that troubles were developing over the building.[25] That evening he set out on his first of three missionary journeys to the Indians, arriving in Makunshe (now Emmaus) on the fateful day. By Wednesday, July 21/August 1, Pyrlaeus' "various letters" reached Bethlehem and the next day the letters were on their way to the Count. More letters followed from the bruised pastor with his description of the affair and apparently

100

his meeting with congregational officials favorable to him. By this time Zinzendorf was with Indians near Tulpehocken, but on his way with others to Philadelphia "because of the current disturbances." Sunday, July 25/August 5 passed quietly as it was the Reformed congregation's turn to use the building. The *Bethlehem Diary* recorded that on Tuesday, July 27/August 7, "Bro. Ludwig, who had visited and fortified the little group of our adherents in Philadelphia, who are being oppressed there, again returned here accompanied by Br. Joh. Bechtel." The tone of the report indicates that the Brethren were not going to fight to repossess the building. By Friday, after ordaining another man to the ministry, Zinzendorf left for what was to be his second journey into Indian country. Here Muhlenberg picked up the story:

> The above-described disturbance occurred on July 18, 1742, old style. About two weeks afterwards [August 1/12], when the Lutherans had gathered to edify themselves with singing and reading in their jointly rented house, the Count himself came in again with his people and wanted to preach. The Lutheran deacons warned him earnestly, however, that he should leave and not disturb them. He withdrew and went away. For some time they tried to reach an amicable agreement and settle the affair peaceably, and to this end some of the elders of the Lutheran congregation, along with one deacon from Providence, even had a meeting with them. The Count, on his part, had commissioned Peter Böhler to speak for him and through him presented a number of written articles to which they were to subscribe. The articles, however, were so curious that they were unable in good conscience to sign them; so the affair remained in process.[26]

The Zinzendorf-Lutherans, as they may be called, filed suit over the affair, and won it in 1743 on the grounds that the Reformed had no right to lock the building because the Lutherans were the legal leaseholders.[27] A squabble about a misdemeanor charge that the Zinzendorf-Lutherans destroyed the lock amounted to nothing. The Count claimed that the congregation of which he was the called pastor was the true and only German Lutheran congregation in the city, and he was the superintendent-inspector of German Lutheran churches and clergy. He then bought a lot between Race and Second Streets from the deal-making William Allen. Beginning in August, 1742 he contracted for the building of a new church called the *Evangelischen-Brüder Kirche*, that is, the Lutheran-Brethren Church. Shortly after construction began, Valentin Kraft arrived, linked up with Stöver, and gained enough acceptance by the Arch Street Lutherans that he appointed some elders and lay deacons.

Zinzendorf, away on his third mission into Indian territory, did not return to Bethlehem until August 24/September 4. On November 6/17, Dominie de Thürnstein announced in Bethlehem that he planned to return to Europe in January, 1743. Eight days later, November 14/25, Pyrlaeus presided at the service that consecrated the new church. Before Zinzendorf left, he had to tie up some loose ends, deal with one more person and be vindicated. On November 25/December 6 the coastal packet, *Savannah*, arrived from Charleston. Pastor Muhlenberg disembarked.

The loose ends included attending to organizational details in the Bethlehem community, taking leave of many friends, and conducting final interviews with several evangelists and other itinerants. At the Sunday evening service, December 20/31, Pyrlaeus sang a Moravian cantata. Zinzendorf delivered his final Bethlehem sermon on the next day, still holding that the Lutheran state church was one of the closest expressions of the apostolic church and could be used by the Brethren, and that the Brethren could find the truth through its doctrines in spite of some erroneous teachings. The last lovefeast led to an emotional farewell with the Brethren singing hymns as the Renewer and his companions crossed the Lehigh River on their way to Philadelphia. Zinzendorf met with some of the leaders of the synods at a location known locally as the Ridge (December 28, 1742/January 8, 1743) to discuss the future of their attempts to transcend theological and organizational differences.

The next evening he delivered his valedictory, the Pennsylvania Testament, at Benezet's home, expressing his disappointment in not having been able to accomplish more in his sojourn among them, his chagrin over the indifference and opposition toward religion among the colonists, and his encouragement that they persevere in their faithful witness, holding before them the vision of the Church of God in the Spirit. Throughout the next day, December 30/January 11 he was occupied not only with arranging for his departure but working on ways to find public and personal vindication for his ministry among most of the Lutherans in the Philadelphia area and handling the pesky matter of a copper cup and record book. He decided to go directly to the latest and most serious representative of the opposition. He invited Muhlenberg to meet him at Stephen Benezet's home that evening.

Endnotes to Chapter Six

1 Revelation 3:7–8 (KJV).

2 See Vogt, pp. 119–122.

3 See Vogt, pp. 52–76 for descriptions of the several groups.

4 "Whereas information has reached us from the island of St. Thomas, of the excitements occasioned there, partly by the mission of certain Moravians, and partly by the arrival of their bishop, the count of Sinsendorf, who has just returned there from St. Eustatius; and as it is rumored that the Gentlemen intends also to go to New Netherland to spread his teachings: the Rev. Classis charges us to send a Pastoral Letter, which has been prepared by our Consistory against the errors of these people, to all the foreign churches. We accordingly send a copy to you, enclosed with this letter, and request you to watch against their errors." Vogt, pp. 134–135, note 50.

5 He later became an opponent of Zinzendorf, often publishing attacks on him.

6 Kelley, p. 219.

7 Beyreuther comments that Zinzendorf misunderstood the revival and religion in America, and came to regard the Great Awakening as *nur ein seelische Feuerwerk*, p. 214.

8 "I expected to be received with love and confidence, but I encountered a great deal of mistrust and suspicion. Is it to be wondered at, that I felt dejected, and that the lukewarmness of my countrymen in Philadelphia depressed me? But I thought: I will keep silent, and not open my mouth. The Lord will help. I traveled through Pennsylvania, but could not speak anywhere, except in Oley. Therefore, I can tell you, my countrymen, in a few words, what I have done in these two months: I traveled and prayed, and wept and bore witness, and sought for peace, and seek it still." Weinlick, p. 141.

9 Weber and Atwood, pp. 33–49.

10 See Vogt, pp. 155–156 for most of the circular letter's text.

11 Spangenberg, p. 299 and Helmich, pp. 16–18.

12 See *A History of the Beginnings*, p. 42.

13 Spangenberg, p. 315.

14 See Reichel, pp. 94–95 and footnote 19 for the list of persons present.

15 Although Moravian sources do not record such a proposal or a personal meeting, it is clear in the confrontation with Muhlenberg that both men and the audience knew of such a proposal and its outcome.

16 Through Zinzendorf's influence, the Bethlehem community began to keep the seventh day as a day of rest, prayer and study in addition to worship on Sunday.

17 *A History of the Beginnings*, p. 56.

18 *Journals*, Vol. 1, p. 75.

19 *A History of the Beginnings*, p. 58.

20 *Bethlehem Diary*, p. 35.

21 *Bethlehem Diary*, p. 39.

22 See Spangenberg, p. 298. Immediately following this description, he cites Muhlenberg's arrival and encounter with the Count.

23 *A History of the Beginnings*, pp. 149–150.

24 *Journals*, Vol. 1, pp. 75–76.

25 *Bethlehem Diary*, p. 45

26 *Journals*, Vol. 1, p. 76.

27 Muhlenberg reflected that the Count had persuaded William Allen that he represented the true Lutheran congregation, who with some of the Reformed leased the building from Allen, and that a minority of malcontents locked the door. Muhlenberg commented further that some Arch Street Lutheran deacons polled their loyalists with the result that they claimed to be the majority and therefore legitimate leaseholders.

Chapter Seven
MUHLENBERG IN PENNSYLVANIA

The *Georgia Packet* was a rough ship and had a rough voyage. The captain, ten crew members and eighteen passengers survived storms, calms, thirst, hunger, ice, heat, rats, anxieties of capture by enemy privateers, and one another. Muhlenberg was quartered in the captain's cabin with seven others, while a five-member family of Salzburg Lutheran refugees, four tailors and a woman shared below-deck steerage with the sailors.[1] From the time they first hoisted the anchor (June 23) to their landing in Charleston (September 22), the crew and most of the passengers cursed, blasphemed, argued, fought, sang lewd songs, gambled, got drunk, and showed cowardice and courage. The passengers suffered seasickness, dysentery, fevers, chills and fear. With exception of the Salzburgers, the others had to endure the chronically faultfinding Muhlenberg. He and the refugees, parents and three children, were the only Germans on board. Usually and in self-defense, the other members of the *Georgia Packet's* company made him the butt of their disdain, ribaldry and mockery for almost the whole ordeal. Yet during their time together, almost all resorted to him for medication, pastoral advice, encouragement and comfort. They asked him to conduct worship with hymns, prayers, and sermons. He turned even casual conversations into earnest exhortations to holy living and salvation. He and the Salzburgers were Godsends to each other. He taught the children most days, gave the family relief from their fetid quarters, comforted them through illnesses, and consoled them when they worried about their future in a strange land. In turn, they were welcome testimonies to him that there still were people faithful to God in an otherwise impious world.

The journey was Muhlenberg's transition from the culturally and spiritually familiar into the shockingly different world of America. Granted, he knew that pious Germans lived in that world, but he had scant information about them, whether the wilderness changed them, and how they would receive him. He did know that he and Zinzendorf would tangle. The voyage was Commoner Muhlenberg's *Bildungsreise*, one far different from that of the Count's or any of the Saxon's other trips. When the Renewer traveled, he almost always had like-minded companions to share the problems, joys, and fellowship. In his earlier life, Muhlenberg showed singular perseverance against significant odds to gain his education and begin his ministry. At important junctures various patrons aided him. To be sure, many in Europe still prayed for him, but now they were an ocean away and had no understanding of what he was about to begin. He was on his own personally and ministerially.

Second, the *Bildungsreise* initiated him into new languages. In an objective sense, he was immersed in rapid, variously accented, common English without Ziegenhagen-furnished translators and advisors. The Salzburgers had lived for a time in Holland, and were of no help to Muhlenberg as he coped with the language every time he spoke, was spoken to and listened to everyone else. Sometimes sincerely and sometimes from pique at the conduct of the others, he hesitated to lead public worship and to preach. Nevertheless, by the end of the voyage, he became fluent enough to understand and be understood. In a second sense, the English-speakers introduced him to more than colloquial speech; they acquainted him with more cursing, blasphemy and gutter-talk than he knew in German. He was shocked by the coarseness of his shipmates. Muhlenberg reflected that up to the voyage, he moved in the sedate and pious circles of family, university, and children at Halle and Grosshennersdorf. The voyage introduced him to foul talk and attitudes that jeered at his religious scruples. He would soon meet Americans — female and male — who took such expressions and conduct even further. By contrast, Zinzendorf had his associates and the Bethlehem brethren as buffers between himself and the majority of the English-speaking settlers. The Count counted on being understood through his courtly conduct, formal Latin, and noble bearing.

The language was different in a third way; it was democratic, secular and even anti-religious. The *Georgia Packet's* English-speakers offered little genuine respect or deference to clergy or nobles. His admonitions went unheeded and were often ridiculed. How different from the German states where ministerial status conferred at least some dignity and attention! He was starting to experience that Anglo-Americans of humble rank argued with, contradicted, interrupted, refuted and disregarded the clergy and church. Soon he experienced being baited in public places about his profession and faith by loudmouthed Americans who seemed cheerfully ignorant of religion in general. Except for some royal officials, there were no nobles in the land who on the basis of birth and blood were seen as the "betters" of others. Those on the way to America and those already there were moving away from the traditional aristocracy derived by lineage and ancestral titles. The emerging aristocracy epitomized in men like Franklin and Allen was marked by shrewdly acquired wealth, opportunistic action, and self-motivation. Muhlenberg was learning a hard lesson as he listened to those who shared the captain's cabin. While he always retained a degree of the Germanic penchant to honor *Obrigkeit* (authority), by December 31, he knew he had to best — or at least report he bested — a Count in open, defiant debate. Zinzendorf never quite reckoned that the commoner who faced him might not submit to someone of higher rank. To be called a liar and be defied before his own entourage was more than Zinzendorf could bear from a "village parson" (*Dorfpfarrer*), as he called his antagonist. The audience in Benezet's parlor murmured against Muhlenberg, but wider audiences addressed by that *Dorfpfarrer* approved what he did.

Before he could get to Philadelphia, Muhlenberg had to trudge to Georgia, and back to Charleston. On leaving the *Georgia Packet*, he sought out and shared fellowship with the city's small, spiritually hungering group of German Lutherans. He apprised his contacts of his mission and began to gather information about conditions in Pennsylvania. He first heard that Valentin Kraft had arrived and was active. It is possible that Muhlenberg knew about Kraft and the reasons for his being deposed from the ministry while Muhlenberg was still in Germany. In those few hours and on his return to Charleston in October, Muhlenberg learned of the Count's problems with the Wesleys and Whitefield, read the available reports from Europe, examined some of the Count's published writings and defenses since Muhlenberg left, and undoubtedly familiarized himself with Tennent's attacks, including a series of slashing sermons delivered and printed in New York in August. The Philadelphia newspaper articles over the past year might not have reached Germany, but they were available in Charleston. Perhaps he had learned of the May speech before the Governor and the Count's use of the name Thürnstein. Whether the Count realized it or not, Muhlenberg was studying him.

By means of several small craft that plied the inland waterway, he and the Salzburgers, with assorted and sometimes drunken fellow travelers, arrived in Savannah (October 1). His reception among the Germans in the city and in the Salzburger settlement at Ebenezer was warm and supportive. Pastors Gronau and Bolzius filled him in about colonial affairs, what they knew of Zinzendorf and the Brethren since the departure of the Moravians to Nazareth, and the breach between Whitefield and the Moravians over predestination. Muhlenberg reflected happily on his visit to Ebenezer. He saw that it was possible to live the Christian life in an orderly and devout manner in America. The pastor-people relationship was loving and supportive. At the same time, he was increasingly aware of the opportunities and risks for mission. The threats of congregations falling into disorder and wrangling in the sputterings of the Great

Awakening were clearly evident among the English-speaking Christians. When Muhlenberg informed Bolzius that Ziegenhagen instructed him to accompany Muhlenberg to Philadelphia, Bolzius was more than surprised.[2] Yet, he made arrangements to comply. The itinerary called for them to travel by inland coastal craft to Charleston, then to take a sea-going sloop to Philadelphia.

The journey to Charleston was uneventful, but the next leg of the trip was delayed for over a month. Eventually, the two pastors agreed that Bolzius ought to return to Georgia, which he did by horseback. The delay caused Muhlenberg anxiety, but he made firm friends among some English and American persons, was attracted by an invitation to be the pastor of the Lutherans in Charleston, and gathered more information about his quarry. He wrote of October 24: "In the evening I accidentally received a printed book in which were described seven conferences which Count Zinzendorf held in Pennsylvania, particularly Germantown, Philadelphia, and New Hannover. Also received a document concerning a tumult which had taken place in an old house on July 18 in Philadelphia between the Reformed, the Moravian Brethren, and the Lutherans. The weak and immature actions which Mr. Zinzendorf exhibited in the conference and the tumult of July 18 grieved me much."[3] But there was no synod at New Hannover. Had he heard of the Count's being there in the aftermath of one of the Tulpehocken disputes with Stöver or, perhaps, if after late August, even Kraft? It seems that the evening's reading strengthened his resolve not to stay among the Germans in Charleston but to proceed quickly to Pennsylvania. At least two of the United Congregations were involved with Zinzendorf; Muhlenberg had to move fast and carefully, otherwise the Count might entrench himself, leave his surrogates in charge, disrupt or destroy the congregations — and Muhlenberg would be adrift in America. Advised that it was safer and faster to travel by sea than by land, he booked passage on an overcrowded sloop and left Charleston on November 12. The voyage was worse than that of the *Georgia Packet*, and the vessel nearly broke apart several times. The crew was like the voyage: "November 14. The wind is very strong, bitter and cold. My sickness increases and makes me vomit day and night. Our ship's company curses to make one's hair stand on end. As long as I was able to speak, I admonished them, but to no avail, for it has already become second nature. To be among such people is a foretaste of hell."[4] They docked at 8:00 A.M., Thursday, November 25 (OS). Muhlenberg had arrived unannounced, alone, sick, weary, and uncertain as to what his next immediate steps ought to be. By that evening he had been filled in on the situations in the United Congregations and Germantown, Zinzendorf's activities and his intention to leave America in January, plus Kraft's machinations, and was on his way by horseback to New Hannover. It was a busy day.

More specifically, Muhlenberg had sought and found his Philadelphia contact, Zwifler. Through him and a cooperative innkeeper, he met one of the deacons (Philip Brand) of the New Hannover congregation who was starting the return ride home that rainy night. The situation was not encouraging. New Hannover was being served by Johann Georg Schmidt (also Schmid), whose regular occupation was as a barber and to whom local people resorted for practical medical treatment. He was also well known to be a heavy drinker and immoral. As far as his pastoral credentials were concerned, members of the congregation knew that he was not ordained, but they liked his fervent preaching. The wife of one of the key lay deacons, Valentin Geiger, was Schmidt's daughter, thereby providing a potential complication for Muhlenberg's task of removing Schmidt from the congregation.

Kraft would take different tactics. A week before Muhlenberg landed in Philadelphia, Kraft sent a report to the Darmstadt Consistory, informing them of his arrangements and expecting the Consistory's approval in the near future. At the same time, he dispatched a letter to Ziegenhagen requesting that the Court Chaplain transmit the funds that had been collected for the United Congregations to Kraft. Both communications to Germany were transmitted by Thomas Mayor, the same man whom Muhlenberg reported snapped the lock of the Arch Street church. Kraft had entered into an unsigned agreement with the Arch Street and Germantown congregations that he would serve as their pastor. In the case of the Arch Street church, he appointed several deacons and elders after the July rupture with those who supported Zinzendorf. The steps Muhlenberg used to dispatch Schmidt and frustrate Kraft are part of the account of how Muhlenberg established himself in the New Hannover and Providence congregations, and can be traced in detail in the *Journals*.[5]

In carrying out those steps, Muhlenberg consciously prepared his assault on Zinzendorf and any of his or his adjunct's claims to have the only Lutheran church in Philadelphia. A number of tactics characteristic of Muhlenberg can be identified in his untangling Kraft and Schmidt from the congregation, gaining the endorsement of the Swedes, and forcing the issue of Zinzendorf's ministerial legitimacy into public view and, through his reports and influence, into print.

The first characteristic tactic was to be as thoroughly knowledgeable as possible about what had happened already and who were his antagonists, their supporters, other persons who had a stake in the situation at hand, and any relevant authorities who might be involved. Muhlenberg was well prepared as he entered the fray. As part of his preparation, he made preliminary contacts with persons who might seem neutral at first, gathering information and impressions from them, and gradually turning them to his side by listening, showing them respect, and letting them become acquainted with him. This took steady, patient work, and encouraged others to build confidence in him. The tactic was in sharp contrast to Kraft's grand claims and flamboyant style.

The second characteristic tactic was closely related; he let his documents speak for themselves and for him. Naturally, those documents included his university certificate, ordination papers, materials from Halle, and Ziegenhagen's attestations. When some in New Hannover, still hurt over the swindler-pastor Schultz, suggested that Muhlenberg had forged the papers, he allayed those doubts through the statement of a respected figure who knew Ziegenhagen's signature. When Schmidt realized that Muhlenberg was fully ordained and qualified, and after hearing him preach, he quietly withdrew from the congregation and accepted (at least for a time) Muhlenberg's authority no matter what Kraft said.[6]

But there soon was another document. While Kraft attempted to make deals with him, blustered in front of congregational officers, and tried to treat Muhlenberg as one of his subordinates, the Halle man worked within the congregational structures at New Hannover and Providence, carried on pastoral work that amazed and gratified members, and brought the lay deacons and elders of the congregations to issue him the local call to be the pastor of those congregations. He went further; he wrote the call document himself and had them sign it on December 25 and December 26 respectively. The terms of the document not only applied to the two country congregations but left room for the Arch Street Lutherans to join them. The document also clearly was anti-Zinzendorf and anti-Moravian:

> We, the Elders and Presbyters and the other Members of the Lutheran Protestant Congregations at New Hannover, Providence and Philadelphia
>
> (1) We testify in God and affirm by Subscription, that we have accepted with a thankful Heart the Rev. Heinrich Melchior Muhlenberg as a lawfull called, ordained, and by our Supplications Sent and represent Minister of the Gospel and the Augsbourg Confession, by the Reverend

Frederick Michael Ziegenhagen his Maiestis German Chaplain and Member of the Society for promoting Christian Knowledge.

(2) We promise to furnish our Minister with all Necessaries what is required for his living in the lawfull Vocation, and to assist him in every good Disposition and Direction which he gives for our and our Children Spiritual Welfare according to the Word I Tim. 5 vers. 17.18, Luc. 10 vers 7.

(3) While we live in the last Days and in perilous Times, we will turn away from Such a Sort of Preachers, which are Lovers of their own Selves, Covetous Boasters proud, Blasphemers, unholy, having a form of Godliness but denying the Power thereof, creeping into Houses and Congregations without Vocation, 2 Tim. 3 vers 1–6 not able to teach others, but to steal, to kill and to destroy the Sheep John X. and we will not Suffer to be administered the holy Baptism and the Lord's Supper in our Congregations by Such a Minister which is not lawfull called, neither Sent or ordained according to the 14 Articul of the Augsbourg-Confession.[7]

Muhlenberg used that document and the others before the Governor, the Swedish Lutheran authorities, Kraft, and, of course, Zinzendorf.

The third characteristic tactic was a variation on the theme of documentary authority; his appeal to the authorities from whom he derived his mission. This was not a blind adherence to the Halle Fathers and Ziegenhagen; it was a shrewd diplomatic strategy. He consistently — and maddeningly for Kraft and probably Zinzendorf, but gratifyingly for the colonial civil and ecclesiastical authorities as well as the Swedes — showed himself to be a man obeying his superiors. The lay leaders of the country congregations and other interested parties urged him to strike a compromise with Schmidt and Kraft so as to divide the pastoral responsibilities among them rather than divide congregational loyalties still further, and Kraft proposed various means by which he would accept Muhlenberg as a partner in his presbyters and consistory. To all he said that he had his instructions, and his documents called on him to carry out those instructions to be the pastor of the three congregations. He could not, he said, disregard those orders or modify them without first receiving further instructions from those who sent him. It bought him time with the congregational lay leaders and they ultimately respected him for his keeping to the terms of the agreements he made in Germany and London. They could reason that he would keep his commitments to them. Besides, he might resemble the other vagabond and imposter pastors if he tailored his ministry to that which was currently convenient. Though appealing to authorities in Europe, Muhlenberg gained the room to discomfort Schmidt and Kraft so that when they departed, he was in the place where he had intended to be. He would use the same tactic in the confrontation with the Count — and the Count reacted as Muhlenberg may have anticipated. As far as Kraft was concerned, such an appeal and the commitment to wait for a letter to cross the ocean and a response to be returned meant that Muhlenberg was out of his hands for at least seven months. In addition, simply Muhlenberg's communication of his situation and Kraft's role would undoubtedly result in Halle's repudiation of the defrocked erstwhile superintendent of the Lutheran church in Pennsylvania. Kraft's options were being shut down.

The fourth characteristic tactic was Muhlenberg's reliance on others to transmit and interpret his documents and his authority. When he entered a tense congregational situation before the calls were extended, he had the lay leaders present his documents and express what they meant. He stepped in when there was a need for clarification or deft emphasis. Those who already were trusted by the general membership were seen as his advocates, and they implicitly became accountable for his credibility. A similar situation arose with regard to his acceptance by the Swedish Lutherans. On December 27, the day after the call to New Providence was signed, he arrived in Philadelphia. Koch was already his supporter. Muhlenberg reported:

> I set out and with God's help covered the remaining twelve miles to Philadelphia. On the way I met old Mr. Kraft who was going into the country. About one o'clock in the afternoon I arrived in Philadelphia to the satisfaction of some friends. About two o'clock we went out to the Swedish church which is situated about two miles from the center of the city. Mr. Tranberg, the Swedish minister, and Mr. Koch were in the church and also another friend, Mr. Schleydorn, who had written to the Germantowners to invite them. Some of them were also present. Since Count Zinzendorf was also just then in the city, he, too, sent his spy to find out what was going to happen.

> The Swedish minister and Mr. Koch extended an invitation to old Kraft yesterday, telling him that they wanted to examine both our calls and testimonials. Mr. Kraft, however, did not want to wait and traveled out in the country. So when I had finished my sermon, the Swedish minister, Mr. Tranberg, asked for my call and testimonials. He had the deacons and the elders and the rest of the male members come forward and read to them

> (1) the letter from the Reverend Court Preacher Zigenhagen, and explained it to them in the English language because they were not so familiar with the German.

(2) He read to the congregation my certificate of ordination at Leipzig and explained it.

(3) He showed them my certificate of matriculation from Göttingen University.

(4) He showed them my certificate from Göttingen University.

(5) The English acceptance signed by the deacons and elders in New Hannover and Providence was also read.

Then Mr. Tranberg said that among the Swedes they would not accept anyone as pastor unless he had a lawful call and a certificate of ordination, otherwise all sorts of confusion would arise.

They were now to declare briefly whether they acknowledged my call and ordination as lawful. The deacons and some others replied that they had as much share in my being sent as New Hannover and Providence. Mr. Koch said that they had accepted old Mr. Kraft as their pastor; did he also have a call to show? They replied that they had not accepted Mr. Kraft as their pastor, nor had they extended him a call because he was unable to present any testimonials from Germany. They said they meant to abide by him who had been sent by the Rev. Court Preacher Zigenhagen at their solicitation. Thereupon they pressed forward and gave their hands to me and Mr. Tranberg.

I had nothing to say on this occasion, but simply followed my instructions. It had to be published to the whole congregation, because I had been sent at their expense out of the collections funds. If they in Philadelphia had let me go and refused to accept me, I would have done my part and remained with the two upper congregations in the country, which themselves were almost too heavy and laborious for one man. But since they claimed a right in Philadelphia, I for my part could not withdraw until I had further instructions from my superiors.[8]

Both Kraft and Zinzendorf had been refused access to the Wicaco pulpit and recognition by the Scandinavian ministers, but Muhlenberg gained both the pulpit and fellowship quickly and decisively. In the process, the officers of the two country congregations publicly repudiated Kraft on the basis of his lack of proper documents. Zinzendorf's "spy" (possibly Böhler or Pyrlaeus) probably reported the reasoning as well as the outcome to the Count. Apparently on the basis of that acceptance and the calls, Muhlenberg was ready to see Governor Thomas and once again the rector of Christ Church. On the day after Tranberg shook his hand (December 27):

I paid my respects to His Excellency, the Governor of Pennsylvania, and showed him the Latin certificate from Göttingen University and also the acceptance which had been subscribed in New Hannover and Providence. His Excellency volunteered every kind office and said that

I should also go to the city magistrate and have myself qualified. I told him that I was already qualified as a subject of my gracious king, having been born in the province of Hannover. He said that there would be no harm in doing it again. In the afternoon I visited the English *minister* of the Episcopal Church who is also the commissary of churches. He said that he had always had very friendly relations with our Lutheran brethren, the Swedish *ministers*. He hoped to continue the same with me.[9]

Muhlenberg lost no time after paying his respects to the Governor, taking the oath, and visiting with the rector at Christ Church. While Muhlenberg connected himself to the wider municipal community, Zinzendorf was in the almost final stage of leaving; he was delivering his lengthy Pennsylvania Testament in Benezet's parlor. On the following day, December 29/January 10, the new pastor of the country congregations conferred with the Arch Street deacons and elders. They gave him their detailed version of the July 18 incident plus tales about Zinzendorf and the items Pyralaeus' supporters took with them. In the course of the day, Muhlenberg's call to be pastor of the third member of the United Congregations was signed.

Muhlenberg had arrived. All he needed was the call from the Arch Street church. That fell into place the next day, December 29, disclosing yet another characteristic: he was a skillful and gracious compromiser. He recognized that the members of the Philadelphia congregation had been through a harrowing time over the past several years. They had been cheated by Schultz, ministered to by Stöver and Zinzendorf, endured the July 18 schism, and accepted Kraft. Stöver had been seen disgracefully and publicly drunk. Kraft was suspected of fathering the child of another man's wife, having a wife in Germany and being engaged to two women in Pennsylvania. Now his star faded and a more stable man was available. But Kraft had pulled them through a difficult period:

Today [December 29] the deacons and elders of the Lutheran congregation [Arch Street] came to me for a meeting. Some of them had been created by Mr. Kraft. One of the deacons who had gone over to the Count and had now returned to us handed over to me the key to a chest containing a small amount of alms, the church vessels, and a church record book. The Count had not expected this man would leave them and come back to us, otherwise he would have taken the key away from him.

I had no desire to discharge the deacons whom Mr. Kraft had created, for it would have given rise to fresh dissension. I therefore decided to renew the appointment of the present deacons and elders and have them confirmed next Sunday. They also signed the acceptance.[10]

A final characteristic tactic is his ability to goad his adversaries into outbursts of anger that served to cause bystanders, whether on the scene directly or present when reading his version of the event, to react negatively to the adversary and positively toward him. Sometimes that tactic involved his being firm and even sarcastic and sometimes quiet so that the opponent's wrath fell on another individual. On December 20, when Kraft, Muhlenberg and the senior deacon of Providence were at Philadelphia, Kraft raged over the deacon's being with Muhlenberg, storming through the inn with shouts and curses. The deacon and others reported the incident when they arrived home, and previously high estimations of Kraft fell. Count Zinzendorf would soon encounter the same tactic.

Did the men have to meet? After all, Zinzendorf was set to leave the colonies, the Arch Street and Race Street churches were not likely to be reunited, and Muhlenberg was accepted in the three congregations. There still was some unfinished business about the July incident. But he and the lay leaders still felt they had to gain possession of the record book or precipitate an action with the Count. Most of all, both men had to meet in order to fulfill their own theological agendas, be vindicated before their different audiences, and set the stage for the future of the Lutherans and Brethren in America. So, as Muhlenberg wrote after naming seven elders of the Arch Street congregation who signed his call:

DECEMBER 29, Wednesday. The eighth elder was still missing and also had gone over to the Zinzendorfers a few months previous. It is not likely that he will return to us, since it is said that the Count has appointed him as one of his preachers. He could never attain to that title among us, for among our people he was only a reader. He is a brewer by profession. This man still has in his possession a church book and a copper cup which he had filched away.

December 30, Thursday. Today I sent two of our deacons to the above-mentioned brewer to demand that he send back our church book and the copper chalice since they belonged to our congregation. He sent back the reply that he had turned them both over to Count Zinzendorf. Then the two deacons wanted to send over to the Count's, but before they reached there, the Count sent Mr. Peter Böhler to me to say that he thought it very strange that when I was in Philadelphia I did not come to visit him. Mr. Böhler entered into a dispute with me concerning their affairs in the presence of our deacons. Finally he said that I should speak with Mr. Thürnstein himself.[11]

On Thursday (morning?), December 30/January 11, Muhlenberg and the Arch Street lay leaders sent deacons David Sackler and Leonhard Herman to the man who was last reported to have the copper cup and church record book taken from Arch Street on July 18. He was the lone elder remaining loyal to the Count. He informed them that he gave the items to the Count. Before the deacons arrived at Benezet's door, where Zinzendorf was lodging, Zinzendorf sent Böhler to remonstrate with Muhlenberg about who really owned the materials and to criticize him for not coming to the Count on arriving in Philadelphia more than a month ago. A *Wortstreit* or argument began until Muhlenberg mentioned that he had read about the Pennsylvania Synods while at Charleston. At that point Böhler gave up arguing, and said that Zinzendorf and Muhlenberg had best meet to settle whatever issues were between them.

Muhlenberg and the two deacons busied themselves in the afternoon. At Koch's urging, the deacons went to Mayor William Till about the book. Muhlenberg dropped the matter of the cup "on account of certain circumstances, and also because it was not very important."[12] The deacons delivered the letter to the Count who made angry comments directed against the arch-Pietist, Muhlenberg. The Count responded to the mayor with a refusal to deliver the book, insisting that he was the pastor and inspector of the only Lutheran church in the city. Unimpressed, the mayor sent another letter. Zinzendorf now agreed to hand over the book that evening. He did not. Instead, "After dinner the Count sent word to me, politely requesting that I should visit him. I went, expecting to speak with the Count alone. When I arrived, however, there was in the room a large gathering of his generals and corporals, the Count presiding at a small table. This was the first time that I saw the Count face to face and I expected to hear something great from the *Reformator Ecclesiae*."[13] The encounter began.

Endnotes to Chapter Seven

1 See *Journals*, Vol. 1, pp. 24–57 for the journey.

2 He probably was dismayed, because of the obvious interruption such a venture would make in the promising work in which he and Gronau were engaged. In addition, winter was rapidly approaching, further Spanish incursions were predicted, and his wife and two children were ill.

3 *Journals*, Vol. 1, p. 63.

4 *Journals*, Vol. 1, p. 64.

5 See especially *Journals*, Vol. 1, pp. 66–75.

6 Later Schmidt joined Kraft and tried to start another congregation. See *Journals,* Vol. 1, p. 158 (in 1747).

7 He then listed the names of the signers. *Journals*, Vol. 1, pp. 73–74.

8 *Journals*, Vol. 1, pp. 74–75.

9 That is, to take the oath of loyalty to King George II.

10 *Journals*, Vol. 1, p. 75.

11 *Journals*, Vol. 1, p. 76.

12 See *Journals*, Vol. 1, p. 81. My reconstruction of the days and the letters is based on unclear versions in the *Journals*, Vol. 1, p. 80 as translated from the *Selbstbiographie*, pp. 152–156. The reconstruction appears to explain a subsequent exchange on December 31/January 12.

13 *Journals*, Vol. 1, p. 76.

Chapter Eight

THE CONFRONTATION

Muhlenberg reported the encounter in his *Journals* and *Selbstbiographie* in almost exactly the same words. It is obviously biased against Zinzendorf and the Moravians, yet accurate enough for an examination of the issues at stake then and later plus insight into the characters of the two men. The accounts are not transcripts of the event but are a digest or condensation. I offer first and without comment the version in the English translation of the *Journals*.[1] Terms provided in German are from the *Selbstbiographie*.[2] I have retained his spelling, but, for the sake of a smoother reading, provided paragraphing as seems appropriate. Following the basic text, I offer a version with comments and observations as to how the argument proceeded and how each sought to out-maneuver and refute the other.

How Muhlenberg set the scene contributes to the manner and flow of the report. He thought he would be speaking to the Count privately, otherwise, as he reflected in the *Selbstbiographie*, he would have taken a couple (*ein Paar*) of his *Vorsteher* (elders) as witnesses (*Zeugen*). He entered the crowded room, comparing it not to a wealthy merchant's parlor but to an auditorium. Zinzendorf, seated at a small table, looked like a presiding judge (*Präses*) and the audience as witnesses to the proceedings. Obviously, Muhlenberg presented himself as a suspect under interrogation. Told to sit at the same table, he faced (*gegen*) the Count, and *ein Examen rigorosum* began:

The Encounter's Basic Text

The Count asked me first about a number of circumstances with regard to Grosshennersdorf in Upper Lusatia. What I knew I answered. Then the following ensued:

Count: On what conditions are you here?

Reply: I have been called and sent through the Rev. Court Preacher Ziegenhagen, who had a commission from the congregation.

Count: What sort of commission did Mr. Ziegenhagen have?

Reply: The three Lutheran congregations in New Hannover, Providence and Philadelphia had been urgently requesting a pastor for several years past. The copies are deposited in Providence and the letters in London, which can be published at any time, if necessary.

Count: When did the congregations last petition for a pastor?

118

Reply: I do not know; I must look it up in the copies.

Count: You must say at once when they wrote the last letter to Mr. Ziegenhagen.

The brewer and several others of his people chimed in and said that the last letter may have reached there about 1739. I did not know, because nothing had been said to me about it.

I replied: I really cannot say just now, and besides, it is of no importance, for I have been called, sent, and accepted. The deacons and elders of the three congregations have signed an acceptance.

Count: Here in Philadelphia no deacons of the Lutheran congregation gave their signatures, for the deacons of the Lutheran congregation are sitting here, and there is no other Lutheran congregation and church here other than the one we have. Haven't you seen the church yet, which was just recently built?

Reply: I know nothing about it, because I am convinced that I preached to Lutheran people and was accepted by them.

Count: They are not Lutherans but rebels, brawlers; and you have become the head of such people and preached to them in the house from which they expelled my adjunct, Pirlaeus. The rebels must come first to us and apologize.

Reply: My dear Count, your people must first come and apologize to our Lutherans because they broke the lock off our church and started the tumult.

Count: That is not true!

Reply: It is true to the extent that they are still involved in a lawsuit over it.

Count: I know of no lawsuit.

Reply: Well, everybody knows what happened last summer, July 18.

Count: Let us stick to the subject. The last time I asked Mr. Zigenhagen how things stood as far as Pennsylvania was concerned, he replied that he could send no preacher there because the congregations were unwilling to stipulate the salary. Now, since Mr. Zigenhagen knew that I had come in here, why did he send you afterwards?

Reply: I was sent to investigate conditions here and to see whether order cannot be established.

Count: Mr. Zigenhagen is an archliar and hypocrite! When I am in his presence, he is meek and humble and submissive; when I am away from him, he inveighs and slanders. This is another spiteful trick which he and Mr. Francke are playing off on me! I shall tell him of it to his face when I get to London.

Reply: My dear Count, it is a shame to speak that way. I have often heard in Germany that you, yourself, were a liar. Am I not forced to believe it?

Count: I have heard that you have read all my writings; did you not read that I have established a Lutheran consistory here in Philadelphia?

Reply: I read in Charleston the report of seven conferences, and through them learned that a certain Mr. Von Thürnstein had caused disturbances in various places, but I did not know that the Count had established a Lutheran consistory.

Count: These are jesuitical tricks.

Reply: I once heard in Germany that you were appointed a Moravian bishop by a Reformed preacher. How does that jibe with your being able to establish a Lutheran consistory?

Count: I am inspector of all Lutheran churches in Pennsylvania and Lutheran pastor in Philadelphia. I have held synods in the country and here, and installed pastors in several places and even deposed a pastor named Stöver.

Reply: Can a Reformed preacher give such authority to you?

Count: Don't you understand canon law? Don't you know that in Wittenberg the foremost theologian was ordained by a Catholic?

Reply: But how is it that sometimes you can be a Moravian bishop and sometimes an inspector and a Lutheran pastor?

Count: I publicly resigned my Episcopal office in Holland in the presence of lords and princes.

Reply: You change frequently.

Count: I have been called as pastor in writing by the Lutheran congregation here in Philadelphia, and likewise my adjunct, Pirlaeus.

Reply: Is your call signed by anybody?

Count: It doesn't need it.

Reply: My call has been signed and I shall trouble myself no further, but just follow the instructions of my superiors in Europe. If this does not please you, you can settle it with them.

Count: But is it not contrary to all fairness and courtesy that after I have been so long in this country that you should not have come to visit me? If you have been sent to investigate matters here, why did you not inquire into our affairs? When a person learns that there is a consistory and an inspector in a place, even if granting that it is illegal, does not one first make inquiries there?

Reply: Even if I had desired to call upon you as a stranger, you would not have been there in any event, for it was said that you were among the Indians. There are all kinds of sects here, and how is it possible for me to run around to all of them? I have enough to do with the Lutherans who have been assigned to me.

Count: I am the Lutheran pastor. Why did you not come to me?

Reply: I had no orders to do so and still have none.

Count: Did Mr. Zigenhagen say that you should pass me by?

Reply: When I was called, I inquired as to how I should conduct myself with regard to the Count and the reply was made that I should have no fear of the Count.

Count: Did Mr. Zigenhagen say that you should pass by the inspector and Lutheran pastor?

Reply: No.[3]

Count: Now just see, my brethren, how this man contradicts himself and lies, since he replies yes and no to the same question.

Reply: Not so, Confrater. Mr. Zigenhagen knew well enough that Count Zinzendorf had gone to Pennsylvania, but he did not know that the Count wanted to be an inspector and Lutheran pastor.

Count: Did you not know that I was inspector and pastor?

Reply: I already knew in Germany that you went to Pennsylvania and intended ….

Count: What did I intend?

Reply: Yes, you intended.

Count: Just speak out. What did I intend?

Reply: I do not know. You yourself said at the conclusion of a reply to Adam Gross's publication, "Brethren, I am now going to Pennsylvania; pray the Saviour to reveal to you what I intend!"

So, who knows what you intended?

Count: As soon as I get to London, I will go to the archbishop and tell him that I established order among the Lutherans here, but that as soon as order was established, Mr. Zigenhagen sent a man who spoiled it all again and brought confusion.

Reply: You may say what you wish, I shall not concern myself with it. Now you have put everything in confusion and, I hope, by God's grace, to establish some order.

Count: Go ahead and do it. If you accomplish anything, it will only serve to increase my church. You have my good wishes. It cannot be denied that you were a Lutheran student in good standing, that you had a pastoral charge, as was reported to me nine months ago from Herrnhut. You have nothing more to do than apologize here, since you made an intrusion here and passed me by.

Reply: Count, the time will come when you will have to beg the pardon of the whole Lutheran church.

Count: What is he saying? He is a young parson [*Pfarrer*], a village parson [*Dorfpfarrer*]!

Reply: You must not become excited, Count.[4]

Count: Make haste to consider and acknowledge that you have done wrong, otherwise I will make the whole thing *public* when I return to Germany.

Reply: When I do wrong before God, I pray for forgiveness, but I owe you no apology in this affair. You may publish in Germany what you please; if you touch me, I shall answer you with the truth. Your affairs are well enough known in Germany.

Count: The things published against me are nothing but pasquils [jokes and lampoons] to which no one will venture to put his name. I am willing to grant you time to reflect and beg my pardon. It merely comes down to a *point d'honneur* and you should not let that sway you.

Reply: You certainly are full of suggestions; in fact you are just what your aunt told me you were.

Count: Hold your tongue as far as my aunt is concerned, or I shall be compelled to expose her.[5]

I could speak quite differently to you if you want me to.

Reply: Go ahead, speak.

Count: Were you not reared at Halle?

Reply: No. I was reared in the province of Hannover, completed my studies at Göttingen, and was also at Halle.

Count: The Hallesians are Pietists; aren't you a Hallesian?

Reply: I am a Lutheran and shall remain so, Count.

Count: Are you such a Lutheran as Mr. Zigenhagen is?

Reply: I was with Mr. Zigenhagen for some time and learned to know his character. I am and hope to become, more and more, such a Lutheran as Mr. Zigenhagen is.

Count: Before the year is out, I shall bring forth more than a hundred witnesses to prove that Mr. Zigenhagen is not a genuine Lutheran.

Reply: Mr. Zigenhagen is certainly not afraid and is not likely to be. I am surprised, my dear Count, at the way you cavil (*häckeln*) at me with your questions and try to hook something on me!

Count: Yes, I am casting a hook (*Haken*) into his conscience!

Reply: Oh, no; you do not touch my conscience, but I gather enough from your questions to know that your heart is not right. If you had a heart or spirit without guile, you would not ask such questions.

Count: You came here to speak to me about a church book and a cup?

Reply: Yes, I wanted to ask you if you would return them or not.

Count: What should we return? They belong to our Lutheran church and congregation. However, if you are so much in want that you need the book and cup, we will present them to you, provided that you sign a receipt which we will make out for you.

Reply: I desire no present from you. I only claim what belongs to us, since the cup and also the book were paid for out of our collections. (Here I stood up.)

Count: Consider well the matter of apologizing; otherwise you will regret it.

Reply: I need no consideration, for I do not acknowledge you as a genuine Lutheran, much less an inspector and Lutheran pastor.

Count: Do you hear that? Now it is clear what the man has in his heart. (The brethren and toadies of the Count assented to everything by nodding their heads and marveled at the Count's ravings as though they were divinely inspired.)

123

Reply: It has also become apparent what you have in your heart. If you are such a genuine Lutheran, why would they not let you preach in the Swedish church?

Count: That was prevented by only one man, the Swedish merchant, Koch.

Reply: Mr. Koch is a deacon (*Vorsteher*) of the Swedish church and he certainly would not have prevented you without the knowledge of the Swedish minister, Mr. Tranberg.

Count: Can you say that Mr. Tranberg refused me?

Reply: I cannot say it positively. Enough you were refused.

Count: There you see, brethren, the man contradicts himself and lies. (Because of the noisy assent of the brethren I was unable to reply. The Count further asserted that I would not preach in the Swedish church more than two or three times before they threw me out just as they had thrown out his adjunct from the old church.)

Reply: I am willing to wait and see. I have nothing further to say except to wish you a happy voyage. Good bye (*Leben Sie wohl*)!

The Encounter with Commentary

1. The Setting and Its Rhetoric

COMMENT: Both men were scholars of the classics, especially the Latin oratorical tradition. Muhlenberg taught others Hebrew, Greek and Latin, and found particular enjoyment in Cicero's speeches and ethical treatises. Zinzendorf knew not only the traditional texts but also the law school courses and jurisprudence. He was thoroughly familiar with the ways that royal investigators and rulers operated. Although he might not have been personally involved in trials, he knew the parry and thrust of questions and answers, and the importance of making a plausible case to those who listened as well as judged matters. Muhlenberg, however, had the hard experience of being hauled into court and having to rely on an advocate to work out a resolution to the charges brought against him and his fellow students. In addition, he successfully refuted and reversed accusations brought against him prior to his departure for London. He knew how to stand up for himself, present evidence in a timely manner, and swing initially ill-disposed authorities to vindicate and even support him. Zinzendorf himself had not been as successful in dealing with his critics and authorities.

124

The encounter's setting was clearly forensic both in Muhlenberg's presentation and Zinzendorf's design. The younger man had expected a private interview that might be restricted to the narrow issue of the items in dispute following the fragmenting of the Arch Street congregation, but he was prepared to expand the discussion. Disconcerted at first, he recovered quickly. As would any classically literate student, he was familiar with Aristotle's *Rhetoric*.[6] Under the heading of forensic rhetoric, the philosopher described types of *apologia* or defense strategies and arguments. One type of *apologia* involved a defense in the context of a hostile set of judges and listeners. The apologist was advised not to appeal to the common sense, fairness, intelligence or compassion of those who opposed and listened. The defender knew beforehand that the judgment would be negative, so the best course was to argue on the basis of higher principles than would be allowed in that particular court, indeed to an unseen future audience. In addition, the apologist was to seek every opportunity to turn the argument against the accusers and the judges, calling their characters, intentions, and deeds into question. In other words, shift from defense to attack, putting the accusers on trial. Slashing comments and insults were to be avoided or only rarely used. Instead, one ought to use innuendo and irony deftly, so as to discomfort and throw the opponent off balance. One way to upset the opposing side was to goad him into losing his temper, making him appear unreasonable and not in control of the facts or the courtroom situation. By diverting the prosecutor's train of thought, the defender could take advantage of the lapse. When forced into a potentially damaging admission, the speaker was to make a quick acknowledgement or find a plausible loophole (such as "I don't have all the information"), then to move to another topic as soon as possible. The apologist's goal under the circumstance of a court stacked against him or his client was not to win in the immediate venue but to leave the courtroom as unscathed and creditable as possible. Vindication would come in other forums, at other times and from other persons.

Zinzendorf, too, cast the encounter in a forensic context. He was the presiding judge and interrogator. He knew something about the person before him, but not much. He attempted several approaches to achieve his purposes. His chief purpose was to break Muhlenberg into acknowledging the Count as an ordained Lutheran pastor, with the authority to be the inspector-superintendent of the Lutheran churches in Pennsylvania. This entailed Muhlenberg recognizing Zinzendorf as the legitimate pastor of the only Lutheran church in Philadelphia. For Muhlenberg to do so would be to regard those who maintained the Arch Street church as rebels, and advise them to ask for forgiveness. Failing that, he wanted Muhlenberg at least to recognize his (Zinzendorf's) authority and those who were ordained by him and under his auspices. That step would have entailed Muhlenberg expressing regret that he had slighted Zinzendorf by not presenting himself to the Count as inspector-superintendent when Muhlenberg arrived in Philadelphia. For Muhlenberg to have acceded to either of these purposes meant that he effectively would repudiate the Halle Fathers, Ziegenhagen and the basis of his mission to America.

Failing either of those purposes, the Count needed to demonstrate to the Brethren and to those gathered in Benezet's parlor that the Hallesians, Ziegenhagen and Muhlenberg were in league against the Count and the vision he and his supporters shared for the future of the *Kirche*. The "Pietists" were the real foes and Muhlenberg was their hastily dispatched and inadequate tool sent to confuse and ruin their ministries and mission. To achieve any of these purposes, Zinzendorf set up a forensic situation and posed his questions with the clear intent to penetrate the witness-defendant's defenses. That meant moving around with pointed questions, probing for weak spots or feinting so as to slip past Muhlenberg's shield of excuses and pretensions. The Count could not and would not yield. No one ought be allowed to shut the door the Savior opened in the new world.

And the contest began.

2. Starting with Small Talk

TEXT: The Count asked me first about a number of circumstances with regard to Grosshennersdorf in Upper Lusatia. What I knew I answered.

COMMENT: Although it had been more than five months since Muhlenberg had seen members of the Zinzendorf family, still any news would have been appreciated. The fact that Count Heinrich was one of Muhlenberg's major patrons could have been a surprise; clearly the recently arrived pastor was well-connected. The fiscal situation at Grosshennersdorf and its sale to her cousin, Baron von Burgsdorf, were probably known to the Count. The conversation did not yet turn to others whom Zinzendorf knew, that is, the Hallesians.

3. The Opening Questions: Who Sent You and Why?

TEXT:

Count: On what conditions are you here?

Reply: I have been called and sent through the Rev. Court Preacher Ziegenhagen, who had a commission from the congregation.

Count: What sort of commission did Mr. Ziegenhagen have?

Reply: The three Lutheran congregations in New Hannover, Providence and Philadelphia had been urgently requesting a pastor for several years past. The copies are deposited in Providence and the letters in London, which can be published at any time, if necessary.

Count: When did the congregations last petition for a pastor?

Reply: I do not know; I must look it up in the copies.

Count: You must say at once when they wrote the last letter to Mr. Ziegenhagen.

The brewer and several others of his people chimed in and said that the last letter may have reached there about 1739. I did not know, because nothing had been said to me about it.

I replied: I really cannot say just now, and besides, it is of no importance, for I have been called, sent, and accepted. The deacons and elders of the three congregations have signed an acceptance.

COMMENT: Zinzendorf is establishing the foundation for his case, making clear to the audience what he already knows. His "spies," as Muhlenberg called them earlier, had shadowed Muhlenberg in Philadelphia, and one was present when his papers were presented to Tranberg. Zinzendorf does not question Muhlenberg's academic and theological credentials or qualifications; he is after the Halle-Ziegenhagen connection, deeming it to be a weak point in the pastor's case, as becomes clear in the follow-up questions. Muhlenberg makes clear from the start that his authorization comes from Ziegenhagen. As far as he is concerned, that is important. Ziegenhagen was his immediate reference point — and source for later emphasis. The Count's follow-up about Ziegenhagen's conditions for sending Muhlenberg opens the way for the criticism of Halle and Ziegenhagen.

Muhlenberg quickly admitted that several years had elapsed since the initial request was made, then moved just as quickly to cite that the request was well documented and official, not generated by a minority faction. The following exchange showed the questioner moving in toward the first weak spot in the defense. Muhlenberg is being mostly honest when he responded that he did not know the date of the last petition, apparently relying on his not knowing it with a degree of precision. The audience, led by the brewer, knows, and provides the approximate date. Muhlenberg includes audience participation in order to emphasize to his audiences the tight situation in which he is operating. Muhlenberg deftly deflected the Count by adding that the exact date really did not matter since Muhlenberg was on the scene and was not only called and sent (matters that dealt with the 1737–1739 petitions), but had a signed acceptance by the three congregations. The stratagem worked. Now Muhlenberg knew that he could disrupt the questioner.

4. The Count's Reaction

TEXT:

Count: Here in Philadelphia no deacons of the Lutheran congregation gave their signatures, for the deacons of the Lutheran congregation are sitting here, and there is no other Lutheran congregation and church here other than the one we have. Haven't you seen the church yet, which was just recently built?

Reply: I know nothing about it, because I am convinced that I preached to Lutheran people and was accepted by them.

Count: They are not Lutherans but rebels, brawlers; and you have become the head of such people and preached to them in the house from which they expelled my adjunct, Pirlaeus. The rebels must come first to us and apologize.

Reply: My dear Count, your people must first come and apologize to our Lutherans because they broke the lock off our church and started the tumult.

Count: That is not true!

Reply: It is true to the extent that they are still involved in a lawsuit over it.

Count: I know of no lawsuit.

Reply: Well, everybody knows what happened last summer, July 18.

COMMENT: Zinzendorf, distracted by Muhlenberg's last comment, moves to defend or at least state his version of the true Philadelphia Lutheran church. He either overlooks or disregards as presently irrelevant or concedes what else Muhlenberg included in his statement: the local calls from New Hannover and Providence. Zinzendorf focuses on the Philadelphia congregation's situation. Is he feeling simultaneously confident about the legitimacy of the Race Street congregation and vulnerable because seven of eight elders have returned to Arch Street? His emotions are also triggered by the ill treatment and dishonor shown by the "rebels" to Pyrlaeus, himself and those who withdrew from Arch Street. He adds that these rebels are the "brawlers" who expelled Pyrlaeus, not a mixed mob of Reformed and disaffected Lutherans or totally Reformed. It is the rebels and brawlers who constitute the gaggle at Arch Street and Muhlenberg is their pastor. The Arch Streeters are not genuine Lutherans at all, and, by implication, neither is their putative pastor.

His question about Muhlenberg not seeing the brand new and recently consecrated Race Street church is edged with sarcasm. How could he miss it? It was virtually around the corner from the rump's ex-slaughterhouse and sometime barn. By insisting that there are no other Lutheran deacons and elders in the city, he gestured rhetorically and probably physically toward his listeners, for the officials were sitting right there. He may have reflected that among the Arch Street leaders were men appointed by the charlatan, Kraft. Actually, Zinzendorf has a strong case at this point, except for the defection of the original elders who returned to Arch Street. He may even be suggesting that Muhlenberg minister to the country congregations, recognize Race Street as the legitimate Lutheran congregation, and agree that Pyrlaeus is its rightful pastor. Similar proposals were put to Muhlenberg in his struggles with Schmidt and Kraft over the past month. Clearly, Muhlenberg could not entertain such an arrangement without recognizing the legitimacy of the Count's basic claims to ministerial and episcopal-like authority.

Muhlenberg cast his response in a two-fold manner and succeeds in blunting the force of the Count's argument. The initial reply is a bland dismissal of the Count's version as irrelevant in the current state of the case coupled with the disingenuous comment that he knows that he preached to Lutherans and was called to be their pastor, with the logical deduction that the Arch Street congregation is the valid Lutheran church in town. The Count, frustrated and angered by the answer, raises his voice and denounces the Arch Streeters and demands that before anything else is arranged in the matter, the Arch Street members must come "to us" and ask for pardon for what they did in July (*Abbitte thun*). At this point, Muhlenberg drops his diffident tone to jab back that if anyone needs to apologize, it is those who left with Pyrlaeus. The reason: they

129

started the fracas by breaking the lock on the door of "our church." Zinzendorf can barely restrain his ire. Muhlenberg pushes him further about the *Prozeß* (trial) that he and/or his supporters are bringing before the civil authorities. The Count's denial is puzzling unless the case was still in a preliminary stage or there was some expectation of settling the matter. Muhlenberg's parting comment infers that the Count's version is not the "true" version of the July incident.

In this exchange the issue of identity and legitimacy surfaces with regard to the congregations. It lurks throughout the encounter, and at the end will reappear in the form of the identity and legitimacy of the Count. Muhlenberg has led the Count away from some of his strongest arguments and needled him into making angry outbursts — shades of his handling of Kraft!

5. The Subject Almost Resumed

TEXT:

Count: Let us stick to the subject. The last time I asked Mr. Zigenhagen how things stood as far as Pennsylvania was concerned, he replied that he could send no preacher there because the congregations were unwilling to stipulate the salary. Now, since Mr. Zigenhagen knew that I had come in here, why did he send you afterwards?

Reply: I was sent to investigate conditions here and to see whether order cannot be established.

Count: Mr. Zigenhagen is an archliar and hypocrite! When I am in his presence, he is meek and humble and submissive; when I am away from him, he inveighs and slanders. This is another spiteful trick which he and Mr. Francke are playing off on me! I shall tell him of it to his face when I get to London.

Reply: My dear Count, it is a shame to speak that way. I have often heard in Germany that you, yourself, were a liar. Am I not forced to believe it?

COMMENT: Zinzendorf returns to the opening series of questions: who sent Muhlenberg and why? Without restating the initial questions directly, the Count recalls his London conversation with Ziegenhagen. The Count has good reason to feel that Ziegenhagen deliberately misled him about Halle's intentions. It is not clear that Zinzendorf mentioned to Ziegenhagen that he (Zinzendorf) would supply that need personally, but he may have, thereby triggering Halle's reflex response in sending

130

Muhlenberg. The Renewer's continued and heated diatribe against Ziegenhagen segues into an attack on his old nemesis, Gotthilf Francke. The ridiculing and hurt tones in his reference to Ziegenhagen's dissembling meekness and submissiveness (really, to Zinzendorf?) but slandering him when his back is turned discloses how deeply wounded Zinzendorf felt. In answer to the direct question, "Why did he send you afterwards?" Muhlenberg prepares for a subsequent round in the encounter. The assumption is that where the Count goes, disorder and confusion are sure to follow — and that the mess was already being made in Pennsylvania through the actions and presence of Zinzendorf and others.

Muhlenberg's closing observation in the exchange is actually a mildly stated but cutting insult that will develop sharper bite at another point. The reference to the Count's reputation in Germany and the charge there that he was a liar will be featured later. Now the Count associates it with the related matter of Muhlenberg's knowledge of the Count and his activities. Muhlenberg's last rejoinder foreshadows two lines of argument that he will pursue later: a reflection on the Count's intemperate behavior, and an allegation about his reputed/disputed honesty. Zinzendorf does not take the bait that will anger him still further — at least not yet.

6. The Encounter's Pivot: Muhlenberg Attacks

TEXT:

Count: I have heard that you have read all my writings; did you not read that I have established a Lutheran consistory here in Philadelphia?

Reply: I read in Charleston the report of seven conferences, and through them learned that a certain Mr. Von Thürnstein had caused disturbances in various places, but I did not know that the Count had established a Lutheran consistory.

Count: These are jesuitical tricks.

Reply: I once heard in Germany that you were appointed a Moravian bishop by a Reformed preacher. How does that jibe with your being able to establish a Lutheran consistory?

Count: I am inspector of all Lutheran churches in Pennsylvania and Lutheran pastor in Philadelphia. I have held synods in the country and here, and installed pastors in several places and even deposed a pastor named Stöver.

Reply: Can a Reformed preacher give such authority to you?

Count: Don't you understand canon law? Don't you know that in Wittenberg the foremost theologian was ordained by a Catholic?

Reply: But how is it that sometimes you can be a Moravian bishop and sometimes an inspector and a Lutheran pastor?

Count: I publicly resigned my Episcopal office in Holland in the presence of lords and princes.

Reply: You change frequently.

Count: I have been called as pastor in writing by the Lutheran congregation here in Philadelphia, and likewise my adjunct, Pirlaeus.

Reply: Is your call signed by anybody?

Count: It doesn't need it.

Reply: My call has been signed and I shall trouble myself no further, but just follow the instructions of my superiors in Europe. If this does not please you, you can settle it with them.

COMMENT: This exchange is the pivot of the whole encounter. Up to now the Count and Muhlenberg sparred with each other. Now the meeting turns nasty, serious and, as far as Muhlenberg understands it, against the Count.

Resuming the questioning, the Count sets up the next phase: Zinzendorf's claim to oversight for the Lutheran congregations and clergy. Again, Muhlenberg avoids using any terms that even hint that Zinzendorf has a Lutheran ecclesiastical organization. At first, he dodges the question, although he undoubtedly knows that Zinzendorf as well as Kraft have established a consistory. Instead, Muhlenberg shifts to the Pennsylvania Synods, mentioning that he read about them in Charleston. He tosses in Zinzendorf's alternate name feigning that he does not know that Thürnstein is Zinzendorf. Thürnstein, he says, is known to have caused "disturbances in various places." Was Muhlenberg's source about the synods one of Anton Gruber's anti-Zinzendorf publications? Muhlenberg has put into the record for his audiences that he made a negative comment about the synods and needled the Count about the use of his title in order to play off on the accusations of confusion and dissembling. Muhlenberg's audience would recall the Freydeck charade.

Zinzendorf's exclamation, "*Jesuitenstreiche!*" is justified. Muhlenberg has been toying with him, and casuistically splitting semantic hairs. Zinzendorf's audience knows that and probably supports the Count's reaction, while Muhlenberg's audience is probably delighted with their man in Philadelphia. Perhaps the Count's forceful use of "Jesuitical" was not only a Protestant expletive but a reaction that hearkened to the ways the Jesuits used to humiliate and force de Noailles to submit to the papacy. Now, here is a Jesuit in Lutheran garb. Zinzendorf seems to be realizing that his opponent is shrewder and more dangerous than he first thought.

Muhlenberg presses the attack, ignoring the question about the consistory, and Zinzendorf falls into the trap. Prefacing his question with what is patently illogical in Saxony and most of the other German states, he asks about Zinzendorf's appointment as a Moravian bishop by a Reformed *Prediger* and then his transformation into an official with authority to establish a Lutheran consistory in British North America. It is highly unlikely that Muhlenberg did not know that Jablonsky was a Moravian bishop and a high church official in the Great Elector's court and that Nitschmann participated, too. The omission makes Zinzendorf appear shallow indeed. Muhlenberg mocks Zinzendorf with the implied insult that it makes no sense and the Count makes no sense but spreads disorder and confusion. Muhlenberg has presented a major Halle and Orthodox criticism of Zinzendorf, perhaps hoping that the audience that night might begin to question the convoluted arrangement.

Zinzendorf is too upset to set the record straight. He resorts to the *de facto* situation and cites that he is exercising authoritative supervision of the churches and clergy. He does not mention that he has been involved in ordinations (an inadvertent omission?) but cites that he has installed pastors and, neatly, mentions deposing one of Muhlenberg's rivals, Stöver. He is also claiming that Muhlenberg needs to work through him because he (Zinzendorf) is the superintendent of the Lutheran churches and pastors with particular reference to Philadelphia. Zinzendorf noted in his statements at Heerndyk that he would center his activities on German Lutherans in Pennsylvania. They were not receiving any help, apart from some books from London. Ziegenhagen gave him every indication that Halle would not be involved with the United Congregations. Zinzendorf, seeing the need, moved into the breach. Now a Jesuitical trickster is playing Francke's malicious tricks (*hämischer Streiche*) on him. The Count has good reason to be angry. He is confirmed in his (correct) view that his Halle foes seek to undermine him and his work for the sake of the Gospel. Muhlenberg has not been sent for Christ's sake but to continue Halle's relentless campaign against him.

Muhlenberg presses the issue of Zinzendorf's superintendent-episcopal character and jurisdiction by asking if a Reformed *Prediger* can bestow such authority on a Lutheran. The Count's rebuke about canon law might reflect his dependence on Jablonsky's and Friedrich Wilhelm's actions based on Prussian civil and canon law. He bolsters his case by pointing toward Luther. Here was the great Reformer who was ordained by a Catholic and then went on to ordain men for the Evangelical church. He tries to regain the initiative by making Muhlenberg appear to be ignorant of the law and history.

Muhlenberg does not back down. He puts Zinzendorf in the worst possible light by caricaturing him as an ecclesiastical chameleon, changing from Moravian bishop to a Lutheran pastor-inspector. Zinzendorf correctly and defensively notes that he publicly lay down (*niedergelegt*) his Moravian *Bischofsamt*. Muhlenberg's dry observation that he changes frequently is sarcastic and presents the Count as unstable, unreliable and of dubious integrity.

Zinzendorf, realizing that it is pointless to proceed along this exchange, shifts to the Philadelphia congregation. If Muhlenberg cannot see and accept the validity of the Count's position on the larger scene, surely he cannot deny Zinzendorf's position in the specific Philadelphia setting. He moves to the obviously proper call extended to him and Pyraelus by the Philadelphia Lutheran congregation. Muhlenberg is unabashed; he pounces. The call is unsigned and, therefore, lacks validity. In Muhlenberg's view, that makes it as binding as an unsigned contract, that is, it is not a genuine call. Zinzendorf's insistence that the omission is not an issue rings hollow; any merchant or lawyer knows Muhlenberg is right. Muhlenberg notes, triumphantly, that his call is signed so he is the legitimate pastor of the Lutheran congregation. He need not argue further. If Zinzendorf wants to quibble, he should take it up with Muhlenberg's superiors in Europe, that is with the Halle Fathers and the Wernigerode Consistory. There is no chance that Zinzendorf will change their minds.

7. The Count Stands on Protocol

TEXT:

Count: But is it not contrary to all fairness and courtesy that after I have been so long in this country that you should not have come to visit me? If you have been sent to investigate matters here, why did you not inquire into our affairs? When a person learns that there is a consistory and an inspector in a place, even if granting that it is illegal, does not one first make inquiries there?

Reply: Even if I had desired to call upon you as a stranger, you would not have been there in any event, for it was said that you were among the Indians. There are all kinds of sects here, and how is it

134

possible for me to run around to all of them? I have enough to do with the Lutherans who have been assigned to me.

Count: I am the Lutheran pastor. Why did you not come to me?

Reply: I had no orders to do so and still have none.

COMMENT: In 1737, on his first visit to England, Zinzendorf offended Ziegenhagen by not paying him a courtesy call at the start of his visit. He compounded the slight by meeting first with Oglethorpe and Archbishop-elect Potter. For someone steeped in courtly protocol, the breach of decorum could only have been deliberate. His business with the General and the Archbishop was more important to him than a tensely polite interview with the Halle man at the St. James Chapel. By approaching Potter, Zinzendorf signaled that he was going over the German Court Chaplain's head. If the Count wanted to derive any benefit from officials in England for the missions in the colonies, it surely would not come from Ziegenhagen. Now, however, Zinzendorf held a position in which he expected his authority to be recognized through such courtesy calls. Not to contact or register with him immediately on arrival was more than discourtesy; it was an insult and a denial of his authority.

Zinzendorf's question also contains a logical as well as reasonable criticism of Muhlenberg. Zinzendorf was Muhlenberg's superior in terms of dignity and social position. If the new arrival was not a crude or general settler but a man of quality, he would have paid his respects to the Count. Moreover, even conceding for the sake of argument that the consistory was illegal and the Count was not really the Lutheran superintendent, if Muhlenberg truly came to investigate "matters here" and not for some more devious purpose, it made sense to start with the Count. Zinzendorf is letting Muhlenberg know that he sees through his flimsy initial answer that he came to survey the situation. Zinzendorf realizes how shrewd the younger man was by going the same day he arrived to the country congregations, establishing himself there, and then insinuating himself into the city schism to challenge the real Lutherans on Race Street and the Count. He heard from his "spies," as Muhlenberg called them, how Muhlenberg undercut Kraft at Wicaco and Arch Street. Now, virtually on the eve of Zinzendorf's departure, he has raised a hue and cry over a record book in order to harass the Count and the true Lutherans. Muhlenberg has lied to the Count and in front of the audience. He really came to America to discredit Zinzendorf and to wreck the mission. The violation of proper protocol has exposed Muhlenberg and those who sent him.

Aristotle advised that when apologists are caught in an embarrassing position, they ought to shift the exchange so as to disrupt the accuser's thought, then retreat to more secure ground. So Muhlenberg somewhat snidely says that even if another stranger wanted to see Zinzendorf, he would not have been able to locate him in the time Muhlenberg has been here. He heard the Count was in Indian country and no one knew when he would return to Philadelphia. That is a partially plausible justification, given the Count's itinerations from Bethlehem. Did listeners note that Muhlenberg never answered the question put to him and that he still did not use terms that acknowledged the Count as a pastor and superintendent or as a fellow Lutheran? Then Muhlenberg sticks in his barbs. He lumps Zinzendorf and his supporters with "all sorts of sects," shrugging that he can not run around to all of them looking for the Count. He twists the statement to wound Zinzendorf even more by saying that he (Muhlenberg) was thoroughly busy with the Lutherans assigned to him, thereby rejecting any involvement the Count-Superintendent would have with him or the country congregations. Then he begins to fall back on his tactic of only following his orders from his superiors. Zinzendorf, possibly flustered by the man's refusal to deal with the damaging question, resorts to his oft-repeated claim to be the German Lutheran pastor in the city. But now he perceives that perhaps Muhlenberg may have been given some specific instructions.

8. Ziegenhagen Re-visited

TEXT:

Count: Did Mr. Zigenhagen say that you should pass me by?

Reply: When I was called, I inquired as to how I should conduct myself with regard to the Count and the reply was made that I should have no fear of the Count.

Count: Did Mr. Zigenhagen say that you should pass by the inspector and Lutheran pastor?

Reply: No.

Count: Now just see, my brethren, how this man contradicts himself and lies, since he replies yes and no to the same question.

Reply: Not so, Confrater. Mr. Zigenhagen knew well enough that Count Zinzendorf had gone to Pennsylvania, but he did not know that the Count wanted to be an inspector and Lutheran pastor.

COMMENT: The exchange is brief and inconclusive. Zinzendorf has already vented some of his anger at the Court Chaplain, but now sees that Ziegenhagen may have played a more insidious part. Did Ziegenhagen instruct Muhlenberg to "pass me by"? The first response is too general, yet is instructive. Before Muhlenberg left for England Counts Henckel and Reuss warned Muhlenberg that dealing with Zinzendorf would be a hard test. Obviously, Muhlenberg and others in Germany had discussed ways of handling the Count. Francke's instructions to Bolzius to accompany Muhlenberg was part of a strategy to terminate the Count's influence in Pennsylvania. Muhlenberg admits that he knew that the Count was in Pennsylvania and asked guidance from Ziegenhagen about relating to him. As Muhlenberg presents Ziegenhagen's response, Zinzendorf seems to have been put in the category of a nuisance. At any rate, Muhlenberg makes no admission that Ziegenhagen gave him instructions about deliberately and insultingly ignoring Zinzendorf the man, nor does he deny it.

Zinzendorf immediately seizes on the distinction and demands to know if Muhlenberg was told to ignore Zinzendorf the pastor and inspector-superintendent. When Muhlenberg answers "No," Zinzendorf jumps on the apparent contradiction. If Muhlenberg was not ordered to snub the inspector-pastor, he is a rude ignoramus. But if he was so instructed, then Ziegenhagen is an arch liar and hypocrite. Muhlenberg responds by distinguishing between his and Ziegenhagen's knowledge that Zinzendorf was somewhere in Pennsylvania and not knowing that the Count "wanted to be" an inspector and pastor. The choice of words is calculated to belittle the Count and to deny him the status he claims. The Count now shifts from Ziegenhagen to Muhlenberg.

9. Intentions and Fraying Tempers

TEXT:

Count: Did you not know that I was inspector and pastor?

Reply: I already knew in Germany that you went to Pennsylvania and intended ....

Count: What did I intend?

Reply: Yes, you intended.

Count: Just speak out. What did I intend?

Reply: I do not know. You yourself said at the conclusion of a reply to Adam Gross's publication, "Brethren, I am now going to Pennsylvania; pray the Saviour to reveal to you what I intend!" So, who knows what you intended?

Count: As soon as I get to London, I will go to the archbishop and

137

tell him that I established order among the Lutherans here, but that as soon as order was established, Mr. Zigenhagen sent a man who spoiled it all again and brought confusion.

Reply: You may say what you wish, I shall not concern myself with it. Now you have put everything in confusion and, I hope, by God's grace, to establish some order.

Count: Go ahead and do it. If you accomplish anything, it will only serve to increase my church. You have my good wishes. It cannot be denied that you were a Lutheran student in good standing, that you had a pastoral charge, as was reported to me nine months ago from Herrnhut. You have nothing more to do than apologize here, since you made an intrusion here and passed me by.

Reply: Count, the time will come when you will have to beg the pardon of the whole Lutheran church.

Count: What is he saying? He is a young parson (Pfarrer), *a village parson* (Dorfpfarrer)!

Reply: You must not become excited, Count.

Count: Make haste to consider and acknowledge that you have done wrong, otherwise I will make the whole thing public when I return to Germany.

Reply: When I do wrong before God, I pray for forgiveness, but I owe you no apology in this affair. You may publish in Germany what you please; if you touch me, I shall answer you with the truth. Your affairs are well enough known in Germany.

Count: The things published against me are nothing but pasquils to which no one will venture to put his name. I am willing to grant you time to reflect and beg my pardon. It merely comes down to a point d'honneur and you should not let that sway you.

Reply: You certainly are full of suggestions; in fact you are just what your aunt told me you were.

Count: Hold your tongue as far as my aunt is concerned, or I shall be compelled to expose her.

I could speak quite differently to you if you want me to.

Reply: Go ahead, speak.

COMMENT: Muhlenberg falters, but his knowledge of the Count's writings steadies him. Zinzendorf now demands to know if the man facing him knew that Zinzendorf was an inspector-superintendent and pastor. The question is loaded, and Muhlenberg decides that it is premature to expose his position on the issue. If he answers yes or no, he opens himself either for a drubbing about rudeness (yes) or a demand that he acknowledge it now (no). Muhlenberg reflects what he knew in Germany about Zinzendorf's journey to America. He could have stopped there, but stumbles into a sentence on the Count's intentions. The Count jumps at the opening, but Muhlenberg recovers. He turns the tables again by quoting the Count against himself, making him sound foolish by the quote that he did not know what he intended.

By now Zinzendorf is exasperated with the eel-like Muhlenberg. He threatens or blusters about his intentions to inform Archbishop Potter of Ziegenhagen's, Halle's and Muhlenberg's duplicitous actions against him, and how they are wrecking the order he has brought to the German Lutherans in the colony. Muhlenberg fires back his standard line that he will bring order out of the present mess.

Zinzendorf continues in the same frame of mind, but realizes that Muhlenberg will stay in Philadelphia after he leaves America. He makes another attempt to break Muhlenberg by saying that all the new arrival has to do is to apologize for intruding on the Count's territory and for not properly acknowledging him. The Count does not include any reference to the Arch Street congregation. The issue has come to a point of honor, Zinzendorf's honor. Muhlenberg's rejection of the proposition is harsh. He predicts that one day the Count will have to beg the pardon of the whole Lutheran church. Again, the Count threatens to expose Muhlenberg publicly, assuming that such a denunciation will ruin the pastor's career. Shifting to a bemused, sarcastic tone, Muhlenberg comments that the Count is getting overheated and is full of suggestions. The Count's reference to Herrnhut discloses that he has already heard about Muhlenberg, but does not disclose what he has heard. Perhaps he learned only that Muhlenberg was at or leaving Grosshennersdorf. Zinzendorf's ire over Halle's sending someone to the United Congregations may imply that he did not know that Muhlenberg was on his way to Pennsylvania. He could have been dispatched to Georgia.

Muhlenberg short-circuits the Count's train of thought by making references to Zinzendorf's reputation in Europe. Zinzendorf flares in the parlor just as he did in print when responding to critics. Having scored with that thrust, Muhlenberg makes the Count furious with his reference to his Aunt Sophie. Muhlenberg has hit a very sore spot. Objectively, it is a thoroughly underhanded tactic, but for the purpose of his *apologia*, it is a brilliant stroke. Now the Count attempts a counter attack.

10. The Count Focuses on Halle and Pietism

TEXT:

Count: Were you not reared at Halle?

Reply: No. I was reared in the province of Hannover, completed my studies at Göttingen, and was also at Halle.

Count: The Hallesians are Pietists; aren't you a Hallesian?

Reply: I am a Lutheran and shall remain so, Count.

Count: Are you such a Lutheran as Mr. Zigenhagen is?

Reply: I was with Mr. Zigenhagen for some time and learned to know his character. I am and hope to become, more and more, such a Lutheran as Mr. Zigenhagen is.

Count: Before the year is out, I shall bring forth more than a hundred witnesses to prove that Mr. Zigenhagen is not a genuine Lutheran.

Reply: Mr. Zigenhagen is certainly not afraid and is not likely to be. I am surprised, my dear Count, at the way you cavil (häckeln) at me with your questions and try to hook something on me!

Count: Yes, I am casting a hook (Haken) into his conscience!

Reply: Oh, no; you do not touch my conscience, but I gather enough from your questions to know that your heart is not right. If you had a heart or spirit without guile, you would not ask such questions.

COMMENT: Given leave to "speak quite differently" to his wiley guest, Zinzendorf tries to lump Halle, Pietism and Muhlenberg together in order to brand the mix as un-Lutheran, legalistic and censorious. He wants to make sure that everyone knows that such persons are hypocrites who have been banned through anti-conventicle laws. The questions and answers effectively put both men in the Pietist camp. The charge being leveled against Muhlenberg includes the fact that the Hallesians are enemies of the Count, the Brethren and genuine Lutheranism in Germany and everywhere else. He is nearly ready to turn to his audience to receive the vindication he has earned. But then he asks Muhlenberg to correlate his Lutheranism with that of Ziegenhagen. Muhlenberg grasps the chance to warm the hearts of his audiences in Europe by praising the man he will always revere. Zinzendorf goes into a hyperbolic attack on the King's preacher and helper of refugee Lutherans. He claims that he will call more than a hundred witnesses to testify against Ziegenhagen's Lutheranism. The outburst allows

Muhlenberg to accuse Zinzendorf of one of Pietism's cardinal sins, that he has an evilly disposed heart, a charge he has been developing for several exchanges.

11. Return to the Presenting Issue

TEXT:

Count: You came here to speak to me about a church book and a cup?

Reply: Yes, I wanted to ask you if you would return them or not.

Count: What should we return? They belong to our Lutheran church and congregation. However, if you are so much in want that you need the book and cup, we will present them to you, provided that you sign a receipt which we will make out for you.

Reply: I desire no present from you. I only claim what belongs to us, since the cup and also the book were paid for out of our collections. (Here I stood up.)

COMMENT: The argument is getting nowhere and it is time to finish the business that prompted Zinzendorf's invitation and the annoying visits of the Arch Street deacons. It is pointless for Zinzendorf to think that Muhlenberg will accept the offer to obtain the cup and the book (with signed receipt!) thereby connoting that the objects belonged to the Race Street Church and that the Lutherans there were bestowing them on the poorer Arch Street group. Muhlenberg wants the items returned because he claims they belong to the genuine Lutheran church, the Arch Street congregation. For either man to yield to the other is out of the question. Muhlenberg begins to terminate the interview by getting up — without permission, of course.

12. The Key Issue Finally Disclosed

TEXT:

Count: Consider well the matter of apologizing; otherwise you will regret it.

Reply: I need no consideration, for I do not acknowledge you as a genuine Lutheran, much less an inspector and Lutheran pastor.

Count: Do you hear that? Now it is clear what the man has in his heart. (The brethren and toadies of the Count assented to everything by nodding their heads and marveled at the Count's ravings as though they were divinely inspired.)

141

Reply: It has also become apparent what you have in your heart. If you are such a genuine Lutheran, why would they not let you preach in the Swedish church?

Count: That was prevented by only one man, the Swedish merchant, Koch.

Reply: Mr. Koch is a deacon (Vorsteher) *of the Swedish church and he certainly would not have prevented you without the knowledge of the Swedish minister, Mr. Tranberg.*

Count: Can you say that Mr. Tranberg refused me?

Reply: I cannot say it positively. Enough you were refused.

COMMENT: Zinzendorf offers Muhlenberg one more chance: apologize or regret it. Now that Muhlenberg is ready to leave, he lets fly what Zinzendorf knew was behind the Halle-man's mission and in his heart: "I do not acknowledge you as a genuine Lutheran, much less an inspector and Lutheran pastor." From 1716 to that moment and even to his dying day, Halle repudiated, thwarted and attacked Zinzendorf. It is the same old story and the same old message he has heard from his family of origin, his in-laws, governmental and high ecclesiastical officials, and one-time friends in Scandinavia, England and Germany. The Brethren accept, honor and love him. The assembly's protest is loud and prolonged. Muhlenberg, unable to resist a further jab, refers to the Swedish church in Philadelphia as evidence that other Lutherans agree in rejecting Zinzendorf as a real Lutheran and pastor. Zinzendorf corrects Muhlenberg on Tranberg's involvement and then attacks Koch. The Count threatens that the Swedes will soon throw Muhlenberg out.[7]

13. Leben Sie Wohl!

TEXT:

Count: There you see, brethren, the man contradicts himself and lies. (Because of the noisy assent of the brethren I was unable to reply. The Count further asserted that I would not preach in the Swedish church more than two or three times before they threw me out just as they had thrown out his adjunct from the old church.)

Reply: I am willing to wait and see. I have nothing further to say except to wish you a happy voyage. Good bye (Leben Sie wohl)*!*

COMMENT: Muhlenberg stays on his feet. Perhaps Zinzendorf rises and they glare at each other. The assembly shouts against Muhlenberg. His *apologia* is over. As he leaves, he claims the last word: "… happy voyage. *Leben Sie wohl!*" Zinzendorf still holds the field and feels vindicated. He has not yielded to that man, those who back him or even a world of critics. Even though he is leaving America, God's Philadelphia-door is open.

Physically, the encounter is over.

Endnotes to Chapter Eight

1 *Journals*, Vol. 1, pp. 76–80.
2 "*Selbstbiographie*," pp. 142–149.
3 "*Selbstbiographie*" reads "Reply: No, the matter had not been considered, and Mr. Ziegenhagen did not know that there was an Inspector and Lutheran pastor here" (my translation). The term *Confrater* does not appear in the *Selbstbiographie* version of Muhlenberg's next response. The answer is simply "*Ja.*"
4 "*Selbstbiographie*," "*Sie müssen nicht in Hitze kommen.*"
5 "*Selbstbiographie*," "*Schweige er von meiner Tante, oder ich werde genöthigt dieselbe zu prostituiren.*" Zinzendorf dropped the formal "*Sie*" in retorting to Muhlenberg, referring to him as "*er*" as if addressing a subordinate. Was he impugning the morality of his maiden aunt Sophie?
6 See Wagner, "A Key Episode."
7 Bryzelius later stated that the Moravians deliberately used him in attempts to undermine Muhlenberg's relationship with the Swedes. Bryzelius was ordained by Zinzendorf, but, in 1760, became a Lutheran and was admitted to the Ministerium as a Lutheran pastor. Muhlenberg implicitly accepted the validity of the Zinzendorfian ordination by not having Bryzelius go through a "regular" ordination. See *Journals*, Vol. 1, pp. 442–446.

Chapter Nine

AFTERMATHS, UNDERSTANDINGS AND IMPLICATIONS

The door closed behind Muhlenberg but the encounter and the controversy were not over. We turn now to selected considerations of the aftermaths, understandings and implications.

Aftermaths

The aftermaths began on December 31/January 12, the morning after the encounter. Muhlenberg, Koch and the Arch Street deacons, Sackler and Herman, went to Mayor Till's office to request his aid in obtaining the church record book. Till was one of the Gentlemen's Party and was elected in the otherwise catastrophic October 1 balloting for the colony's Assembly and various city offices. Allen, Turner, Till and their allies realized they needed German votes to break the Friends' domination of the Assembly. Intimidation had failed miserably. Zinzendorf clearly was not the leader to whom they could turn; he was too controversial and he was leaving within days. His adjunct, Pyrlaeus, did not have the stature or the support of enough persons inside and outside the city. While Benezet was an important figure, he was not a German. Koch was a more impressive figure and was highly regarded by most of the Germans in the city. Muhlenberg had the right documents, personal demeanor and leadership capacities. In addition, Zinzendorf's response to the mayor on the previous day and his failure to deliver the book as promised did not sit well with Till.

The mayor responded to the request that morning with a more strongly worded message to Zinzendorf insisting that the book belonging to the German Lutherans, as represented by the deacons, be given to those men. Again, the Count gave an evasive reply through Böhler that angered the mayor. He wrote now for the third time, threatening legal action. Zinzendorf claimed, in answer, that he did not have the item. It is clear that by frustrating the mayor, Zinzendorf risked being detained, but he knew that the Race Street congregation's claim to be the true Lutheran church in Philadelphia would be weakened if he surrendered the record book.

That evening, at 7:30 p.m., Zinzendorf preached his farewell sermon (*Abschiedsrede*) at the Race Street Lutheran church. While he spoke, Koch and Muhlenberg dined with Mayor Till. The locations of the two protagonists that evening foreshadows Muhlenberg's acceptance as a leader among the Germans by the English-speaking power elite. The Swedish deacon and the German pastor mollified an angry mayor, and dropped the request for the book altogether. Perhaps they realized that their case was weak and that Allen would testify he had leased the building to the only Lutheran church in town. Plainly, however, Zinzendorf left a poor impression on Till and his associates. James Logan, one of Allen's associates and probably the most highly regarded intellect in the city, wrote later that the Count "appears a mere knight-errant in religion, scarce less that Don Quixote was in chivalry!...[he wished after Zinzendorf left] I could say any thing concerning him to satisfaction, but his conduct lost him all credit here, being now regarded by his own few Moravians." The Swedish visitor to Philadelphia, Peter Kalm, reported in 1748 that Zinzendorf's "uncommon behavior here persuaded many Englishmen of rank that he was disordered in his head."[1]

The Count and his entourage left Philadelphia around 9:00 p.m. that night. After dinner, Muhlenberg and Koch went to the Wicaco church where the former conducted a service and preached to his Arch Street flock. When he arrived at his Philadelphia rooms, he was given a letter from Zinzendorf really intended for Tranberg. The Count wanted the last word. In it, he "charges me with heresy and urges that I be driven out of the Swedish church, and if they do not do so, he threatens to bring charges against the Swedish church council before his Reverence, the Archbishop of Upsala."[2] Was the Count serious? Did he forget that Tranberg knew that the Swedish government had issued a rescript against him and that most of his former Swedish friends repudiated him?

The Renewer journeyed to New York City, then took his chartered ship to England (January 8/20), and arrived at Dover on February 17/28. There he had to face what he had resisted for so long: the Brethren were declaring themselves as an independent religious community in Britain and the Prussian monarch had already done the same in his realm. In addition, new developments were afoot. His son, Christian Renatus, and others were moving into what the Moravians call their "Sifting Period." The mission to America was left to be led (and capably so) by Böhler, and the soon-to-arrive Spangenberg.

Muhlenberg had another immediate problem: Valentin Kraft. Recognized now by the city authorities, the Swedes and the United Congregations, he was free to take on Kraft. On Sunday, January 2, Kraft attempted to preach at the German service held at Wicaco. The Swedes refused him access. He and a group of his supporters from the Germantown congregation tried to enter the Arch Street building. Muhlenberg earlier and quite cleverly had taken possession of the keys with the understanding that he was to decide who could enter the building.

He refused to let Kraft enter. By Tuesday, Kraft was gone — for the present. Muhlenberg had no more serious rivals in the United Congregations.

A second immediate aftermath was the continuation of the rivalry and competition between the Race and Arch Street congregations. Neither side sought a reconciliation and each thought the worst of the other. By the end of the winter of 1743, Muhlenberg and the lay leaders had negotiated with Allen for a site and began constructing a new church. It was dedicated on October 20, 1743. Perhaps the rivalry between the congregations and the settlement of the lawsuit (February, 1743) pushed the financing and construction to completion. The court decided that Allen had indeed leased the building to the Lutherans and not to the Reformed. It was, therefore, permissible for a Lutheran deacon to lock the door. One set of Lutherans had admonished the set led by Pyrlaeus about entering the building. But since both sets were Lutherans in the still unified congregation, the Pyrlaeus-led set had the right to break the lock. The court found that the members of the Reformed congregation perpetrated the violence, and they were fined. Case closed. The Arch Street congregation dropped attempts to get the book and other items. Ironically, the presenting cause of the encounter was no longer on Muhlenberg's agenda. He had accomplished what he came for: the thwarting of Zinzendorf and being called to the United Congregations.

In 1743 the Philadelphia and overall Pennsylvania situation changed. The Swedish Lutheran pastor, Laurentius Thorstonsen Theophilus Nyberg, was sent to Wicaco. Nyberg had Moravian tendencies before he came to Philadelphia and grew steadily closer to the Brethren. Koch complained so loudly to the Archbishop of Upsala and royal authorities that they dismissed Nyberg from Wicaco. Nyberg joined the Moravians and became one of their most popular preachers and Muhlenberg's bitter enemy.

Count Zinzendorf provided for the continuation of his vision for new ways to evangelize the non-believers and to organize believers. The Pennsylvania Plan still motivated him and those dedicated to his vision. In the Pennsylvania Testament and the *Abschiedsrede*, he addressed those who would carry on in the future. The sermon's announced text was Mark 14:8, the same as his final sermon-presentation for his examination for the Stralsund Consistory, "She did what she was able." In his heart-felt sermon, he stressed the inward nature of the Christian life and the knowledge of the God who searches human hearts. The woman who anointed Jesus' feet did what she was able for her Lord, and he praised her for it, saying that wherever the Gospel would be proclaimed, her witness would be made known to the world. Others, looking at the event externally, murmured at what seemed so useless and wasteful. Jesus, however, had looked upon her heart, knew that she did what she was able, and on the basis of her intention to thank and serve God, praised her. He continued that discipled living was not a matter of human deeds and accomplishments, but was a matter of intention and will. He made the obvious applications to his ministry in Pennsylvania and to his listeners' futures with the Savior. The important point was to proclaim the Gospel of the Lamb's blood and grace.

The theme of inward intention allowed him to speak of other *Religionen* and the many types of Christian groups. He was convinced that all *Religionen* had at their core the intent to seek and praise God. There was, therefore, a common and potentially unifying principle that could be discerned and sought in each particular tradition and organization. God in human form showed the nucleus of that core to be God's justifying grace in the blood and wounds of the Savior. So, Christ was already present, although unseen, in all *Religionen*. This was a strategy for evangelism among the Indians and even the unbelieving Pennsylvanians. It was also a means to understand the relationships among squabbling Christian groups. In each group and not in any one group alone there were persons whom the Count, in good Pietist fashion, called the Children of God (*Gotteskinder*). In the endtime, these scattered but yet whole people would be brought together as the fulfilled *Gemeine Gottes im Geist* (community of God in the Spirit). In the present, the *Gotteskinder* in a *Religionen* formed a *Gemeinlein* (little communities of the faithful) in the *Religionen*. For the present it was neither necessary nor advisable to pull persons from their Christian *Religionen* into yet another big organization. God would bring the consummation in God's good time.

He then said that the Bethlehem settlement was not to be considered a Moravian community. Moravians, Lutherans, Reformed, sabbatarians and adult baptizers all were there. Bethlehem was to be the *Gemeine ohne Name*, the community without a name. That was not meant to be an identity-less entity. He pointed to the Revelation to John. God knew and would bestow the name on the individuals who were to be saved and on the new Jerusalem. For now, humble Bethlehem foreshadowed that eschatological Jerusalem. The mission of the Bethlehem-based *Gotteskinder* was not to establish a separate *Religion*, but to go to and into the other *Religionen* with the message and ministry of the crucified Lamb by whose blood humans are saved. That strategy was understood

147

in Bethlehem, but regarded by Muhlenberg as a Zinzendorfian-Moravian plot to seduce believers and congregations into becoming Moravians.

In the *Abschiedsrede* Zinzendorf reflected that he did what he was able in a land that that was simultaneously anti-religious and overly religious. The latter was evidenced by sectarianism and the former by indifference and atheism. He did what he could and felt satisfied with what had been accomplished and dissatisfied with not having done more. There was plenty yet to do. Others, in Pauline terms, would come after him, and still others after them. He did not care if his name was forgotten as long as the Gospel was proclaimed. Did he include Muhlenberg among those who would come after him? Perhaps. But his letter written to the Swedish officials earlier that day and delivered to Muhlenberg's rooms that night breaths a different spirit. He also warned in the sermon of those who would attempt to ruin the work that had been accomplished. In his closing prayers, he praised the Savior, saying that Christ was now at home in Pennsylvania as Lord of the land among Indians and Europeans and would remain there until the fulfillment of all things in his second coming. Almost overcome with emotion and not wanting to disrupt the rest of the service, he left the Race Street church and soon departed from Philadelphia.

The sermon and the ideas it contained had a powerful and mixed aftermath. The *Gemeine ohne Name* was led by Böhler until he returned to England and Spangenberg arrived to assume overall leadership (1744). From the Bethlehem side, it was legitimate to ordain persons for ministry in the Lutheran and Reformed *Religionen* and to send them to serve in congregations of those churches. The Reformed and Muhlenberg-led Lutheran clergy took such acts as treacherous and subversive. Both sides exchanged hostile words and deeds as congregations split, lawsuits were lodged, and the Gospel was stymied. The anti-Zinzendorf Lutherans and Reformed insisted on their own confessional and ecclesiastical positions. Muhlenberg's *Journals* contain pages of complaint, accusation and recrimination against the Moravians.

It would be a relief to report the permanence of a comment discovered in the *Bethlehem Diary* for June 24, 1744:

> Br. Döling told us that the Rev. Pastor Muhlenberg in the early sermon on the preceding Sunday had warned his people not to slander the Moravian Brethren any longer or to sin against them. What he had done hitherto should not be done any more. It went as far as writing to Sweden regarding them in an effort to make thorough inquiry whether they were tolerated there and considered orthodox. It is said

Muhlenberg's own *Vorsteher*, Köppele, has been powerfully awakened by Pastor Neuberg [Nyberg] and comprehends the matter. And Butcher Jacob is said to have talked with Mr. Muhlenberg and stated why he attends the services of the Moravian Brethren. And when he answered, "My dear Mr. Muhlenberg, just look at our people; one boozes, the other whores, the third spends his time in other public vices. And in our Church things are done so frivolously and coldly. But since I have worshiped with the Moravians and seen their orderliness, quietness, love for each other and have heard their preaching, my heart has sensed something entirely different, so that I cannot forget it." Thereupon, Muhlenberg is said to have embraced him and told him, "Good, hold on to this grace...." We consider this mere Jesuit trickery.[3]

Did this really happen? Unfortunately, there are no extant journals from Muhlenberg for 1744. In March, 1745 he reported that Bryzelius, then still a Moravian, assailed him for being a Halle Pietist. Throughout 1745–1747 he and Nyberg maintained a running battle of recriminations. Perhaps the report and the skeptical comment that concluded it reflected Muhlenberg's tactic of not speaking directly to an issue when he felt that an abrupt comment would not be helpful at that time. In 1745, as the result of an argument with Nyberg, Muhlenberg wrote to the Halle authorities, requesting them to consider the question of whether Lutherans and Moravians could work together.[4] He expanded that request by suggesting that "unbiased" universities in Sweden and the German Tübingen be consulted. This was scarcely a neutral inquiry because Tübingen had turned against Zinzendorf and the Swedes were about to issue an even more condemnatory rescript against the Count. Ironically, Muhlenberg and those associated with him were often accused of being crypto-Moravians. Actually, their pastoral practices, preaching styles, theological concerns and ministering care were closer than either was willing to admit.

The third and fourth aftermaths are more positive. In the encounter Zinzendorf threatened to expose the Hallesians and Muhlenberg publicly when he returned to Europe. His protests to Archbishop Potter over the recognition of the Moravians as a separate religious community appear to have outweighed his complaints about the Hallesians, but did not eliminate Potter's support of the Brethren in British North America. Instead of confronting the Hallesians directly, a perhaps more reflective Count wrote Francke a conciliatory letter (1746) expressing his "ecumenical love" for the man and Zinzendorf's prayers that he would enjoy that Sabbath rest now enjoyed by the cloud of blessed witnesses. In other reflections, the Count was turning to further study of the Augsburg Confession and attempting to control his *Jähzorn* (anger or rage).[5]

The final aftermath came through a January, 1747 letter from the deacons of the Race Street church. The officers wanted to know what their present relationship was to the Count. Was he still their senior pastor and inspector-superintendent of Lutheran churches in Pennsylvania? They reflected the *Abschiedsrede* as they wrote, "We are also glad that Herr Muhlenberg has come to the land….[We ask you] to bless now from afar our work among the Lutherans in Pennsylvania which lies so close to your heart and because the harvest will be so great, so help us with still more faithful laborers."[6] Zinzendorf responded by surrendering his functions in the congregation and as inspector-superintendent of the colony's German Lutheran congregations.

Understandings

The survey of the encounter's aftermaths prepares for developing four historical understandings and suggests three implications. The first understanding is the most obvious: the controversy was intensely personal. Two devout, dedicated and very different men faced each across that table. Whether consciously or not Zinzendorf was fulfilling a qualified version of his family's motto: he would yield to no one when convinced that he was following God's will. He was a creatively inspired person who was opposed by authority figures throughout his life and he reacted to that opposition with dogged resistance. No matter which way he turned, a relative, tutor, teacher, cleric, governmental official, critic, and sometimes friend sought to counter his will and mission. The fact that he was a nobleman, raised with powerful senses of entitlement to deference and obligation to serve, compounded his conviction that God called him to a special vocation. His personality attracted others — at least initially — to join him in causes that he championed, and he was able to provide starting points to carry on those causes. The purposes may have been more sweeping than could be achieved, yet he had the vigor to inspire and lead. The Count handled adversity with courage, but also with indignation often expressed through anger, his *Jähzorn*. He also had energy and zeal that outstripped his fiscal resources and management skills. Never given to understatement, he had the pen of a poet and a treasury of images and metaphors. Zinzendorf's sense of the future was more certain and far-reaching than that of his contemporaries. This led him, as during that December evening, into conflicts with those who had other and more immediate visions.

Muhlenberg was the antithesis of his counterpart in the controversy. He was a commoner from a small town who struggled to get his education and status. The man from Einbeck was reluctant to discuss in detail his own spiritual journey. His journals disclose a self-controlled, spiritually modest person. He knew disappointment, worry, privation, delay and misunderstanding from the bottom up, that is, from his meager social origins to Countess von Gersdorf's defaulting on his salary to life in America. When his circumstances seemed most dire, a patron or benefactor emerged to assist him. Muhlenberg never forgot their help, and he developed a strong sense of loyalty to those who aided him. Hard experience taught him how to stand up for himself and his purposes not by flaunting but by confronting authorities from within the structures that initially were arrayed against him. Far from being a calculating or scheming man, he was, nevertheless, shrewd. He saw the possibilities within a situation and pursued existing procedures in order to fulfill his mission. He may be characterized as a creative strategist, sufficiently patient to let situations develop without overtly interfering in them, and careful enough to nudge them in his direction as opportunities were presented. His abilities, toughness and prospects were consistently underestimated by others, so he surprised his critics when he spoke and acted. Muhlenberg knew loneliness, yet made friends quickly and gained their support, especially when they realized his goals could be aligned with theirs. Tactically flexible, he kept his goals in view, moving toward them sometimes by implicit compromises and, as Zinzendorf discovered, quick thinking and a sharp tongue.

As Zinzendorf styled himself as a preacher-prophet-apostle and perhaps abbé for the world, Muhlenberg was content to start as a pastor to three struggling congregations torn by dissension and problematic leaders. The controversy took much of its polemical tone and shape from the personalities of the men who encountered each other.

A second element in understanding the controversy is to see that each man represented a different way Christians have of describing how God and humans relate to each other. What may be called a psychological contrast set the pair at odds. Muhlenberg's personal experience of God's working salvation in him, while not described in confessional detail, was congruent with the basic Spener-Halle "order of salvation," that is, election, vocation, illumination, conversion, regeneration, justification, mystical union, renovation, preservation, and glorification. While one is hard pressed to find Muhlenberg referring to *unio* and *glorificatio*, the other factors are present in what he told of himself and what he proclaimed to others. He did not question the Halle pattern, and seems to have operated in pastoral counseling, preaching and teaching within those parameters. The Halle Fathers saw the pattern as God's universal and invariable program for saving men and women. Within that program, they and their man in Pennsylvania underscored the need for repentance. Here they followed Luther straight from the opening of the Ninety-five Theses. Repentance was a critically important part of the Halle ethos. Although Muhlenberg entered that ethos as a university educated adult, he never questioned repentance as the central psychological factor in the human response to God.

Zinzendorf had a different and miserable experience at Halle. As a child and youth, he bore the brunt of his relatives' and Halle's staff's attempts to break his will. For him, the Halle pattern was oppressive and did not move a person beyond repentance. Certainly he shared the bleak Lutheran view of fallen humanity and the absolute inability of a person to do anything saving before God. But the Count grew in his conviction that while repentance was necessary, Halle's fixation on it weakened the Lutheran insistence on justification by faith through grace as bestowed in the sufferings, death and resurrection of Jesus. Instead of centering on repentance, Zinzendorf concentrated on the liberating power of Christ's atonement as the dynamic for justified believers to live as *Gotteskinder*.

Was this simply a matter of balance that made little difference? Muhlenberg did not think so. Repeatedly, when criticizing the Count and the Brethren, repentance was at the center of his objections. In a 1747 debate with Nyberg, Muhlenberg wrote, "The awakened souls seemed to be hungry and liked my preaching, except that they could not endure the words 'Law', 'repentance', even though I expounded them clearly on the basis of Luther's Catechism and the rest of the symbolical books."[7] In a similar context, he reported, "The words and substance of the Law, repentance, faith and sanctification are objects of contempt among beginners as well as the more advanced [who are prone to be what Muhlenberg called "Zinzendorfians."]. Their faith rests for the most part on trifling fancies and sensual feelings and not upon the sole saving Word of the prophets and apostles."[8] Zinzendorf appears to have occupied a position between the pessimism of Lutheran and Calvinist anthropology which required deep life-long repentance and the Wesleys' developing understanding of Christian perfection through the Spirit's work of sanctifying grace. Zinzendorf thereby became a target for both sides.

A related psychological difference is the contrast in their reliance on supporting communities of believers. Zinzendorf flourished and was animated by the presence and interchanges with others. He both generated as well as became an integral participant in fellowships of devout persons. He reflected that trait from his childhood remembrance concerning Tante Netty through his leadership in the Moravian settlements. He understood the Christian life to be communal. He may have assumed that the groups in which he was a member and came to lead would eventually be emulated by the wider society. When that did not happen, his disappointment could turn to frustration and anger.

Muhlenberg, on the other hand, was accustomed to being and acting alone. He did not set up new communities or create covenantal groups. He attempted to bring order to and to provide leadership for congregations. His reference and supportive community was an ocean away. He was adept at cultivating support from others, e.g., Tranberg, Koch and the United Congregations' lay leaders. Still, he maintained a reserved, separate self-understanding. Curiously, while Zinzendorf's Bethlehem established hours for prayer, Bible study and community meetings — a Pietist's dream, Muhlenberg did not even propose the formation of prayer and study circles in the congregations under his jurisdiction. He stressed, instead, the roles of ordained pastors to preach, teach and administer the sacraments.

So, on December 30, Muhlenberg was able to overcome his surprise when he saw a crowded room, and he had the presence of mind to appeal to his superiors in Hannover. For his part, it was natural for Zinzendorf to sit in the midst of a community that respected and agreed with him. Further, the Count's animus toward the Halle authorities and Ziegenhagen reflected his past experiences with them and his correct conclusion that Muhlenberg was sent to shut the door the Count struggled to keep open. Muhlenberg firmly accepted the Halle Fathers' and Ziegenhagen's understandings of the Christian experience and their determination to stop Zinzendorf.

A third means to aid understanding the controversy is that the men had contrasting views of a critical issue on Lutheran theology: the nature and authority of the Lutheran Confessions. Both claimed to be "confessional Lutherans," thoroughly loyal to the teaching therein as well as to the heritage of Martin Luther. Indeed, a continual accusation leveled by the Zinzendorf Lutherans against the Muhlenberg-connected Lutherans was that the latter were not genuine Lutherans but deviants from the true faith. The term "Pietist" was equated to "Hallesian" and both became the Zinzendorfers antitheses to "Lutheran." The sullying of "Pietist" occurred independently of Herrnhut, and the Brethren employed it effectively against the "Halle men" in Pennsylvania. Muhlenberg, obviously, could not disassociate himself from his mentors and patrons, and saw the uselessness of trying to rehabilitate the word. He sought instead to limit the damage inflicted by his detractors. Zinzendorf understood himself as sharing in the heritage of Wittenberg and its connections to the Orthodoxists. The significant differences between Zinzendorf and Muhlenberg over the Confessions were part of wider theological debates among German Lutherans and to a lesser extent among their Scandinavian counterparts. Muhlenberg may be regarded as representative of what I term here "Confessional Exclusivism," and Zinzendorf of "Confessional Inclusivism." Muhlenberg shared the attitude of the late sixteenth and seventeenth century Lutheran divines who gave the *Confessions* and Luther's writings an exalted status, claiming that these were the proper interpretations of the Scriptures and the so-called ecumenical creeds. This position was advanced and spread through the development of the Formula of Concord and the publication (with subscription forced upon German Lutheran pastors) in 1580. Philip Melanchthon, the chief compiler-editor of the Augsburg Confession, subsequent to its original presentation to Emperor Charles V and the members of the Diet at Augsburg (1530), developed several altered texts or *variata* that his critics claimed made untenable concessions to the Calvinists.

Confessional Exclusivists insisted on as literal interpretation as possible of the documents, especially of the Augsburg Confession (also called the Augustana). They would not admit any authoritative use for the Lutheran church's doctrine and practices beyond Scripture, Creeds, Confessions and Luther's writings. The theological task for pastors and laity, as they saw it, was to adhere closely to those standards for the sake of the Lutheran church's integrity, survival and good order. Muhlenberg shared that understanding and stated it bluntly in the call documents he prepared for himself and others throughout his ministry. Without strict confessional conformity, he concluded, the Lutheran mission and ministry in North America or anywhere else would founder. On that basis, Muhlenberg could have friendships with Reformed and other Christians, but refused to share in communion and to preach from one another's pulpits. If, as the seventh article of the Augustana maintains, the true unity of the church is manifested in the Gospel being "preached harmoniously (*Einträchtiglich*) according to a pure understanding and the sacraments are administered in conformity with the divine Word," the Confessional Exclusivists could not enter the deepest levels of fellowship with those whom they considered as not having the requisite pure understanding of the Gospel and who did not properly administer the sacraments. The bewildering array of sects, experimental religious communities, vagabond and imposter preachers, despisers of revealed religion and atheists coupled to the inability and reluctance of governmental authorities to intervene in religious affairs convinced Muhlenberg and those like him that strict adherence to the Confessions was absolutely necessary if the Lutheran church was to survive, let alone flourish.

In that light, Muhlenberg could only be aghast at what he already knew about the Count and what he came to know about his and the Brethren's work in Pennsylvania. In his view the seven Pennsylvania Synods were not aids to mission but spreaders of confusion, dissension and disappointment. They were bound to fail because they were not confessionally grounded. For the same reason, in the encounter Muhlenberg struck at the Count being appointed a bishop for the Moravians by a Reformed preacher, and, seemingly on that basis, claimed superintendency over Lutherans. Muhlenberg knew that Zinzendorf participated in ordinations of men for the Brethren in Germany, but he must have been shocked by his presumption to ordain persons for ministry in the Lutheran and Reformed churches in British North America. That was not only invasive but anti-Confessional. It was a recipe for confusion and schism.

Zinzendorf clearly had a different view. He was a Confessional Inclusivist. His understanding of the one, holy, catholic and apostolic Church (*Kirche*) as an invisible fellowship of the children of God had Lutheran confessional sources. He regarded the historically and culturally conditioned visible institutions, the *Religionen*, as fallible but necessary and useful instruments of what would ultimately give way in the eschaton to the *Kirche*. The Church of God in the Spirit and the *Gemeine ohne Namen* were genuine attempts to model that coming reality. They were outposts or *Gemeinlein* of the Kingdom. The Lutheran Confessions, as was true of Lutheran theology at its core, were valid and authentic and the best expressions of the Christian faith. Other confessions, too, had their validity and authenticity. Moreover, the cherished Lutheran documents were meant to be guides, not a new Scripture. It was quite within the Lutheran tradition to revise the Augsburg Confession and even to find room for other interpretations within them. So, Zinzendorf, in the name of Christ's desire to have one flock following the one Shepherd, concluded that faithful Lutherans ought not keep what was considered outdated and irrelevant by later circumstances. There-fore, he felt it proper to refuse to subscribe to the condemnations in the Augsburg Confession.

By the same reasoning, the Confessions were not a new canon law. The Augustana, Article 14 on the calling of persons to the ministry applied to ordinary circumstances, but it was not to be imposed rigidly or as the only way to provide for the ministry of Word and Sacraments. The Lutheran church might have the best teachings, but not all of its teachings and practices reached to that level, and some were flawed. To construe Article 14 as universal and invariable smacked of the kind of legalism he detested at Halle and found unacceptable among the Orthodoxists. Ultimately, such an interpretation was unbiblical and un-Lutheran. No community of believers ever called Luther to be its pastor. No one consecrated him as a bishop or superintendent, but he carried out congregational visitations, assigned pastors to congregations, and presided at ordinations. Paul and Stephanas' family — even Rabbi Jesus — did not conform to Article 14, yet they practiced a full ministry. The Confessions, therefore, were open, not closed, documents. They provided essential principles but were far from being a new canon or a new canon law.

Zinzendorf's reading of Article 7 on the church's unity reached behind the controversies among Lutherans in the latter half of the sixteenth century. The Augsburg Confession was intended to lay the ground for Christian unity, or at least for the doctrinal agreement between Evangelicals and Roman Catholics. The Augustana, in attempting to protect the witness and survival of the Evangelical movement, clearly wanted to avoid the stultifying effects of uniformity in expressions and practices. In that critically important sense, the Augsburg Confession was profoundly ecumenical. This was clear in the Confession's position that rites need not be the same among Christian communities. Zinzendorf, as did Spener, wanted a spiritual rapprochement of Lutherans with Reformed. Again, he reached behind the polemics that heated the relations and rhetoric of mid-to-late sixteenth century spokespersons in Geneva, Zurich and Wittenberg. The Count had the courage and temerity to advocate for the validity of Reformed confessions, while giving priority to the Augustana. He extended his qualified confessional openness to adult baptizers, sabbatarians, separatists and illuminati. While he may have been disappointed that the seven synods did not achieve more, he could regard them as starting points for future work. As far as providing for the ministry of the Reformed and Lutheran churches, Zinzendorf could appeal to his sense of call to be the apostle-proclaimer to the whole world, not simply to one *Religion*. Who else was going to step into the breach? Halle put a price tag on the urgent requests of the United Congregations for a minister, the Swedes did not send men who planned to stay, and the Reformed were slow to respond. America was mission territory for settlers, slaves and the indigenous peoples. Paul and Barnabas did not wait for invitations or formal calls or salary negotiations to be completed. They followed the Spirit's leading and people heard and responded. Zinzendorf had the courage and call to respond and then to provide for the continuance of the work.

One of Muhlenberg's observations in a critical time five years after the encounter can be read from the perspectives of both confessional stances:

> When the head, namely Count Zinzendorf, and his brethren are in Russia, their faith is in exact accord with the articles of the Greek Church. When they are in Catholic countries, they believe and live as the Pope and councils teach. When they are in Switzerland, they believe and live in accord with the Synod of Bern. When they are in Sweden, they believe in accord with the Augsburg Confession, and when they are in England, they believe and are in exact accord with the [Thirty-Nine] Articles of the Episcopal Church. How can one say of such toadeaters that they are Christ's true followers?[9]

Muhlenberg perceived Zinzendorf and the Brethren as theological chameleons who would take on any color in order to ensnare unwary Christians. It is no accident that he often cited texts from the Gospel of John about hirelings and thieves and from the Pastoral Epistles about false teachers who speak pleasantly but lead the gullible to damnation. Zinzendorf would say, as he did in the *Abschiedsrede*, that God's saving truth was present in all *Religionen* and we have the task of discovering and bringing that truth out of the divine treasury. He and the Brethren had enough of one *Religion's* claim to have exclusive rights to truth. That was the preamble to heartache and persecution.

The final means for our consideration to understand the controversy is to recognize that the men and the positions they embodied had different ecclesiologies. Zinzendorf's *Gemeine Gottes im Geist* and *Gemeine ohne Namen* relied on an eschatological vision of the *Kirche* that sounded some Leade-Philadelphiaist overtones but essentially was grounded in his Pietist understandings of the invisible (*unsichtbare*) *Kirche*. His Philadelphia-Open Door was a brave vision that attempted to take advantage of America as the land of new beginnings that were harbingers of Jesus' imminent return. In light of that return, he preached about the post-Pentecost apostolic community in Jerusalem, looking forward to the consummation when the new and mighty Jerusalem would appear as Christ's Bride. In the apostolic Jerusalem, believers shared bread, prayers, property and ministered to the needy. Their lives and their faithful witness were the evangelical outreaches to the world. The grim examples of Ananias and Sapphira (Acts 5:11–14) forecast the dismal fate of those who violated the community's sanctity. Zinzendorf was convinced that America was a unique place and a God-given opportunity to renew and reconstruct the Christian community. It would be a sacrilege to perpetuate in the New World the old corruptions, errors and divisions that stalked Europe. New structures and approaches were needed. He was certain that through the times and conditions God was authorizing those ordinations and sending fisher-evangelists and workers into the American physical and religious wilderness. The best way to constitute the church in this raw land was as a mission society and as a ministering community for the life of the world. Still, we were not in the mighty Jerusalem to come but in lowly Bethlehem — and Nazareth and Emmaus. And there was work to do in congregations that were struggling for survival.

Muhlenberg's personal disposition and mission was not founded on newness but continuity. His task later became his motto: *ecclesia plantanda*, plant the church! While the prospects seemed slim at times, he was committed not only to thwart the Count and the Brethren but to have the German Lutheran church take root in American soil, grow, blossom and bear fruit. Planted trees do not walk through doors. They need steady, reliable and skilled attention and nurture. The church, present in congregations where the Gospel was harmoniously preached and taught and the sacraments rightly administered, was the proper setting for the work of the Spirit to call, gather, enlighten and sanctify believers as they come to know Jesus. A regularly called and properly ordained ministry was essential for the planting and growth of the church.

Given that outlook, Muhlenberg could not do otherwise than to oppose Zinzendorf. He also realized that the German Lutherans, with few exceptions, emigrated not in communal groups but as families. Most fanned out into the countryside; indeed, the colony was mostly countryside with a few large towns such as Philadelphia and Lancaster. Unlike the agricultural pattern of rural Germany where farmers settled together in villages and walked to their fields, the American pattern was for individual families to live on their land far from neighbors. Congregational activities were not central to the settlers' lives; survival and work were. The

158

Brethren had the *Gemeinlein* spiritual resources of Bethlehem and Nazareth. The German Lutheran and Reformed congregations, consequently, had a different ecclesiological structure. The congregations were more like occasional associations of neighbors who gathered for worship and special events such as funerals. These associations were held together rarely by resident pastors and mostly by circuit-riding ministers and lay leaders. The laity was more independent and less tractable in those congregations than anyone had known in Germany. They also were susceptible to the wiles and ministrations of itinerant pastors of unproven credentials, abilities and honesty.

Muhlenberg would grow increasingly insistent on developing a cadre of proven pastors, catechists and teachers. He also realized that Halle-style institutions located in one central place would not fit the American scene. In addition, he had heard and seen enough of communal groups such as that in Ephrata and Bethlehem. Zinzendorf saw the promise of a future dedicated to mission and the development of close-knit Christian communities. He had to work with the realities of scattered, struggling congregations in the midst of an indifferent and often hostile society.

Implications

Three implications of the controversy, its aftermaths and understandings are reflected in the question Muhlenberg asked the Halle Fathers in the course of his argument with Nyberg. Nyberg argued that it was possible to be a Moravian and a Lutheran. Muhlenberg was convinced that it was impossible. He queried, with a slight adaptation for present purposes: "Do the Moravian Brethren and Lutherans of the present day come so close to each other in their doctrine and practice so that we can unite our ministries, help each other in churches and schools, and teach in common?" Essentially this is the eighteenth century version of the twenty-first century issue of "full communion" between churches.

The first implication is that theological discourses and arguments, like religious experiences, are profoundly personal. The personalities, backgrounds, cultural conditioning and historical settings of the individuals involved are essential factors in the exchanges they share. In order to understand and to draw the implications of the contents of their intellectual transactions, we need to factor in who they are, where they have been, and what their perspectives are. It is not too much to say that we who listen and watch them have the vantage point from which we may know more about them than they know about each other. We are able to reopen Benezet's door to listen and relisten to the words, tones and

159

settings. Such consideration of the person-quality of religious engagement is not only for the past. We have the opportunity to ask who we are as we listen, what has happened to us, and how we may see ourselves in light of what those in the past have given us.

A key factor of the Moravian method of engaging in theological conversations is to begin with and to explore throughout the discourse the personal elements and the *Lebenslauf* (life-journey), or more accurately the *Glaubenslauf* (faith-journey), of those who are involved. As we reheard the controversy, we recognized their journeys, and have the opportunity to search ourselves and our own commitments and understandings.

A second implication is how we have heard the contrasting understandings of the roles of formal theological discourse in, with and through the build-up to and the controversy itself. Here the intra-Lutheran struggles of Orthodoxy and Pietism with Confessional Exclusivism and Inclusivism indicate that theologizing is inescapable. There are theological agendas and standards both beneath as well as on the surface. What are the theological roles of the Scripture, creeds, confessions, liturgies, biblical hermeneutics, and organizational structures? How can we articulate these clearly to others and ourselves? With what authority do we invest them and at what peril do we ignore them? Zinzendorf left the room and America and was drawn into the "Sifting Period." Muhlenberg's championship of the Lutheran Confessions was virtually forgotten and even repudiated two generations later, and today attitudes toward those documents contribute to Lutheran disunity. If theologizing is inescapable, then how can the passions and intellectual vigor called forth be set in the framework of frank, yet respectful speaking and listening?

A third implication drawn from the controversy is that it was about the mission of the Christian Gospel. While the protagonists understood the political and ecclesiastical forces that drove them into the room, they also realized that the subject was the future of their cultural version of the Christian church in an alien land. Zinzendorf already was acutely conscious of the impulse to reach out to the wider society. As Muhlenberg became acclimated to America, he recognized that the ministry of the Gospel went beyond German Lutherans. Could these divergent theological and ecclesiological positions join, in spite of their reservations and contrasts, to share the ministry of mission? Muhlenberg may have implied acceptance by accepting into the Ministerium persons ordained under Zinzendorf's and the Brethren's auspices as well as others without requiring what he would have considered a "regular" ordination. He saw, by implication, that there was one ministry in the *Kirche*. The implication is that such a ministry can extend into other areas of mission and service.

Muhlenberg's eighteenth-century question was answered in 1998 and 1999 with a rousing "yes!" when the Evangelical Lutheran Church in America and the Northern and Southern Provinces of the Moravian Church in America voted to enter full communion with each other. This act does not close Benezet's door but opens it for understanding. This act presents to the two churches the opportunity to face the open door set before all Christians, to listen to the Savior calling us to go with him, and to encourage us to follow our Shepherd together.

Endnotes to Chapter Nine

1 Kelley, pp. 219 and 222.
2 *Journals*, Vol. 1, p. 83.
3 Unpublished manuscript, provided and translated by Prof. Otto Dreydoppel, Jr.
4 *Journals*, Vol. 1, p. 109. See pp. 150–170 for reports of the continual disagreements between Muhlenberg and the Moravians.
5 See Beyreuther, pp. 229–230 and Wagner, "A Key Episode."
6 Beyreuther, p. 213, author's translation.
7 *Journals*, Vol. 1, p. 155.
8 *Journals*, Vol. 1, p. 158.
9 *Journals*, Vol. 1, p. 159.

Bibliography of Works Cited

The Bethlehem Diary. MSS in Moravian Archives, Bethlehem.

Beyreuther, Eric. *Zinzendorf und die Christenheit, 1732-1760*. Marburg an der Lahn: Verlag der Francke Buchhandlung, 1961.

Bodling, Kurt A. "A Century of Muhlenberg Biographies: An Analysis." **Concordia Historical Institute Quarterly**, Vol. 71, part 2 (1998), pp. 86-93.

Cheetham, Nicholas. *A History of the Popes*. New York: Dorset Press, 1982.

Durnbaugh, Donald. *Fruit of the Vine: A History of the Brethren, 1708-1995*. Elgin: Brethren Press, 1997.

Erb, Peter, ed. *Johann Conrad Beissel and the Ephrata Community: Mystical and Historical Texts*. Lewiston: Edwin Mellen Press, 1985.

————. *Pietists: Selected Writings*. New York: Paulist Press, 1983.

Freeman, Arthur. *An Ecumenical Theology of the Heart: The Theology of Count Nicholas Ludwig von Zinzendorf*. Bethlehem: Board of Communications, Moravian Church in America, 1998.

Geissler, Suzanne. *Lutheranism and Anglicanism in Colonial New Jersey: An Early Ecumenical Experiment in New Sweden*. Lewiston: Edwin Mellen Press, 1988.

Glatfelter, Charles H. *Pastors and People: German Lutheran and Reformed Churches in the Pennsylvania Field, 1717-1793*. Two vols. Breinigsville, Pa: The Pennsylvania German Society, 1980.

Hamilton, J. Taylor and Kenneth G. Hamilton. *History of the Moravian Church: The Renewed Unitas Fratrum, 1722-1957*. Bethlehem: Moravian Church in America, 1967.

Hamilton, J. Taylor. *A History of the Church known as the Moravian Church or Unitas Fratrum, or the Unity of the Brethren During the Eighteenth and Nineteenth Centuries*. Bethlehem: Times Publishing Co., 1900.

Hamilton, Kenneth G., trans. and ed. *The Bethlehem Diary, Volume 1, 1742-1744*. Bethlehem: Archives of the Moravian Church, 1971.

Hamilton, Kenneth G. and Lothar Madeheim, trans., Vernon H. Nelson, Otto Dreydoppel, Jr. and Doris Rohland Yob, eds. *The Bethlehem Diary, Vol. II, 1744-1745*. Bethlehem: The Moravian Archives, 2001.

Harle, Craig, David Haugaard, Jeffrey Scheib, Carolyn Peters, and Joseph Foster. *Lawmaking and Legislators in Pennsylvania: A Biographical Dictionary, Vol. 2, 1710-1766*. Philadelphia: University of Pennsylvania Press, 1997.

Hart, Simon and Harry Kreider. *Lutheran Church in New York and New Jersey, 1722-1760: Lutheran Records in the Ministerial Archives of the Staatsarchiv, Hamburg, Germany*. Ann Arbor: United Lutheran Synod of New York and New England, 1962.

Havens, Mary. "Zinzendorf and the 'Augsburg Confession'." Ph.D. diss., Princeton Theological Seminary, 1990.

Helmich, Carl, Jr. "An Inquiry into the Character, Scope and Objectives of the Pennsylvania Synods, 1742." Typescript, Moravian College and Theological Seminary, 1953.

Herberman, Charles, *et alia*, eds. *Catholic Encyclopedia*. New York: Robert Appleton, 1911, Vol. 11.

Jacobs, Henry Eyster. *Lutherans: The American Church History Series*. New York: Christian Literature Co., 1993.

Jordan, Albert F. "The Chronicle of Peter Böhler Who Led John and Charles Wesley to the Full Light of the Gospel." **Transactions of the Moravian Historical Society**, Vol. XXII, part 2 (1960), pp. 100-178.

Kelley, Joseph J. *Pennsylvania: The Colonial Years, 1681-1776.* Garden City: Doubleday, 1980.

Kistler, Ruth Marie. "William Allen: Founder of Allentown, Colonial Jurist, Industrialist and Loyalist." **Lehigh County Historical Society Proceedings**, Vol. 24 (1962).

Kleiner, John, ed. *Henry Melchior Muhlenberg: The Roots of 250 Years of Organized Lutheranism in North America. Essays In Memory of Helmut T. Lehmann.* Lewiston: Edwin Mellen Press, 1998.

Kolb, Robert and Timothy Wengert. *The Book of Concord: The Confessions of the Evangelical Lutheran Church.* Minneapolis: Fortress Press, 2000.

Kostbarkeiten aus dem Herrnhuter Unitätsarchiv. Bad Boll, Herrnhut und Zeist: Herrnhut Druck und Verlag Haus, 1999.

Lehmann, Helmut and Jaroslav Pelikan, eds. *Luther's Works: American Edition.* St. Louis and Philadelphia: Concordia Press and Muhlenberg/Fortress Press, beginning 1957.

Lehmann, Helmut T. "Missioner Extraordinary." **Concordia Historical Institute Quarterly**, Vol. 71, part 2 (1998), pp. 56-71.

McManners, John. *Church and Society in Eighteenth Century France.* Vol. 1: *The Clerical Establishment and Its Social Ramifications.* Oxford: Clarendon Press, 1998.

Muhlenberg, Henry M. *Die Korrespondenz Heinrich Melchior Muhlenberg aus der Anfangszeit des deutschen Luthertums in Nordamerika.* Berlin: DeGruyter, 1986.

———. *The Correspondence of Henry Melchior Muhlenberg*, Vol. 1, *1740-47.* Translated and edited by John Kleiner and Helmut Lehmann. Camden, Maine: Picton Press, 1993.

———. *Selbstbiographie, 1711-1743. Aus dem Missionsarchive der Franckischen Stiftungen zu Halle.* With additions and clarifications by Dr. W. Germann. Allentown: Brobst, Diehl, 1881.

———. *The Journals of Henry Melchior Muhlenberg*, 3 vols. Translated by Theodore Tappert and John Doberstein. Originally printed Philadelphia: The Evangelical Ministerium of Pennsylvania and Adjacent States and Muhlenberg Press, 1942. Reprinted Evansville, Indiana: Lutheran Historical Society of Eastern Pennsylvania and Whipporwill Publications, 1982.

Neisser, Georg. *A History of the Beginnings of Moravian Work in America, January 1732 to 1741.* Translated by William N. Schwarze and Samuel H. Gapp. Bethlehem: Archives of the Moravian Church, 1955.

Nelson, Clifford E. *The Lutherans in North America.* Rev. ed., Philadelphia: Fortress, 1990.

Nielsen, Sigurd. *Der Toleranzgedanke bei Zinzendorf: Ursprung, Entwicklung und Eigenart seiner Toleranz,* Vol. 1. Hamburg: Ludwig Appel Verlag, no date.

Podmore, Colin. *Anglican-Moravian Conversations: The Fetter Lane Common Statement with Essays in Moravian and Anglican History.* London: The Council for Christian Unity of the Church of England, 1996.

———. *The Moravian Church in England, 1728-1760.* Oxford: Clarendon Press, 1998.

Preus, Robert. *The Theology of Post-Reformation Lutheranism: A Study of Theological Prologomena.* 2 vols. St. Louis: Concordia, 1970.

Reichel, Levin Theodore. "The Early History of the Church of the United Brethren *(Unitas Fratrum)*, Commonly Called Moravians in North America, A.D. 1734-1748." **Transactions of the Moravian Historical Society**, Vol. III (1888).

Říčan, Rudolf. *The History of the Unity of the Brethren: A Protestant Hussite Church in Bohemia and Moravia.* Translated by C. Daniel Crews. Bethlehem: Moravian Church in America, 1992.

Ritter, Abraham. *History of the Moravian Church in Philadelphia.* Philadelphia: Hayes and Zell, 1857.

Salomon, A. *"La Catholicité Du Monde Chrétien d'après la correspondence inedite du comte Louis de Zinzendorf avec le cardinal Noailles et les évêques appellants, 1719-1728."* The work appears in **Cahiers de la Revue d'histoire et de philosophe religieuses**, number 17. Paris: Librairie Félix Alcan, 1929.

Sawyer, Edwin Albert. "The Religious Experience of Colonial American Moravians." **Transactions of the Moravian Historical Society**, Vol. XVIII (1961).

Schmidt, Martin and Wilhelm Jannasch, eds. *Das Zeitalter des Pietismus.* Bremen: Carl Schünemann Verlag, 1965.

Snyder, Howard Albert. "Pietism, Moravianism, and Methodism as Renewal Movements: A Comparative and Thematic Study." Ph.D. diss., University of Notre Dame, 1983.

Soderlund, Jean R., ed. *William Penn and the Founding of Pennsylvania: A Documentary History.* Philadelphia: University of Pennsylvania Press, 1983.

Spangenberg, August Gottlieb. *The Life of Nicholas Ludwig Count Zinzendorf.* Translated by Samuel Jackson. London: Samuel Holdsworth, 1838. German original 1772-75.

Spener, Philip J. *Pia Desideria: or Heartfelt Desire for a God-Pleasing Improvement of the True Protestant Church.* Translated and edited by Theodore Tappert. Philadelphia: Fortress, 1964.

Stoeffler, Ernst. "Pietism — The Message, Early Manifestation, and Significance." **Contemporary Perspectives On Pietism**, a special edition of the **Covenant Quarterly** (February/May, 1976), pp. 3-24.

————. *The Rise of Evangelical Pietism.* Leiden: Brill, 1965.

Tappert, Theodore, trans. and ed. *The Book of Concord.* Philadelphia: Fortress Press, 1959.

Thayer, Theodore. *Pennsylvania Politics and the Growth of Democracy, 1740-1776.* Harrisburg: Pennsylvania Historical and Museum Commission, 1953.

Tyerman, L. *Life and Times of the Rev. John Wesley, M.A.,* Vol. 1. New York: Harper and Brothers, 1870.

Van der Zee, Henri and Barbara Van der Zee. *William and Mary.* New York: Alfred Knopf, 1973.

Vogt, Peter. "Zinzendorf and the 'Pennsylvania Synods' of 1742: The First Ecumenical Conferences on the North America Continent." Masters thesis, Moravian Theological Seminary, 1992

Wagner, Walter H. "A Key Episode in American Lutheranism: Muhlenberg's and Zinzendorf's Encounter." **Concordia Historical Institute Quarterly**, Vol. 71, part 2 (1998), pages 72-85.

Wagner, Walter H. and Arthur Freeman. *Following Our Shepherd to Full Communion: Report of the Bilateral Dialogue of the Moravian Church in America and the Evangelical Lutheran Church in America.* Minneapolis: Augsburg-Fortress, 1998.

Weber, Julie Tomberlin, trans. and Craig Atwood, ed. *A Collection of Sermons from Zinzendorf's Pennsylvania Journey.* Bethlehem: Moravian Church in America, 2001.

Weinlick, John. *Count Zinzendorf: The Story of his Life and Leadership in the Renewed Moravian Church.* Nashville: Abingdon, 1956.

Wesley, John. *The Works of John Wesley,* Vol. 19, 1738-43. Edited by Reginald W. Ward and Richard Heitzenrater. Nashville: Abingdon, 1990.

Zeiser, Samuel. "Ecclesiolae in Ecclesia and Ecclesia Plantanda: Conflicting Approaches to Mission among the German Protestants in Colonial Pennsylvania." S.T.M. thesis, Lutheran Theological Seminary at Philadelphia, 1989.

Zinzendorf, Nicholas Ludwig von. *Hauptschriften.* Edited by Eric Beyreuther and Gerhard Meyer. Hildesheim: Georg Olms Verlagsbuchhandlung, 1963.

Index

abbé 44–46, 48, 55, 151
Abschiedsrede 55, 144, 146, 148, 150, 157
Act of Settlement 4, 9
adventist 24
Aldersgate 65, 66
Allen, William 33–37, 39, 96, 101, 104, 106, 144–146
Amsterdam Classis 31, 38, 90
Amsterdam Consistory 27, 28
Ancient Moravian Church 50, 57
Anglican 6–10, 17, 22, 24, 25, 28, 33, 96
Anglo-Dutch Wars 6
Anne 5, 7, 9
Antes, Heinrich 91, 92
Anthony Ulrich 53
Anton , Paul 16, 21
apologia 125, 139, 142
Appellants 45, 46
Arch Street 26, 31, 32, 93, 95–101, 104, 109, 110, 114–116, 125, 126, 129, 135, 139, 141, 144–146
Arndt, Johann 16
Arnold, Gottfried 18, 19, 21
Association of the Skippack Brethren 90
Augsburg Confession 3, 12, 16, 21, 43, 50, 55, 57, 61, 62, 65, 70, 73, 150, 154–157
Augustus III 4, 54, 59, 62, 65, 66, 91
Augustus the Strong (Augustus II) 4, 47, 53, 54, 59, 61

Bavaria 2–5
Beauval, Samuel de 46
Bechtel, Johann 32, 91, 92, 101
Beissel, Johann Conrad 19–21
Benezet, Judith 99
Benezet, Stephen i, ii, iv, 25, 40, 91, 95, 102, 107, 114, 116, 126, 144, 159, 161
Benezet, Susanna 99
Bengel, Johann Albrecht 15
Benigna 71, 72, 91
Berkenmeyer, Wilhelm Christopher 27–29
Berthelsdorf 40, 47–50, 52, 53, 58, 65, 85

Bethlehem iii, iv, 89–91, 94, 95, 98–100, 102, 103, 106, 136, 147, 148, 153, 158, 159
Beyer, Andreas 51
Beyreuther, Eric 57, 103
Bildungsreise 44, 46, 47, 105, 106
Boehme, Jacob 18, 21
Bohemia 3, 5, 10, 49
Böhler, Peter 65, 90, 98, 99, 101, 113, 115, 116, 144, 145, 148
Böhm, Johann Philip 31, 32, 38, 93, 96–99
Bohme, Anton Wilhelm 7, 16
Böhnisch, Georg 59
Bolzius, Johann Martin 86, 107, 108, 137
Book of Concord 12, 16, 21, 82
Brand, Philip 109
Breithaupt, Justus 16
Britain iii, 2, 4–10, 16, 23, 29, 34, 35, 64, 68, 71, 75, 94, 96, 145
British Evangelicalism 25
British North America ii, iii, 7, 10, 17, 19, 23, 64, 66, 68, 71, 90, 133, 149, 155
Bryzelius, Paul 97, 143, 149
Bucks County 33, 34
Büttner, Gottlieb 93

Canstein Bible Institute 40
Canstein, Carl Hildebrandt von 40
Cassel 62
Castell, Theodora von 47
Catherine of Bragauza 6
Charles Edward Louis Philip Casimir ("Bonnie Prince Charlie") 9
Charles I of England 6, 22
Charles II of Spain 3
Charles II, Charles Stuart of England 6–8, 22
Charles V, Emperor 154
Charles VI, Emperor 4, 53
Charles VII, Emperor 5
Charles X Gustav of Sweden 2
Charles XI of Sweden 2
Charles XII of Sweden 2

Charleston 24, 102, 105, 107, 108, 116, 120, 131, 132
Charter of Pennsylvania 22
Chief Elder 68, 71
Christian VI of Denmark 53, 62
Christiana 28, 97
Church of God in the Spirit 90, 93, 94, 97, 102, 155
Church of the Brethren 19
Clausthal 79
Clement XI, Pope 44, 45
Comenius, Amos 74
Congregationalist 24
Country Party 32, 35, 36
Covenant of the Four Brethren 47, 89

Danish West Indies 10, 53, 61, 66, 71, 90
Darmstadt Consistory 29, 30, 109
David, Christian 47, 49, 51
Declaration of Rights 8, 9
Delaware 6, 7, 27, 28, 38
Denmark 2, 5, 7, 47, 49, 51–53
Dober, Leonhard 53, 68
Dresden 5, 13, 37, 47–49, 53–56
Dresden Consistory 13, 54, 55, 70
Dresden Socrates 48, 53
Dunkers 92
Dylander, Johannes 28

Ebenezer (Georgia) 86, 107
Ebersdorf 19, 46–48, 53, 54, 56, 62
ecclesiolae 18, 50, 67, 94
Edeling, Christian Ludwig 41
Edict of Toleration 9
Einbeck 78, 80, 151
English Civil War 2, 6
Ephrata 20, 159
evangelical 7, 11, 18, 25, 41, 57, 64, 65, 76, 87, 158
Evangelical Lutheran Church in America ii, 161

Falckner's Swamp 19
Fetter Lane 65, 71, 96
Fetter Lane Society 59, 67, 68

First Sea Congregation 98, 99
Florida 5, 23, 24
Forks of the Delaware 91
Formula of Concord 12, 21, 154
Foundry Society 68, 96
Frame of Government 7, 22, 38
Francis I, Emperor 44
Francis Stephen, Duke of Lorraine 4, 5
Francke, August Hermann 7, 15, 16, 19, 21, 120, 130, 131, 133, 137, 149
Francke, Gotthilf 42, 52, 83, 86, 131
Franconia 3, 40
Frankfurt am Main 15, 63
Franklin, Benjamin 25, 96, 106
Frederick I of Prussia 2–4
Frederick II the Great 4
Frederick III 3
Frederick of Hessen 2
Frederick Wilhelm 3
French Camisards 20
Fresenius, Johann 29
Friedrich Wilhelm 13
Friedrich Wilhelm I of Prussia 61, 63, 133
full communion ii, 159, 161

Geiger, Valentin 109
Gemeine 68, 69, 89, 92, 98, 147, 148, 155, 157
Gemeine ohne Name 147, 148, 155, 157
Geneva 5, 68, 156
Gentleman's Party 32–33
Georg Ludwig (of Hannover) 5–7, 9, 10, 78
George I of England 10, 78
George II of England 10, 37, 117
Georgia 5, 23–25, 34, 59–61, 65, 66, 86, 107, 108, 139
Georgia Packet 88, 105–107, 108
Germantown 26, 27, 29, 32, 38, 91–93, 98
Gersdorf, Charlotte Justine von 40–41
Gersdorf, Georg Ernst von 53
Gersdorf, Henriette Sophie von 17, 18, 40, 41, 77, 82, 83, 86, 122, 138, 139, 143, 151
Gersdorf, Nicholas von 40

Gnesio-Lutherans 12, 13, 21
Gordon, Patrick 30, 33
Görlitz 47, 49
Gotha Synod 68
Göttingen 79, 80, 85, 86, 88, 113, 123, 140
Gray's Inn Walk 71
Great Awakening ii, 25, 68, 103, 107–108
Great Northern War 2, 3
Gregorian Calendar iii
Greifswald 2, 55
Grosshennersdorf 5, 18, 41, 82, 83, 86, 106, 118, 126, 139
Gruber, Johann Adam 90

Halle 7, 15–20, 29–31, 38, 40–42, 48, 51, 52, 54, 59, 60, 64, 66–68, 72, 76–78, 82, 83, 85, 86, 88, 90, 106, 110–112, 122, 126, 127, 130, 133–135, 139, 140, 142, 149, 151–153, 156, 157, 159
Hallesche Nachrichten v, 77
Hallesian 13, 29, 31, 40, 41, 48, 51, 52, 77, 80, 81, 123, 126, 140, 149, 153
Hamilton, Andrew 32–36, 38, 96
Hannover 4–7, 9, 10, 24, 37, 65, 75, 78, 81, 85, 86, 114, 123, 140, 153
Hapsburg 4
Heerndyk 64, 70, 95, 133
Heidelberg 38
Heinrich, XXIV Count Reuss-Köstritz 47, 82, 86
Heitz, Johann Georg 47
Henckel, Edmund 86, 137
Henkel, Anton Jacob 29
Henrietta, Anne 5, 6
Henrietta Maria 6
Henriette Catherine 40, 41
Herman, Leonhard 116, 144
Herrnhaag 63, 69, 89, 92
Herrnhut 26, 47–57, 60–63, 65, 66, 69, 72, 73, 83, 85, 89, 90, 122, 138, 139, 153
Herrnhuters 49, 50, 52, 54, 59–63, 67
Hirtenbrief 66–68, 90
Hohenau, Ernst Christoph Hochmann von 19

Holland 4, 5, 16, 62, 63, 68, 70, 85, 106, 120, 132
Holy Roman Empire 2, 3, 40
Huldenberg, Baron 61, 62
Hungary 3, 5, 51
Hutton, James 65, 71

illuminati 1, 24, 156
Innocent XI, Pope 44
inspector, election 32, 34, 36
inspector, Halle 82
inspector, Lutheran 13, 31, 95, 101, 116, 120, 121, 123, 125, 126, 131, 132, 134, 136–138, 141–143, 150

Jablonsky, Daniel Ernst 61, 63, 65, 74, 133
James I of England 5, 6
Jan Sobieski (John III of Poland) 3
Jansenism 44, 45
Jansenius, Cornelius 44
Jednota Bratrská 60
Jena 51, 66, 72
Jesuit 18, 44, 45, 51, 133, 149
jesuitical 120, 131, 132
John III of Poland 3
Joseph I, Emperor 4
Journals, Muhlenberg's iii, v, 76–78, 84, 109, 118, 148
Julian Calendar iii

Kalm, Peter 145
Karl Alexander, Duke of Württemberg 55, 56
Keith, William 33
Kirche 69, 89, 92, 101, 126, 155, 157, 161
Koch, Peter 28, 96, 97, 112, 113, 116, 124, 142, 144–146, 153
Kraft, Valentin 31, 38, 101, 107–115, 117, 129, 130, 132, 135, 145, 146
Kuhlenkamp, Dr. Gerardus 66

Labadie, Jean de 18, 21
Lange, Joachim 16, 21
Langemack, Gregorius 55, 73
Leade, Jane 18, 19, 21, 157

Lehigh County 34
Lehigh Valley 89, 91
Leipzig 19, 113
Leipzig Consistory 88
Leo X, Pope 44
Leopold I, Emperor 2, 3, 40
Logan, James 145
London Conference 71
Löscher, Valentin 13, 20, 42, 43, 47, 48, 55, 56, 62, 65
Louis XIV of France 2, 3, 6, 8, 44, 45, 72
Lusatia 2, 40, 41, 53, 82, 86, 118, 126
Luther i, 11–13, 16, 43, 69, 73, 134, 152, 153, 156
Lutheran Orthodoxy 11–13, 15

Mack, Alexander 19, 21
Malander, Olaf 28, 97
Maria of Modena 8
Maria Theresa 4, 5
Marienborn 63, 66, 68, 89
Mary II of England 4, 8, 9
Mary Henriette Sophia 6
Mayor, Thomas 100, 109
Melanchthon, Philip 12, 13, 21, 154
Mennonite 24, 92
Merlan, Johanna Eleanora von 19
Meurer, Philip 93
Michaelis, Johann 16
Ministerium 38, 82, 143, 160
Moravia 3, 10, 49, 51
Moravian Church in America ii, 161
Mount Airy 34, 38, 39
Muhlenberg, Heinrich Melchoir i–iv, 1, 5, 7, 16, 18, 20–22, 24–26, 28–31, 37–41, 55, 59, 71, 72, 75–88, 93, 98–116, 118, 124–146, 148–155, 157–161
Muhlenberg, Nicolas 78
Münchhausen, High Sheriff von 81

Natzmer, Dubislaw Gneomar von 41, 65
Nazareth 25, 89, 91, 94, 107, 158, 159
Neustadt 79, 84
New Hannover i, 26, 29–31, 93, 108–110, 113, 118, 127, 129

New Jersey 6, 7, 27, 28, 91
New Style calendar iii, v, 91
New Sweden 3, 23, 26, 27
New York 6, 24, 27, 31, 36, 90, 91, 107, 145
Ninety-five Theses 11, 152
Nitschmann 51, 53, 60, 61, 65, 93, 97, 133
Noailles, Louis-Antoine de 45, 46, 72, 133
Non-Jurors 9
Northampton County 34
Nyberg, Laurentius Thorstonsen Theophilus 146, 149, 152, 159

Oetinger, Friedrich Christoph 15
Oglethorpe, General James 23, 63
Old Style calendar iii, v, 55, 59, 65, 86, 87, 95, 98, 101, 108
Oley 92, 93, 103
Oporin, Joachim 80
ordination 12, 13, 28, 29, 31, 38, 54–56, 58, 60, 61, 67, 70, 72, 73, 76, 84, 88, 94, 97, 110, 113, 133, 143, 155, 156, 158, 160
Orthodoxists 12, 13, 15, 16, 20, 21, 48, 154, 156
Ottoman 2, 3, 9

Paedagogium 17
Paris 44, 46, 72
Pastoralis Offici 45
Paul V, Pope 44
Peace of Nysted 3
Peace of Westphalia 1–3, 15, 18, 50, 52, 60
Penn, William 6, 7, 22, 24, 38
Penn, Hannah 33
Penns Neck 28
Pennsylvania i–iv, 5–7, 10, 15, 18–20, 22–25, 27–33, 35, 37, 59, 65–68, 75, 83, 85, 86, 90, 91, 95, 102, 103, 105, 107, 108, 112–114, 119–121, 125, 130, 131, 133, 136, 137, 139, 146–148, 150, 152, 154, 155
Pennsylvania Plan 89, 146
Pennsylvania Religion 24, 91
Pennsylvania Synod iii, 92, 116, 132, 155

170

Pennsylvania Testament 102, 114, 146
Petersen, Johann 19
Philadelphia i–iv, 15, 18–21, 23, 25–34, 36–38, 52, 55, 69, 75, 86, 88–91, 94, 95, 97–103, 107–110, 112–116, 118–120, 125–129, 131–134, 136, 139, 142–146, 148, 157, 158
Philadelphia Movement 18, 21
Philip V of Spain 3
Philippists 12, 13
Pia Desideria 16
Pietism 3, 11–16, 18–20, 25, 29, 31, 41, 43, 48, 51, 77, 81, 84, 140, 141, 160
Pietists 12, 14, 15, 18, 21, 51, 76, 77, 80, 123, 126, 140
Pilgergemeine 63
Pilgerruh 61
Pilgrim Congregation 5, 63
Plumstead, Clement 36
Poland 2–4, 10, 60, 61
Pomerania 2
Potter, John 63, 64, 71, 73, 74, 96, 135, 139, 149
Pragmatic Sanction 4
Presbyterian 24, 25, 33, 34, 94
Preus, Robert 12, 13, 21
Prominent Gentlemen 33
Providence i, 21, 26, 29, 30, 31, 38, 79, 93, 101, 109, 110, 112, 113, 115, 118, 127, 129
Provincial Assembly 32, 33
Prussia 2– 6, 10, 27, 60, 63, 65, 94, 134, 145
Pyrlaeus, Johann 93–95, 99, 100, 102, 113, 119, 120, 128, 129, 132, 144, 146

Quaker 7, 23, 24, 32, 35, 36, 95
Quesnel, Pasquier 45

Race Street 93, 115, 129, 135, 141, 144, 148, 150
Radical Pietism 15, 18
Ratio Disciplinae 50, 72
Reading 19, 20, 29, 92
Reformed 1, 10, 18, 24, 26–28, 31, 32, 37, 38, 44, 50, 60, 64– 69, 72, 90, 92, 93,

96–98, 100, 101, 104, 108, 120, 129, 131, 133, 146–148, 154–157, 159
Religionen 69, 89, 90, 95, 147, 148, 155, 157
Renewed Moravian Church 63
repentance 11, 14, 78, 94, 152
Reuss 81, 82, 86, 137
Reuss, Erdmuth Dorothea von 19, 47
Richter, Abraham Ehrenfried 55, 73
Ronneburg castle 62, 63
Ross, Eneas 96
Rothe, Johann Andreas 47–50, 53
Rudman, Andrew 26
Russia 2, 5, 61, 157

sabbatarian 24, 97, 156
Sackler, David 116, 144
Salzburg 10, 23, 49, 60, 86, 105
Sardinia 4
Savannah 102
Saxony 2–5, 10, 27, 40, 43, 46, 47, 53, 65, 86, 95, 133
Schaeffer, Melchior 47–49, 73
Schmidt, Johann Georg 109–111, 117, 129
Schultz, Johann Christian 29, 30, 110, 114
Schwenkfelders 24, 90, 97
Sea Congregation 98, 99
Selbstbiographie v, 75, 76, 80, 82, 118, 143
Seyffert, Anton Sr. 93
Sibeth, Carol Joachimus 55
Sifting Period 145, 160
Silesia 3, 5, 47, 49, 50, 51, 73, 82
Sitkovius, Christian 60, 61, 65
Skippack 19, 90, 92
Small Catechism 12, 21, 81
Sober, John 36
Society for the Propagation of Christian Knowledge (SPCK) 7, 16, 21, 52, 74, 83
Sophia of Brunswick-Hannover 5, 9
South Carolina 23, 24
Spain 2–5, 35
Spangenberg, August i, 51, 54–57, 59, 60, 90, 92, 94, 99, 145, 148

Spener, Philip Jacob 15–18, 151, 156
St. Croix 53
St. Georg cloister 56
St. James Chapel 7, 16, 78, 85
St. Thomas 53, 58, 103
Steinhofer, Friedrich Christoph 53, 56
Stephanas 56, 57, 70, 156
Stoeffler, Ernst 13
Stöver 29–31, 38, 93, 97, 101, 108, 114, 120, 131, 133
Stöver, Jr., Johann Casper 29–31, 38
Stöver, Sr., Johann Casper 29, 30
Stralsund 2, 55, 85, 91, 97, 146
Stuart, James Francis Edward 8
Stuttgart 57, 58, 95
superintendent 13, 15, 31, 42, 47, 48, 54, 55, 62, 82, 84, 95, 101, 112, 125, 126, 133, 135–138, 150, 156 (see also inspector)
Sweden 2, 3, 5, 10, 28, 47, 49, 61, 148, 149, 157
Swedenborg 54

Tennent, Gilbert 25, 91, 94, 96, 107
Test Acts 7
Thirty Years War 1, 2, 6, 78
Thomas, George 34–37, 91, 95, 96, 113
Thomasius, Christian 16
Thuringia 46, 48
Thürnstein, Louis i, 40, 91, 92, 94, 95, 98, 102, 107, 115, 120, 131, 132
Till, William 36, 37, 116, 144, 145
Tollstadius, Lars 26, 38, 97
Tranberg, Peter 28, 96, 97, 112, 113, 124, 127, 142, 145, 153
Trappe 38
Treaty of Carlowitz 3
Treaty of Utrecht 4
True Christianity 16
Tübingen 15, 95, 149
Tulpehocken 20, 29, 31, 38
Turner, Joseph 33–36, 144

Ulrich, Anthony 53
Ulrika Eleonora 2

Unaltered Augsburg Confession 12, 65
Unigenitus 45, 46
United Congregations 30, 64, 83, 90, 93, 108, 109, 114, 133, 139, 145, 146, 153, 157
United Provinces 7, 8, 44, 66
University of Wittenberg 13, 42
Unschuldige Nachrichten 13
Upper Lusatia 40, 41, 53, 82, 86, 118, 126
Utrecht 4, 44

Vienna 3, 4, 9
Vineam Domini 45
Viscount Perceval, Earl of Egmont 60
Vorsteher 72, 118, 124, 142, 149

Waiblinger, Johann Georg 61, 97
Walking Purchase 34
War of Jenkin's Ear 35
War of the Austrian Succession ii, 5, 10, 75
War of the Polish Succession 4
Wars of the Spanish Succession 2, 3
Watteville, Friedrich von (also Friedrich de) 42, 46–48, 66, 67
Weinlick 46
Weiser, Conrad 20
Wernigerode, Christian Ernst zu Stolberg- 59, 83
Wernigerode Consistory 134
Wesley brothers 64, 65, 94, 96, 107, 152
Wesley, Charles 63
Wesley, John 60, 65–68, 71, 74
Westphalia 1–3, 5, 50
Wetteravia 62
Whitefield, George 25, 34, 90, 91, 94, 96, 107
Wicaco 27, 28, 135
Wiegner, Christoph 90
William III of England 2, 4, 6, 8, 9
William of Orange 2, 8
Windrufwa, Andreas 28
Wriede, Gottlieb 51
Württemberg 15, 55, 56, 86

Young Pretender 9, 37

Zellerfelde 79

Ziegenhagen, Friedrich Michael 7, 16, 17,
    30, 52, 59, 60, 63, 64, 73, 75, 77, 78,
    85–88, 90, 106, 108–111, 118, 119,
    121-123, 126, 127, 130, 131, 133,
    135–140, 143, 153

Zinzendorf, Nicholas Ludwig von i–iv, 5,
    7, 15, 17–22, 25–29, 31, 37, 38, 40–
    63, 65–74, 76–78, 81–83, 85, 86, 88–
    99, 101–103, 105–109, 111–116,
    118, 121, 124–146, 148–160

Zinzendorf, Benigna 71

Zinzendorf, Christian Renatus 72, 145

Zinzendorf, Georg Ludwig 40, 41, 72

Zinzendorf, Maximilian Erasmus von 40

Zinzendorf, Otto Christian 40

Zinzendorfians 52, 152

Zwifler, Johann David 86, 109

173